Potential of Precedent in the Statutory Legal Order

Lex et Res Publica
Polish Legal and Political Studies
Edited by Anna Jaro

Volume 12

Zur Qualitätssicherung und Peer Review der vorliegenden Publikation

Die Qualität der in dieser Reihe erscheinenden Arbeiten wird vor der Publikation durch die Herausgeberin der Reihe geprüft.

Notes on the quality assurance and peer review of this publication

Prior to publication, the quality of the work published in this series is reviewed by the editor of the series.

Leszek Leszczyński / Bartosz Liżewski / Adam Szot (eds.)

Potential of Precedent in the Statutory Legal Order

PETER LANG

Bibliographic Information published by the Deutsche Nationalbibliothek
The Deutsche Nationalbibliothek lists this publication
in the Deutsche Nationalbibliografie; detailed bibliographic
data is available in the internet at http://dnb.d-nb.de.

Library of Congress Cataloging-in-Publication Data
A CIP catalog record for this book has been applied for at the
Library of Congress.

This publication is a result of the research project No. 2013/11/B/HS5/03821
entitled "Potential of Precedent Argumentation in the Polish Legal Order
(A Theoretical and Comparative Approach)", financed by the National Science Center
(Narodowe Centrum Nauki) in Poland.

NATIONAL SCIENCE CENTRE
POLAND

Reviewed by Prof. Alexander Bröstl
Cover Design: © Olaf Gloeckler, Atelier Platen, Friedberg

ISSN 2191-3250
ISBN 978-3-631-79018-2 (Print)
E-ISBN 978-3-631-79019-9 (E-Book)
E-ISBN 978-3-631-79020-5 (EPUB)
E-ISBN 978-3-631-79021-2 (MOBI)
DOI 10.3726/b15625

Peter Lang – Berlin · Bern · Bruxelles · New York ·
Oxford · Warszawa · Wien

This publication has been peer reviewed

www.peterlang.com

Contents

Part Three: Comparisons and Optimizations

Introduction

1. This book contains works on the current role and potential of precedential practice in statutory law systems. The majority of these articles are based on relevant European studies and on Polish judicial decisions. Specific features of *common law* systems are treated as a point of comparative or adaptive reference both with respect to the very 'act' of resorting to prior judicial decisions and to granting the same possible features of precedential practice. What binds the works presented in this volume is a strong conviction that the potential of precedential practice in judicial decisions taken in statutory law countries shows an ever-increasing trend which manifests itself in various branches of the law and on different decision-making levels.

The role and the potential of this practice is shown from various points of view, expressed in three parts.

Part One focuses on the aspects that fall within the terms of reference of the theory of law. In addition to discussing the grounds for and manners of implementing prior judicial decisions in court cases at hand, attempts are made at determining the role of prior decisions in making interpretations by way of validation arguments and the *ratio decidendi* reconstruction as well at determining their role in establishing normative grounds for current decision-making processes. Special attention is given to a comprehensive comparison of the *ratio decidendi* and *per analogiam* reasoning.

Part Two comprises analyses of ways in which prior decisions are implemented and referred in justifications to judgments by the European Court of Justice, in the application of the European Convention for the Protection of Human Rights and Fundamental Freedoms by the European Court of Human Rights. Relevant analyses are also made with respect to the Polish judicial decisions regarding the constitutional, administrative, civil, and criminal laws.

Part Three focuses, largely on a comparative basis, on determining the potential of the precedent in judicial practice of statutory law systems. The application of the *stare decisis* as used in the American judicial practice is considered with a view to determining the potential of the precedent in the light of precedent-based argumentation and the characteristic features of the decision-making process and justification of judgments in the statutory law systems.

2. The authors of the studies presented in this volume adopt a classic understanding of the legal precedent. According to the relevant definition, a precedent is "an adjudged case or decision of a court, considered as furnishing an example

or authority for identical or similar case afterwards arising or a similar question of law (...). A rule of law established for the first time by the court for a particular type of case and thereafter referred to in deciding similar cases (...). A course of conduct once followed which may serve as a guide for future conduct"[1] or "decision that functions as a model for later decisions"[2] as well as "decision which serves as a guide for present action"[3], or, the most generally, as "decision... that has a special legal significance... being regarded as having practical... authority over the content of the law"[4].

Irrespective of the above terminological convention, the notion of "a precedent" is replaced in many articles with "another" or "a prior" decision of the application of law, and the term of "precedential practice" is used interchangeably with "the implementation", "reference to" or "resorting to" another (prior) decision, depending on whether reasoning is discussed or the arguments which justify the decision taken. Given the precise focus of the works presented, which, by nature, triggers repeatability of numerous references, there is a great deal of ellipsis. This is best illustrated in references made to the term "decision" (as in "the implementation of the decision"), which denotes a reference to the content of the decision as well as its justification in order to demonstrate the type of reasoning employed in the decision-making process that leads to issuing a given decision.

Editors: Leszek Leszczyński, Bartosz Liżewski, Adam Szot

---

1 H.C. Black, *Black's Law Dictionary. Definitions of the Terms and Phrases of American and English Jurisprudence, Ancient and Modern*, 7th ed., West Publishing Co, St. Paul 1990, p. 1176.

2 D.N. McCormick, R.S. Summers, *Introduction*, [in:] *Interpreting Precedent. A Comparative Study*, eds. eidem, Dartmouth 1997, pp. 1–2.

3 N. Duxbury, *The Nature and Authority of Precedent*, Cambridge 2008, p. 1.

4 Cf. G. Lamond, *Precedent and Analogy in Legal Reasoning*, The Stanford Encyclopedia of Philosophy, [online:] http://plato.stanford.edu/entries/legal-reas-prec/ [available: 26.10.2016], pp. 1–2.

Part One: A Point of Theory

Leszek Leszczyński

Precedent as an Argument of Judicial Interpretation

Abstract: The precedent in the judicial application of law is not an independent but an important interpretation argument for the judicial application of law, first of all in the context of cooperation with legal regulations, which are the basic carriers of law here. In a judicial interpretation, an earlier decision may become a validation argument, which is subject to a separate reconstruction in order to determine the pattern of behaviour contained in a more or less clearly articulated *ratio decidendi* of such a decision. This pattern participates in the construction of a normative basis for decisions, entering into various relations with legal regulations and legal principles and open (extra-legal) criteria used in a given decision-making process. Thus, it becomes an element of the content of the judicial decision, defining both the qualification of the facts and its normative consequences, as well as the argumentation of the reasons for the decision, which is important for future decision-making processes.

Keywords: judicial interpretation, validation argument, normative base of decision, justification of decision

The use of a prior ruling in the current decision-making process leads to reconstructing (deriving) a model of behaviour contained in this ruling (*ratio decidendi*), which then enters in different relations and becomes an element of the normative basis of a decision currently made. All these types of reasoning show differences in relation to the measures concerning legal provisions in so far as the text components of the provision, the text of the decision, and its justification[1] differ.

1 Cf. D.N. MacCormick, *Why Cases Have Rationes and What These Are*, [in:] *Precedent in Law*, ed. L. Goldstein, Oxford 1991; Z. Bankowski, D.N. MacCormick, L. Morawski, A. Ruiz Miguel, *Rationales for Precedent*, [in:] *Interpreting Precedent. A Comparative Study*, eds. D.N. MacCormick, R.S. Summers, Dartmouth 1997, pp. 481–502. For the Polish judicial practice cf.: L. Morawski, M. Zirk-Sadowski, *Precedent in Poland*, [in:] *Interpreting Precedent*…, op. cit., pp. 242–245.

1 Reconstruction of *ratio decidendi*

1.1 Theoretical Model

(1) Separating *ratio decidendi*[2] from a decision and its justification is based on two assumptions related to some extent to the nature of precedent. The first one relates to the typical understanding of the precedent. Here, it is assumed that the precedent is not the whole decision but its *ratio decidendi*. Thus, both the possibility and ability to make a distinction between the *ratio decidendi* and the *obiter dicta* are necessary conditions of precedent[3]. Whereas the second assumption means deliberate use of the *ratio* in 'one's own' decision-making process. A condition of argumentation from precedent is not identification or reconstruction of the *ratio* but its appropriate application in the current decision-making process[4].

(2) The *ratio* can be determined in two ways, which include some detailed additional variants. The first one involves identifying the *ratio* with the statement included in the summary of a ruling that is culled out from the text of the reasoning and underlined by the adjudicating panel. It is usually a literal quote of a given passage of the reasoning. The second variant, which is applied in the absence of such an underlined summary, involves a more 'original' reconstruction of the *ratio* from the entire text of the reasoning in as many as three forms, i.e. either from one passage, two or more or even the whole reasoning as the condensed form of the whole text.

In the case of the first method, it is important that underlining the passage be done at the request of the judge-rapporteur as a result of the 'decision' of the whole adjudicating panel, not the publisher of the decision. Then it is more likely to reflect the intent of the Court as to marking the most important arguments for a given ruling. Although it does not automatically prompt one to use such argumentation, it definitely goes into this direction. This way means a more faithful

---

2 The role of identifying the *ratio* in relation to the case law cf. e.g.: R. Cross, *Precedent in English Law*, 2nd ed., Oxford 1968, p. 31 et seq.; N. Duxbury, *The Nature and Authority of Precedent*, Cambridge 2008, p. 58 et seq., esp. pp. 67–110; L. Alexander, E. Sherwin, *Judges as Rule Makers*, [in:] *Common Law Theory*, ed. D.E. Edlin, Cambridge 2007, p. 45 et seq.; G. Marshall, *What is Binding in a Precedent*, [in:] *Interpreting Precedent…*, op. cit., p. 510 et seq. The role of *ratio decidendi* in the statutory law system cf. R. Siltala, *A Theory of Precedent. From Analytical Positivism to a Post-Analytical Philosophy of Law*, Oxford–Portland 2000, p. 85 et seq.

3 Cf. R. Siltala, op. cit., pp. 65–67; G. Marshall, op. cit., pp. 515–516.

4 Cf. J. Levin, *How Judges Reason. The Logic of Adjudication*, New York 1992, pp. 137–150.

reference to the solution adopted in the decision that has been applied. At the same time, it potentially introduces some sort of automatism which may limit the activity of the Court to merely citing such a summary in the judicial reasoning of the decision that has been pronounced.

The second and more complex method requires that the adjudicating panel be more active, and it favours a more adaptive application of the model in the court's decision-making process. Even though the lack of indication of the principal summary or summaries of a ruling does not eliminate the possibility of identifying the *ratio*, it does make it more difficult. Such an indication, apart from the method of culling out the *ratio* mentioned above, may be achieved when the passages of a decision begin with the 'summaries' generalized to match the 'systematics'. No indication of the principal summary may result in some uncertainty as to 'discovering' the right summary that is in some sense 'hidden' in the text of an often long judicial justification. This may, in turn, lead to an error in identifying the passage that is significant in one's decision-making process especially in terms of the weight of a given passage with respect to the presented argumentation.

Such a method of determining the *ratio* may also be employed in the context of a specific scenario when the current adjudicating panel will treat as the *ratio decidendi* another passage of the reasoning than the one indicated in the form of separate theses or combine that other passage with the summary culled out by the adjudicating panel that undertook the prior decision.

Widening the margin of the potential lack of 'argumentative compatibility' between both decision-making processes occurs when the content of the *ratio* is based on different passages of the justification, especially various sections of the justifications of more than one decision. Such action also includes identifying the relationship between the passages of the argumentation adapted in one's own decision-making process with some conflicts between them which cannot be avoided.

Yet another option in reconstructing the *ratio* can be seen when the Court 'decodes' the model of behaviour from the whole reasoning on its own and adjudicates without recourse to the culled out summary or to a particular passage or specific passages of the reasoning. Decision-makers face the most difficult task that may lead them to a wider 'margin of uncertainty' – the risk of making a mistake – when they select to 'condense' the contents of the judicial reasoning in the current decision-making process. This effect could also appear in the previous options of the latter reconstruction scenario; nonetheless, in the event of recourse to a wider text, the scale of activity as well as the risk of error clearly increase. The scope of this activity, and thereby the level of difficulty, is even broader when collating and condensing means the use of more than one judicial reasoning of the applied decisions.

(3) Regardless of which method mentioned above is used, the process of determining the *ratio decidendi* involves appropriate generalization of the content of the summary or the passage of the judicial reasoning. It is the generalization of a lower degree than the one which is employed when a certain model of behaviour worded in a legal provision is reconstructed.

The process of applying the *ratio* is not therefore 'from detail to detail' in the sense of a simple and 'parallel' comparison of the contents of both decisions, i.e. the one already made and the one being made. It is, in fact, complex reasoning and, in principle, it includes three stages. Following the first stage of identifying the specific 'summary of the ruling to be applied' there is reasoning 'from detail to the general' where the text of the identified summary of the ruling that can be applied is transformed into the reconstructed and generalized *ratio decidendi*. Next comes the stage of transformation into the reasoning 'from the general to details' where the generalized *ratio decidendi* evolves into the '*ratio* that is reduced' to the contents of the decision currently being taken.

Such reasoning can undergo modification, which reinforces creativity of the decision-makers if the *ratio* is constructed by them 'individually' from the whole justification or justifications of more than one decision. Then, especially in the latter case, between the second and third stages indicated above one should insert an additional operation involving reasoning 'from general to general' which would include the construction of 'one's own' appropriately 'condensed' *ratio*, or alternatively the *ratio* additionally collated with other already generalized *rationes*.

The fundamental basis in reconstruction of the *ratio* involves syntactic rules. Such reconstruction does not directly refer to the features of the syntax of legal provisions but to the syntax of the language of the decision. The latter is different from the text of legal provisions in several ways among which one should indicate its bigger size and explanatory nature of the judicial reasoning or its eristic (argumentative), yet not 'imperative' style in the justification.

An important role at this stage of operative interpretation is also played by the functional rules whose position increase in each case and is based on the 'need' to use prior decisions. However, the role of the systemic-structural rules of interpretation is reduced while the role of the systemic-axiological rules of interpretation, which should always be taken into account as a reference of the *ratio* to the legal principles, remains rather unchanged.

Some modifications of the above model occur when the reconstruction of the *ratio decidendi* is based on several decisions. Systemic or quasi-systemic rules are used as context rules since a few precedents may create a 'micro-system', i.e. a conglomerate of decisions that are associated with one another also in the form of mutual impact of the contents of reconstructed models of behaviour.

(4). Clarification of the meaning of expressions used in the applied decision or in the text of the justification being a component of the reconstruction stage, is based on the fundamental role of semantic rules. The context rules of interpretation are syntactic rules (since a phrase is an element of the statement that constitutes the *ratio decidendi)* as well as functional rules. The systemic-structural argument is raised when the meaning of a term is linked with a particular place of the institution which is involved in the decision-making process in the legal system.

The clarification of the meanings of the names and phrases set forth in a decision shows a certain characteristic which stems from the fact that the text of the sentence of a decision or its reasoning shows a different dimension of language precision. E.g., it does not require the involvement of as many linguists as in the case of drafting the legislative regulations. Even if one believes that the author of the reasoning and the adjudicating panel took special care in the wording of the text, one must assume that the precision of the text of the reasoning comes from the linguistic knowledge and experience of the judge who has significantly less time to complete their task. This aspect also concerns the semantics of the phrases contained in the justifications of the resolutions passed by extended panels despite greater care taken in wording. Undoubtedly, the phrases used in judicial reasoning are based more on the juridical context resulting from the use of one's own professional experience in pronouncing decisions and the meaning of the phrases established in their course especially if a given phrase appears in the summary of the ruling, drafted primarily for the purpose of publication of decision.

It is possible that the reasoning of the applied decision will include a judicial definition of a term, which will update the rule of taking in account the established meaning with the use of such definition in the current decision-making process. At the same time, one must remember that such a definition will not be as precise as it usually happens in the case of definitions in a legal act.

1.2 Elements of Optimization

The above description of the reconstruction of the *ratio decidendi* allows for putting forward several proposals to optimize the reasoning in the decision-making process within the statutory law system[5].

5 Cf. for common law order: M.A. Eisenberg, *The Principles of Legal Reasoning in the Common Law*, [in:] *Common Law Theory*, op. cit., passim; J. Komarek, *Reasoning with*

(1) Reconstruction of a model of behaviour, i.e. a norm that is to be applied (*ratio decidendi*), from a prior judicial decision should take into account the style of the text of judicial practice that is different from a 'normative' language. It is also vital when it takes the form of a clearly formulated summary of the ruling. The degree of precision which, despite frequently demonstrated certain similarity to the text of the provision, is practically lower than in the case of the text of legal regulations. One should be especially aware of the distinctiveness of both 'language styles' in two cases. One is when this model is reconstructed from a passage of the reasoning that was not formally culled out. The other case relates to a scenario when the reconstruction, which practically means the construction of such a model, is condensed from the whole justification, which is directly linked with the ability to substantively 'condense' longer texts (argumentation). It all gets more difficult if in any of the above types of reconstruction more than one justification is considered.

(2) The process of reconstructing a norm from the *ratio decidendi* includes establishing the scope of normalisation and application. Despite the necessary generalisation of the *ratio*, such a process should be directly contrasted with the facts of the case and be conducted in the context of direct adaptation of the *ratio* to the specific needs of the current decision-making process. In particular, this applies to the *ratio* from the decisions recognized as the basic ones, i.e. the most closely related to the current decision-making process.

(3) The distinctiveness of the languages of a legal provision and the text of a decision should also be taken into account in terms of the clarification of the meaning of individual names, words, and terms used in the justification of the applied decision. When drafting the reasoning of a decision and apart from the condition of semantic precision, one must also be aware that complete semantic correctness is more challenging as compared to the legislative process. This problem is less often found in relation to the phrases that constitute the elements of a clearly marked summary, especially in the decisions of the courts of the highest instance, and, in particular, when the decisions take the form of a resolution passed by extended panels.

Previous Decisions. Beyond the Doctrine of Precedent, "American Journal of Comparative Law" 2013, no. 1, passim; M.M. Moore, *Precedent, Induction and Ethical Generalization*, [in:] *Precedent in Law*, op. cit.; J.M. Marshall, *Precedent and Interpretation in the American Common Law System*, [in:] *Wykładnia operatywna prawa – perspektywa teoretyczna i dogmatyczna*, eds. L. Leszczyński, A. Szot, Toruń 2017, pp. 74–84.

(4) When performing both syntactic and semantic operational determination one should take into account that the decision might be written in foreign languages (the judgements of the European Court of Human Rights or foreign courts[6]). What is more, there could also be a need to compare the decisions officially translated into Polish with the rulings in other official, working or similar language versions, which should happen in the case of using Court of Justice of the European Union rulings by the courts of the European Union Member States[7].

2 *Ratio* in the Process of Building the Basis of the Current Decision

2.1 Theoretical Model

2.1.1 Standard Course

(1) The most important role of the *rationes decidendi* in the reasoning of the current decision-making process reveals at the stage of constructing the normative foundation of a decision. It creates a basis made from various models reconstructed at the earlier stage. As the rules reconstructed from other decisions do not serve as independent components of the basis of the current decision at this stage, they interact with the rules reconstructed from legislative provisions and open criteria (like rules of rightness, good customs, etc.).

If one wanted to capture more specific roles of other decisions, one would need to make a distinction between three basic scenarios. The first involves combining one rule 'from a decision' (*ratio decidendi*) with one or more rules from legal provisions, whereas the second and third scenarios involve putting together several rules usually reconstructed from various decisions. In the second scenario they take the form of single *rationes* referring to various concepts in the decision-making process that play the role – either individually or 'separately' – of an element supplementary to the rules reconstructed from legal provisions. The third scenario involves the rules that are already compared and linked and take

6 Cf. S. Bertea, C. Sarra, *Foreign Precedents in Judicial Argument. A Theoretical Account*, "European Journal of Legal Studies", [online:] http://cejsh.icm.edu.pl/cejsh/element/bwmeta1.element.ojs-doi-10_17951_sil_2018_27_1_13/c/6580-4974.pdf [available: 25.10.2017].

7 It seems that the official translation of a CJEU judgement into the national language needs to be compared with other versions, including one of the main languages, and with the one that is the closest in relation to that national language.

the form of a somewhat combined *ratio decidendi* that will in turn be linked to the models reconstructed from legal provisions.

Making a distinction between such scenarios allows for the recognition of different roles of the rules reconstructed from prior decisions and the scope of their impact on the content of the current decision.

The second and third scenarios typically reinforce the participation of the *rationes decidendi* as compared to the inclusion of a single *ratio* (the first scenario). In most cases, the combined rule (*ratio*) used in the third scenario, which comes from more than one decision, is potentially the strongest. It seems to be valid especially in the statutory law system where the number of such combined *rationes* can in a way substitute the Anglo-Saxon rule of direct and decisive impact of the *ratio* from a single decision based on precedent[8].

Combining *rationes* from various decisions in the second scenario involves some use of systemic and structural rules. However, the relations in terms of hierarchy and scope in the case of combining rules from provisions is greater. Both types of rules may be treated equally or they may be put together in an 'asymmetric' way. In the latter case, an 'incomplete' *ratio decidendi* which plays the fundamental role in constructing the basis is 'inferentially' supplemented with a *ratio* from a different decision connected with the first one in terms of the subject-matter.

The situation is slightly different when the *ratio decidendi* serves as reinforcement of using an open criterion, e.g. the principle of equity and its role in constructing the basis of the current decision. Due to the lack of a normative content in a general clause referring to such criterion, courts do not seem to feel pressured to link their reasoning exclusively or mainly with legal provisions. The fact that such criterion is indicated in the provisions without specifying its contents means that reference to the case law in a form of particular decisions may determine uniform content of such criterion with respect to the specific decision-making process. Therefore, axiological argumentation is subject to 'objectivisation' at least in the context of searching its bases in more established findings of case law (precedential practice) when the role of non-system criteria in the construction of the basis of the decision is strengthened. Consequently, putting together open criteria and models of behaviour axiologically reconstructed from other decisions as construction elements of a normative basis of a decision reinforces the role of the latter by making it almost the only

8 Cf. e.g.: L. Alexander, E. Sherwin, op. cit., p. 45 et seq.; N. Duxbury, op. cit., p. 58 et seq., esp. pp. 67–110.

role in determining the impact of the open criteria on the final shape of the normative basis of a decision.

(2). The process of combining several rules of behaviour from different decisions – constructing the concept of collective *ratio decidendi* – leads to wider generalization of the *ratio* than in the case of basing its reconstruction on one decision only. All the more, such reasoning should not be presented as 'from detail to detail'. The need to generalize the *ratio decidendi* contained in several decisions translates into greater freedom for the interpreter. Also in this case, generalization does not reach the level of a norm contained in a legal provision even though it does go beyond the generalisation applied when interpreting one *ratio.*

Thus, the three-stage reasoning becomes the four-stage reasoning. The identification of a specific *ratio* and the reasoning 'from detail to the general' within the reconstruction of each *ratio decidendi* from each applied decision is then followed by its 'collective construction' through putting together the elements of a few *rationes.* 'Collective construction' happens before finally imposing such *ratio* on the facts established ('from the general to the specific') and is possible, thanks to the use of the above-mentioned quasi-systemic arguments. The third (additional) stage makes the whole process more complex. The said generalization of this part of the basis of the current decision which is based on another decision widens the margin of decision, i.e. the space for interpretation by reaching a higher level of generalization than in the case of the reconstruction from one decision only. Furthermore, one should also link the level of generalization and the scope of the said margin with the way of reconstructing the *ratio,* in particular by making a distinction between situations where the *ratio* is reconstructed from a marked summary of the ruling, a summary that is a passage of a justification or when the *ratio* is condensed ('squeezed out') from such text. The level of generalization is therefore higher and the scope of the margin wider, the more *rationes* 'reconstructed' from the whole reasoning of the decision participate in the collective *ratio.*

(3) When one or more than one *ratio decidendi* are compounded with the rules reconstructed from the provisions and open criteria at this stage of operative interpretation, they have an impact on the relationships between the rules applied in interpretation. Consequently, the role of systemic-structural rules is more important when the *rationes* are combined with rules from legal provisions. In turn, when such link is also created between open criteria, it strengthens the role of axiological rules alone or together with systemic rules[9]. In such situations,

---

9 The role of case law in defining the contents and the role of open criteria cf.: L. Leszczyński, *Stosowanie generalnych klauzul odsyłających,* Kraków 2001, pp. 7 et seq., 337 et seq.

the basis of a decision is built based on a wider scope of the rules of interpretation which may include systemic-axiological rules if the principles of law are also considered. The participation of the *ratio* associated with the rules from legal provisions as to the subject matter may – in the context of these relationships – be treated as a kind of inferential (instrumental or axiological) supplementation of the basis with its missing elements that is built for the purpose of a specific decision of applying law mainly on the grounds of those provisions.

Nevertheless, the basic role should be assigned to the functional rules, which involves the inclusion of the arguments from the function that is to be realized in the construction of the basis of a decision when the rules from other decisions are applied. Since this is conducted within the scope that does not limit the essential role of systemic-structural arguments in relation to the participation of the models from legal provisions, one should rather speak of co-working of both rules in such proportion as they in fact participate in the construction of the collective basis of the decision that is currently being taken.

The general feature of strengthening the role of the functional rules should also be confronted with the type of norms that build such a basis. The most limited role of these rules is assumed when competence bases are built unless that competence is linked to the 'task norm' which itself generates a strong role of an argument from a function. Such a role strengthens gradually from the construction of the most precise basis of detailed procedural norms through procedural principles of law until substantive bases. In the last group, the role strengthens also with respect to qualification and consequential bases.

2.1.2 Conflict Course

The participation of the *rationes decidendi* in the construction of the basis of current decision may lead to some conflict between them and the rules decoded from legal provisions as well as between different *rationes decidendi*.

(1) A typical solution of the conflict between *rationes* and the rules from legal provisions in a statutory law system may not be based on the thesis that the *ratio decidendi* has priority over the rule expressed in a legal provision. Such a thesis might be found in the *common law* systems[10], which clearly reflects the power of precedent in the whole jurisprudence and in separate decisions[11].

---

10 Cf. A. Barak, *The Judge in a Democracy*, Princeton 2008, pp. 16–17, 78–80, 273–276 (e.g. in the context of the senior–junior partnership).

11 Here, "court rules" among many established by the courts may be 'helpful' (cf. A.M. Ludwikowska, *System prawa Stanów Zjednoczonych. Prawo i prawnicy, struktura władzy, spory prawne*, Toruń 1999, p. 75). Cf. I.C. Kamiński, *Źródła prawa w systemie*

It is possible to reach such an interpretative compromise that would remove the conflict between those rules by appropriate juxtaposition (weighing) of their normative content. Such action does not deny the characteristics of such legal order, though may weaken the position of the rules reconstructed from legal provisions. Such weakening however may be limited by a certain selection of arguments put forward in judicial reasoning and the style of its presentation, which shifts the stress in the reasoning of the decision and its making process.

Resolving the conflict is – in a limited scope – based on the systemic conflict of law rules. In general, here one applies a rule typical for the statutory law system, i.e. the rule of *lex superior* which says that a legal provision overrides a decision. Whereas the rule of *lex specialis* cannot work here because in every case it would mean the priority of a less generalized *ratio* which has a closer connection with the current decision-making process. When arriving at a compromise, the rule of *lex posterior* may in fact play a role here if an element of a deep social change or the time difference between an 'old' provision and 'new' ruling or rulings justified the modification of such provision.

In the process of resolving the conflict we could use axiological rules of the conflict moving into the direction of the modification of the rule from the provision based on the argument of a closer relationship of the decision modifying such provision with the principle of law[12]. Though we would have to do it carefully and within a limited scope. However, in the statutory law system removing such conflict may not take the form of direct recognition of another decision as the principle of law or a conviction that a decision is axiologically more significant than a legal provision.

(2) Including several *rationes decidendi* in the process of building the basis of a decision may lead to a conflict among them. Consequently, the conflict may be resolved by finding interpretative compromise and removing certain decisions which are potential construction elements of the decision currently being taken. Such measures will be accompanied by reasoning typical in removing conflicts between the rules reconstructed from legal provisions with regard to some distinctiveness resulting, e.g. from the lack of systemic relationships between rationes.

---

common law, "Rejent" 2016, no. 3, pp. 21–26 to read more about this relationship in British case law.

12 In the EU law, where the rules of law are mainly linked with the summaries of the most important judgements of the Court of Justice, the position of this argument is stronger.

Maintaining the 'controlled adequacy', one may consider the significance of the rule of priority of '*ratio superior*' or '*ratio specialis*'. The former means the priority of the *ratio* associated with the position of the court delivering its decision or the type of ruling from which the *ratio* is reconstructed. The latter means the priority of the *ratio* more closely associated with the subject matter considered in the current decision-making process. Whereas, the rule of '*ratio posterior*' would not always be analogous to the *lex posterior* rules as the priority could be assigned both to the older *ratio* as the 'first in line' (or 'earlier in line') and consequently the more established one as well as to the newer *ratio* as a more current one.

In the process of removing the conflict between different *rationes*, one may, to some extent, use axiological arguments albeit recognizing one of the conflicting *rationes* as a principle will not be easy to justify apart from the already-mentioned EU law in which some CJEU rulings are recognized as the notions of the principle of law[13]. However, referring to the argument of priority of one of the conflicting *rationes* based on its close relationship with the principle or basing such priority on a social or even personal axiological preference may be possible though it will not take the form of regular measures of interpretation in the statutory law order.

In general, resolving conflicts between particular *rationes decidendi*, despite the fact that such action may not even be noticed, seems to happen much more seldom in the case of applying them in a statutory law system as compared to resolving conflicts between the rules from legal provisions.

2.2 Elements of Optimization

The key components of the optimizing model of using the *ratio decidendi* in the construction of the normative basis of a judicial decision include both the standard and conflict course.

(1) The essence of this stage of operative interpretation is to transform the norms to be applied that were reconstructed at the preceding stage into the normative basis of a decision. Such a transformation, which involves appropriate combination of the rules, should include the *rationes decidendi*. What is more, many different norms should be employed, since the 'interpretation basket'

13 Cf. L.N. Brown, T. Kennedy, *The Court of Justice of the European Communities*, 5th ed., London 2000, pp. 345–367; K. McAuliffe, *Precedent at the Court of Justice of the European Union. The Linguistic Aspect*, "Current Legal Issues" 2013, no. 15; A. Kalisz, L. Leszczyński, *Zasady prawa w stosowaniu prawa wspólnotowego*, "Europejski Przegląd Sądowy" 2005, no. 1, pp. 23 et seq., 26–27.

includes competence, procedural, and substantive norms. As it results from validation findings, the construction of the basis of a decision must assume the supplementary role of such models in the statutory law system. Bearing the above in mind, it is vital that putting the established *rationes decidendi* in such a role be real and not only formal as the latter would probably translate into a mere 'ornamental' reference of such decisions in judicial reasoning and written justification.

(2) Establishing the scope of participation of prior decisions should take place at the beginning of this stage of interpretation. If decision makers realize the need of the real participation of the *rationes decidendi* at an early stage, they will be able to establish correctly the scope of insufficiency – a kind of 'interpretation gap' – of this part of normative basis that was built on the grounds of legal provisions. Consequently, they would be able to determine the scope of the supplementation or modification based on the applied prior decisions with potential 'co-application' of the open criteria referred to in the provisions. This concerns all aspects of the participation of other decisions. They include the identification of the legal provisions applied in a given process, the reconstruction of the rules of behaviour as well as the construction of the final normative basis of the decision taking account of both the normative material and the case law. The scope of using other decisions depends on the 'power' of the case law in the form of already established jurisprudence and particular prior decisions[14].

(3) The norms reconstructed from prior decisions should play an active role in the construction of the normative basis of the current decision when it is necessary to inferentially supplement the rules given in legal provisions including

---

14 Cf. R. Von Moschzisher, *Stare decisis in Courts of Last Resort*, "Harvard Law Review" 1924, no. 37; W.N. Eskridge Jr., *Overruling Statutory Precedent*, "The Georgetown Law Journal" 1988, no. 76; E.H. Caminker, *Why Must Inferior Courts Obey Superior Court Precedents*, "Stanford Law Review" 1994, no. 46; R. Bronaugh, *Persuasive Precedent*, [in:] *Precedent in Law*, op. cit. As for the U.S. Supreme Court jurisdiction cf.: F. Schauer, *Has Precedent Ever Really Mattered in the Supreme Court?*, "Georgia State University Law Review" 2007, vol. 24, iss. 2; W.A. Edmundson, *Schauer on Precedent in the U.S. Supreme Court*, "Georgia State University Law Review" 2007, vol. 24, iss. 2; E.J. Segall, *Is the Roberts Court Really a Court?*, "Stetson Law Review" 2011, vol. 40; J.M. Walker Jr., *The Role of Precedent in the United States. How Do Precedents Lose Their Binding Effect?*, [online:] https://cgc.law.stanford.edu/commentaries/15-john-walker/ [available: 10.09.2016]; T.R. Lee, *Stare Decisis in Historical Perspective. From the Formating Era to the Renquist Court*, "Vanderbilt Law Review" 1999, vol. 52; C.J. Peters, *Originalism, Stare Decisis and Constitutional Authority*, [in:] *Precedent in the United States Supreme Court*, ed. C.J. Peters, Dordrecht 2013; F. Schauer, *Stare Decisis and the Selection Effect*, [in:] *Precedent in the United States Supreme Court*, op. cit.

instrumental and axiological inference. The special use of the fundamental rule of inference, i.e. *per analogiam iuris* in the process of the construction of the basis should be based on the rulings that establish the axiological content of a principle of law – especially if such content is not given in the provisions – and the ways of inferring a norm from the content of such principle. In the construction of the normative basis of a decision the *rationes* may also be active in defining the role of classic reasoning *per analogiam legis*[15].

(4) *Rationes decidendi* should play an active role in the aspect of constructing the normative basis of a decision that is linked to the need of resolving a conflict between the rules reconstructed from legal provisions that are combined at this stage of interpretation. Case law may be used through the reference to the axiological or functional rules. What is more, the said role should increase irrespective of whether it concerns the determination of the 'interpretative compromise' or refusal to use one of the conflicting rules. The same also applies to the conflict between the decisions only, to the conflict between open criteria of the general reference clauses and, to some extent, to the conflict between these various models. Nevertheless, resolving the conflict between judicial decisions and legal provisions should be done carefully, as it means entering into a dispute with the legislator.

(5) The role of the norms reconstructed from prior decisions in the construction of the current normative basis of a decision should increase in each case of 'normative opening' given in the regulations. This aspect mainly concerns the participation of open criteria both in the context of taking account of axiological content and determining the so-called axiological border within which the principles and open criteria can operate simultaneously. Another valid point is related with the participation of such open normative constructions as theologically conditioned programme-norms, task-norms or axiologically grounded norms of human rights. In every case where the normative content is less clearly defined in a provision, judicature and its precedential practice may – on the basis of legal discourse and also with reference to non-systemic factors – determine these contents and their participation in the construction of the normative basis of a judicial decision.

---

15 Cf. G. Lamond, *Precedent and Analogy in Legal Reasoning*, "The Stanford Encyclopedia of Philosophy", [online:] http://plato.stanford.edu/entries/legal-reas-prec/ [available: 26.10.2016].

3 Reduction in Decision-making

The model of reasoning at the stage of reduction of the result of operative interpretation to the content of decision may also generate some reference to the arguments derived from other decisions proportionally to the role of the *ratio* in the construction of the basis of a decision. It is valid in the case of reductions of both the qualification and the consequence bases. The former means normative qualification of the established facts (where case law sometimes allows for introducing elements of the so-called principle of opportunity), while the latter involves defining normative consequences of a given qualification of facts (where it can be associated with, usually established by the courts of the highest instance on the basis of case law, a kind of 'policy of sanctioning' as to the method of reacting to certain phenomena, e.g. within the scope of a specific type of crime).

Optimization of such reduction should link each reconstructed *ratio* with particular factual findings of the current decisional process similar to the current ones on which it was built. The above relationship also applies to the situations in which the *ratio* is associated not with establishing or qualifying the factual findings understood as social facts but with establishing the contents and qualification of 'legal facts' in a form of a contract, of an administrative decision in the framework of the judicial control of administration, of a judgement in cassation proceedings or of a normative act in the judicial review of constitutionality. Only when the normative model applied in the construction of the normative basis of a decision comes from a prior 'abstract decision', e.g. a resolution passed by an expanded panel in the court of last instance, may the specification in the form of a link with a qualified factual or legal status be limited due to the higher level of generalization of such decision.

4 Conclusions

Relying on other judicial decisions in making a judicial interpretation, even if the role of legal provisions continues to be dominant, does introduce new elements to legal reasoning.

On the one hand, this approach helps perceive characteristic features of the reconstruction of patterns of behaviour in previous judicial decisions – in many cases resulting from linguistic diversity – and determine the meanings of phrases contained therein (with respect to such operations on legal provisions). On the other hand, this approach reinforces the role of prior judicial decisions at the stage of constructing the normative basis for the decision at hand before determining its final content.

Various relations established among the arguments from prior judicial decisions and other arguments and open criteria reinforce the role of functional principles in operative interpretation linking the same in many cases with axiological rules. It follows that by supplementing and, at times, adjusting the effects of linguistic and systemic rules of interpretation, these relations make the interpretation as well as the processes of law application more flexible.

If the application of an argument from a prior decision is linked with properly disclosed arguments in the justification of the decision, which indicate the adaptability of the content of the prior decision to the current decision-making process, the precedential nature of a specific action and its binding force[16] will increase accordingly. And where such an application is related to the actual repeatability of such actions and manners of reasoning in judicial practice at large, judicial practice will acquire the features of precedential practice. This, in turn, will reinforce the link between flexibility and uniformity of the application of law, an element essential for the proper operation of a legal system.

16 Cf. A. Peczenik, *Binding Force of Precedent*, [in:] *Interpreting Precedent…*, op. cit., pp. 461–480; J. Roland, *How stare decisis Subverts the Law*, [online:] http://www.constitution.org/col/0610staredrift.htm [available: 15.05.2016].

Andrzej Korybski

Analogy as a Basis of Precedential Reasoning

Abstract: In Anglo-Saxon legal literature, the problem of logical basis of precedential reasoning is treated as one of the key research issues. Divergent concepts are put forward. The first of them states that analogy is the basis of precedential reasoning. Another one is based on the assumption that a similar reasoning and precedential reasoning are separate and are based on different assumptions. These concepts are analysed and discussed in the article. Logical characteristics of each reasoning and cultural roots are taken into account. Attention is paid to the fundamental convergence of functions of the compared legal reasonings, and at the same time to the differences in argumentation per analogiam legis and precedential reasoning based on the assumption of binding force of precedent. There are also formulated conclusions concerning the limitations and conditions concerning the possible use of the Anglo-Saxon theory of precedent to the statutory legal orders.

Keywords: analogy, analogia legis, precedential reasoning

1 Introductory Remarks

The development of the European Union's legal order is to a large extent based on specific and precedential rulings of the Court of Justice of the EU. It also gives the European legal doctrine the task to consider at least a partial use of the Anglo-Saxon construct of precedent in the legal orders of Continental countries. Analyses undertaken by the literature on the subject focus predominantly on defining the meaning of precedent and *per rationem decidendi* reasoning as well as showing some possible ways of applying this type of reasoning (including, in particular, the practice of so-called non-binding precedent[1]). The question of the relationship and distinctive features of precedential reasoning and *a simili* reasonings, which are rooted in statutory law cultures, is yet to be addressed. It is particularly important to analyse and see if the uniqueness of the European legal culture (with the features of the EU's legal order) can facilitate the adoption of the construct of binding precedent along with *stare decisis,* or, alternatively, if the construct is impossible to adopt and, possibly, even redundant due to the sufficient role played by analogous reasoning in statutory law interpretation.

1 See: L. Leszczyński, *Zagadnienia teorii stosowania prawa. Doktryna i tezy orzecznictwa,* Kraków 2001, pp. 303–331.

Analysing the possibility to apply the Anglo-Saxon construct of precedent requires, in the first place, the following actions:

1) defining the meaning and function of each of the above-mentioned types of reasoning against the backdrop of uniqueness of the legal culture where the given type of reasoning was shaped and characterized by the doctrine. The first task is to provide a general description of analogous reasonings, followed by *per analogiam legis* (which, chronologically speaking, precedes the former and stems from the Roman legal tradition); and precedential reasoning as well as the construct of precedent in the form which it has taken in the Anglo-Saxon legal culture;
2) formulating conclusions as regards the relationship and the differences between the types of reasoning, including an analysis of the function of each of the types of reasoning in particular legal orders;
3) analysing the scope of use (including the function of precedent in statutory legal orders) and barriers which hinder or narrow down the possibility of inclusion of precedential reasoning in legal practice.

2 The Essence of Analogy

Finding similarities in significant features (attributes, characteristics, etc.) is the essence and the decisive factor determining the function of analogous reasoning in legal doctrine and practice. Analogous reasoning is a universal thinking pattern which is applied by humanity[2]. Analogous reasoning is also an important complement of two other logical reasoning patterns: deduction and induction. It must be noted at this point that in general logic, analogy is included in the pool of probabilistic reasonings and is placed very closely to inductive reasonings[3]. The presentation of the basic reasoning types indicates that there is an association between the so-called incomplete inductive reasoning and analogous reasoning. Although inductive reasoning usually follows the pattern "from a particular statement to a general statement" (which is more or less likely), the

2 More: F. Macagno, D. Walton, *Argument of Analogy in Law. The Classical Tradition, and Recent Theories*, "Philosophy and Rhetoric" 2009, vol. 42, no. 2, pp. 154–167. In Polish literature: T. Barszcz, *Struktura* argumentum a simili, Lublin 2015, passim.

3 S. Hanson, *Legal Method and Reasoning, Cavendish Publishing Ltd.*, Routledge 2012, p. 2016–2018, S. Brewer, *Exemplary Reasoning. Semantics, Pragmatics, and the Rational Force of Legal Argument by Analogy*, "Harvard Law Review" 1996, vol. 109, no. 5, pp. 947–977. In Polish literature see also: Z. Ziembiński, *Logika praktyczna*, 26th ed., Warszawa 2004, pp. 190–191, 243.

foundation of analogy is the pattern of "from a particular detail to another similar (or the same) detail"[4].

Analogous reasoning takes place in every culture and in every legal order. It often is an indispensable basis for choosing the right behaviours (decisions) and actions that follow decisions. In legal thinking processes, analogous reasoning leads to a conclusion which justifies the repetitive nature of a normative qualification of a case already resolved (through an earlier legal decision), or interpreted (through an earlier act of interpretation of legal regulations). If there is a large number of cases, the repetition of results acquired through analogy in a given legal order may lead to the identification of a rule which will facilitate the decision-making process in similar cases, or the interpretation of legal provisions before deciding on the normative basis of the decision. Therefore, analogous reasoning may, in the right legal-practical circumstances of the given legal order, lead to inductive conclusions. In the legal cultures which have developed the principle of equal treatment of subjects of law, analogy has become one of the most important argumentation tools to support equal treatment of entities/subjects representing the same type.

Representatives of social and life sciences (including, in particular, the sciences focusing on humans, such as neuropsychology) agree that *per analogiam* reasonings are based on:

1) identification of at least two objects in a given reality which social subjects intend to compare due to their expectations (needs, interests, ambitions). These objects need to be compared precisely because of the same needs (the aim of the comparison);
2) making certain arrangements on the scope of comparison; here, the point of departure are expectations, as expectation define the set of comparable features, characteristics, etc. Defining the scope and the criteria for the comparison facilitates the performance of a substantial description of the compared objects, which also includes the differences between the objects, not just the similarities. This is important for analogous reasoning in the doctrine and in legal practice, as it justifies not only analogy based on statutes and acts of law (*analogia legis*), but also reasoning based on the contrary (*argumentum a contrario*).

Analogy is a notion juxtaposed with unambiguousness and ambiguousness because it makes it possible to indicate both significant similarities between

4 Z. Ziembiński, op. cit., p. 313.

the objects (which allows for their identification as belonging to one class) and significant differences (which justifies their positioning in different classes). Analogous reasoning in philosophical studies pertains to cognition, i.e. concluding about certain features or attributes of elements of the objects subjected to comparison. Analogous reasoning in axiologically entangled social science also consists in making normative qualifications of the compared behaviours and their impact on social life. The point of departure for such qualifications can be a socially adopted behavioural pattern for the particular situation, or the existence of a previous normative qualification of the behaviour as precedential behaviour. It is worthwhile noting at this point that behaviourally justified use of analogy is deeply rooted in social awareness. It is also reflected in the expectation of individuals (but also whole communities) who require the same subjects to be treated in the same way in similar circumstances. That is why analogy is such an important tool for the verification of justness and fairness of legal regulations.

Compared against the other reasoning types of deduction or induction, analogy offers no conclusions and is limited to identification of similar features (attributes, elements, etc.) shared by two comparable objects (phenomena, states, artefacts, processes, activities). In the literature on general logic authors draw our attention to the fact that analogy is not based on logical implication, unlike deduction. Correctness of analogous reasoning depends on the likelihood of the explicitly or implicitly adopted inductive assumptions[5]. The correctness predominantly depends on the right selection of the objects to be compared; the relationships between incomparable objects cannot be subjected to analogous reasoning. It also depends on a skilful separation of significant (substantial) characteristics from accidental characteristics of the compared objects. An important feature of analogous reasoning in social sciences, differentiating it from deductive (formal) and inductive (empirical) reasoning, is the possibility of including the concepts and values of justness and fairness into analogous reasoning. These values are assigned key importance when deciding about the essence of law and its social functions. Looking for just resolutions (decisions) is based on finding similarities (analogy) between the compared states, processes, activities, etc. Consequently, it is defined as searching for the right measure or pattern for qualifying decisions or activities as just or not just. These qualifications also build on the basis of the same measures applied for decisions or activities with particular essential features. The possibility to support analogy with values such as equality

5 Quoted after: ibidem, p. 191. See also: L.C. Becker, *Analogy in Legal Reasoning*, "Ethics" 1973, vol. 83, no. 3, pp. 248–255.

before law, justice, fairness of law is, with reference to the legal doctrine and practice, particularly clear in the case of *analogia iuris* reasoning.

In summary: essence of analogy is the formulation of hypothetical conclusions (which depends on the strength of inductive statements concerning the similarities between objects) which pertain to the consequences of the similarities. Of these two compared objects (states, processes, activities, etc.), one needs to have been examined (described, analysed, interpreted), with its significant features identified. The essence of the comparison of objects of social life is the application of the same (equally justified, equal, just, fair, etc.) measure as the one which has been applied in the case of the object constituting the basis for the comparison.

As a result of analogous reasoning we acquire the so-called observative statement, i.e. a sentence which presents the likelihood of what followed from the observation of the fragment of reality where the objects reside. The statement (developed as a result of analogous reasoning) is, importantly, included in a broader and coherent whole of descriptive statements which describe and explain the given fragment of reality. The statement is a hypothetical one, and the probability of its truthfulness depends on the logical value of the statement which is the assumed premise in the process[6]. In each of the above patterns there is an assumption (tacit, as in pattern 1, or explicit, as in pattern 2) that each object with features *a, b … n* belongs to class X of objects; the assumption is based on the premise that a number of observed objects with features *a, b … n* have a specific function within a broader system of states, things, phenomena, processes, etc. or serve a specific purpose (value).

A significant feature of analogous reasoning in statutory law culture is the assumption that the function, objective or value of a given legal regulation (institution, branch of law or an entire legal system as a broader fragment of reality to which legal phenomena refer) is decided upon by the so-called rational legislator, a specific construct of legal thinking, whereby the mode of defining the will of the legislator depends on the adopted theory of interpretation of law. That is why legal analogous reasoning is one of the key issues in interpretation of law in statutory law cultures, and one of the fundamental topos of legal argumentation. The association of law with language leads to analogy as other reasoning types, has its logical foundation and is part of the legal dogmatic method as the method applied by jurisprudence.

6 S. Brewer, op. cit., p. 951–954.

3 Features of *per analogiam legis* Reasoning

A simili, per analogiam reasoning types constitute a part of the European legal interpretation and legal reasonings doctrine and are treated as a particularly significant element of professional training of lawyers[7]. However, there are discrepancies in the positioning of the reasoning types which result from the differences in understanding of the function and essence of these reasoning in interpretation of law. We can include analogy in the body of functional interpretation rules, i.e. we can position it beyond legal conclusions[8] and treat it as the so-called interpretation directive. Analogy can also be treated as a special and distinct part of interpretation of law, defined as legal inferences. In the light of the description of analogous reasoning presented above, this approach can only be defended if the notion of "legal inference" is granted its specific meaning which is different than the notion of drawing conclusions on the basis of general logic.

Regardless of these terminological discrepancies there is an agreement as to the historical roots of analogous reasoning which stems from the Roman legal culture and is reflected in canonical Latin formulations and maxims which are still regarded as fundamental legal knowledge. Compared against the tradition of Roman private law and its approach to analogy, the construct of precedent is at least a dozen centuries younger and is associated with the development of English monarch-made law. In some interpretations, claim that analogous reasoning in the form of analogy based on statutory law (in short: *analogia legis*), is the type of reasoning specific for statutory law cultures, not significant in the Anglo-Saxon legal culture[9].

Including *analogia legis* in functional interpretation is linked to the assumption that *analogia legis* is a tool to fine-tune legal norms which are interpreted based on an unclear legal provision. Functional interpretation takes place when,

---

7 These reasoning types are a fundamental part of introductory law and logic coursebooks for students of law. In the Polish literature on the subject the coursebooks are based on the previously quoted work of Z. Ziembiński; see also: *Wprowadzenie do nauk prawnych. Leksykon tematyczny*, ed. A. Bator, Warszawa 2006, pp. 289–293; J. Jabłońska-Bonca, K. Zeidler, *Prawnik a sztuka retoryki i negocjacji*, 2nd ed., amended and supplemented, Warszawa 2016, pp. 286–289.

8 Apart from the coursebook by Z. Ziembiński see also: S. Wronkowska, *Podstawowe pojęcia prawa i prawoznawstwa*, 2nd ed., amended, Poznań 2003, pp. 82–83.

9 This seems to be the assumption of many representatives of Polish legal doctrine of 20th century which refer back to the work of German Roman Law experts and legal theorists. See: J. Nowacki, Analogia legis. *Zagadnienia teoretycznoprawne*, Łódź 1964, passim.

after application of the rules of logical and linguistic interpretation and systemic directives, the interpreting entity has not acquired a sufficient level of clarity as to the addressee, behaviour patterns of circumstances de-coded from the particular provision (or provision). If that is the case, the scope of application and/or the normative scope of the norm is not precisely defined[10]. However, the role of *analogia legis* is perceived similarly by clarifying the concept of interpretation of law. In order to apply *analogia legis* it is of key importance to identify the *ratio legis* of the interpreted provision and the arguments which prove the reasons behind comparing an unclear provision with another provision which does not produce any doubts for its interpreters although it is based on the same *ratio*. The application of analogy makes it possible to decide on certain semantic issues or even to fill the linguistic gap which results from a lack of words to describe at least one of the content elements of the interpreted norm[11].

Analogia legis argument is therefore a special type of *argumentum a simili* and refers to similarity of circumstances, features of addressees or features of the behaviour pattern[12]. The foundation, however, is always identification of the same *ratio legis* for each of the compared norms. This means that it would not be justified to apply analogy if the assumption of a reasonable lawmaker is rejected. Discovery of lack of similarity between the compared norms or provisions from which the norms are interpreter, creates a possibility to use a different type of legal reasoning known as *argumentum a contrario*. If the principles of logical and linguistic interpretation as well as systemic interpretation lead to the identification of a clear and doubt-free scope of application and normative scope of the interpreted norm, what still must be done is to verify the alignment of the content of the norm with the system of values assigned to the entire branch or even the entire system of law. If no such consistency or alignment is found, the so-called narrow interpretation or broad interpretation of the provisions may be applied, and in extreme cases *praeter legem* or *contra legem* interpretations can be used[13].

Application of analogy is only possible in situations of linguistic (semantic) unambiguity of the norm which constitutes the point of reference, and the norm's

10 Here, I adopt the assumptions of the derivative concept of interpretation of law (see: Z. Ziembiński, op. cit., p. 191, 243; M. Zieliński, *Wykładnia prawa. Zasady, reguły, wskazówki*, extended 3rd, Warszawa 2006, passim).

11 See: Z. Ziembiński, op. cit., p. 243.

12 In the Polish literature S. Wronkowska (op. cit., p. 83) takes a different approach, distinguishing *a simili* reasoning from *analogia legis*.

13 More: K. Płeszka, *Wykładnia rozszerzająca*, Warszawa 2010, passim.

appropriate axiological justification which excludes the possibility of application of broadened or narrow interpretation. For those in favour of treating analogy as a set of rules of functional interpretation, it is of key importance to assume that analogy should fit within the text of the compared provisions and the language of the norms decoded from the provisions. Going beyond the text of the provision (which happens in the case of broadened or narrow interpretation) has features of legislative activity of the court (*sui generis*) to complement the acts of law, with the aim of ensuring axiological coherence of a given branch of law or the entire legal system. That is why going beyond the text of the provisions may – in the case of statutory law based on the division of power with separate legislative power – give rise to justified doubts.

Inclusion of the analogia legis not to legal interpretation, but to legal argumentation is based on the assumption that reasoning a simili goes beyond the text of the given legal act, and the result of this reasoning creates a new legal norm. According to this approach, the use of analogy is composed of the following three stages of reasoning:

1) defining the unclear or ambiguous elements of the provision (provisions) with reference to a factual state of things; such unclear elements are in particular unclear (incomplete) description of the characteristics of the addressee, circumstances or behavioural pattern of the addressee;
2) defining the scope of the clearly formulated provision (provisions) which identifies the addressee, circumstances or behaviour patterns in situations significantly similar to the one in question, with incomplete or unclearly regulated behaviours in given facts of a case;
3) deciding that the similarity between both situations regulated by law justifies a reference of the same legal consequences (legal qualification) to a non-regulated factual state of things as in the case of clearly and completely regulated factual state[14].

In this case, too, the foundation of statutory reasoning is rooted in the rule presented in the following maxim: *Ubi eadem legis ratio, ibi eadem legis dispositio.* The compared legally regulated situations (one is regulated in a way which raises no linguistic doubts, the other is regulated in an incomplete or unclear way), therefore, share the same *ratio legis*, and the justification for the use of analogy is

14 See: L. Morawski, Wstęp do prawoznawstwa, Toruń 2000, p. 188–190.. A similar description of *analogia legis* is presented in the publication: *Wprowadzenie do nauk prawnych*, op. cit., pp. 288–293 (entry author: Z. Pulka).

the assumption of reasonable lawmaker understood as a functional and targeted consequence of encoding normative content in legal provisions. If the lawmaker has regulated clearly one type of factual circumstances with the right assignment of *ratio legis*, then it is obvious that by doing so the lawmaker allowed for the application or transfer of the same provision to a different (but significantly similar) factual state with the same *ratio*. Analogy is a tool to fill gaps in legislation by means of the three-stage conclusion-drawing process presented above. The application of analogy, therefore, goes beyond the language of an unclearly formulated provision (provisions) and beyond the framework of functional interpretation[15]. If we conclude that a legal norm is binding and regulates clearly some state of things which is defined in the relevant provisions in an unambiguous way, then we must conclude that another norm is also binding which is not explicitly stated in the provisions and which pertains to a significantly similar state of things (i.e. the addressee and the circumstances) and contains a prescribed behaviour pattern directed to a similar addressee in similar circumstances[16].

In statutory legal orders, *analogia legis* is also one of the instruments which ensure the consistency of relative uniformity of judicial decisions[17]. Shaping the consistency of court rulings (or in its softer version – a consistent approach to rulings of certain types) can therefore be seen as one of the most important functions of *analogia legis* in legal orders which is fundamental for guaranteeing the rationality of expectations and predictability (as to the mode of issuance and content of legal decisions pertaining to the same or similar cases). Consequently, it is also fundamental for guaranteeing the certainty of law. It is worth noting at this point that there is one feature which differentiates *analogia legis* from precedential reasoning (presented below): *analogia legis* is treated as an instrument to ensure cohesion of the axiological foundation of law (which is decided upon by the lawmaker), not as a way to "socialize" rulings, while such socialization is characteristic for the Anglo-Saxon legal culture.

4 Precedential Reasonings

Anglo-Saxon literature presenting the essence of precedential reasoning and the construct of precedent is at least as rich as the Continental body of legal literature

15 In: L. Morawski, op. cit., p. 189.

16 In: *Wprowadzenie do nauk prawnych*, op. cit., p. 290.

17 See more in: L. Leszczyński, *Zagadnienia teorii stosowania prawa…*, op. cit., pp. 49–61.

devoted to interpretation of law[18]. Precedent doctrine plays a similar role in Anglo-Saxon jurisprudence as theory of interpretation of law in Continental jurisprudence. The role of both these doctrines is to extract generic legal norms and interpret their content precisely so as they can serve as a basis for future legal decisions (in particular for future court rulings). Although representatives of the Anglo-Saxon doctrine agree on to the fundamental assumptions behind the construct of precedent, they do not fully agree on the possible types of precedential reasoning and the role of precedential court rulings in the shaping of the content of future (later) rulings.

At the foundation of precedential reasoning lies the discovery of similarity between the state of things that an already existing court decision pertains to and the state of things in a different (later) case which is to be decided upon by the court. The practice and doctrine of precedent refer to the court decisions which have been introduced to the legal order and exist in it in the form of recorded and documented rulings[19]. In the Anglo-Saxon construct of precedent, *stare decisis* rule is of fundamental importance. Over a few hundred years since the advent of precedential practices, the rule has become not only a cultural but also a formally binding requirement for correctness of judge-made decisions in the Anglo-Saxon legal order.

Stare decisis[20] principle is not understood consistently in particular Anglo-Saxon legal orders, particularly as regards the court is bound by previous, precedential court decisions. It seems that the assumption of lower courts being bound by decisions of higher courts is not questions, and a great majority of precedential rulings come from courts of appeal. However, depending on the systemic structure of the state (particularly its federal or homogeneous form) the constructs of binding courts of first instance with decisions of higher courts are varied. In the American doctrine it is assumed that lower state courts are bound by decisions of higher state courts (i.e. courts of appeal). Federal courts,

---

18 Compare: G. Rivlin, *Understanding the Law*, 5th ed., Oxford 2009, in particular p. 30, pp. 162–174; specialist monographies and articles in theory of law published over the recent years can be counted in dozens (e.g. J.F. Horty, *Rules and Reasons in the Theory of Precedent*, "Legal Theory" 2011, vol. 17, no. 1, pp. 1–33 – and the quoted literature).

19 In: R.S. Barker, *The Concept of Precedent and its Significance in the Constitutional Law of the United States*, Pittsburgh 2010, [online:] https://works.bepress.com/robert_barker/7/download/ [available: 1.12.2016].

20 "*Stare decisis*" is a shortened version of the maxim which reads in full *Stare decisis et non movere quieta;* one must stand by the things decided, without violating the normal state of things shaped by such decisions.

in turn, are bound by the decisions of federal courts of appeal for the given district (*Federal Court of Appeals*). Nevertheless, courts (regardless of their type) are not bound by the decisions of the Supreme Court. In the United Kingdom, it is accepted that the *English Court of Appeals* is bound by the decisions made by the *House of Lords*, which acts as the Supreme Court. In general, however, *stare decisis* means that lower-instance courts do not have the power to overrule precedential decisions of higher courts. When a lower court is not willing to apply a previously made and legally binding court decision made by a higher court it must prove that there is significant difference between the situation it is looking into and the precedential situation decided upon previously by the higher court.

Stare decisis rule, therefore, pertains only to binding lower courts with the rulings by higher courts made in similar cases. It must also be added that the court which issued the precedential ruling is itself bound by the ruling in any later cases, as long as that later case is similar to the precedential case. *Per rationem decidendi* reasoning does not, however, lead to the assumption that a higher court may be bound by a precedential ruling of a lower court; it is a rule that rulings of lower courts may acquire the status of precedent only after they are upheld by relevant decisions made by higher courts.

In the Anglo-Saxon doctrine of precedent, the following arguments in favour of the need for precedential reasoning are presented: (1) appropriate shaping of the content of legal order which ensures fairness of court rulings as the most important element of the legal order (*consistency*); (2) guaranteed predictability of individual and social expectations as to court decisions to be made in similar cases (*rational expectations*); (3) ensuring institutional replicability of court decisions (*replicability*) with concurrent possibility of flexible adaptations of the legal order through its alignment with some significant social and awareness changes, leading to (4) support for lawmaking implemented by legislative and executive bodies as well as correcting statutory law (*need for law-making*). A legal order ought to have a lasting and fair foundation in the form of values which are indispensable for the social and ethical legitimacy of the order. Courts are the fundamental tool for the shaping and protection of social and moral foundations of legal order. Therefore, law is to be fair and equal. This means, in the first place, that law ought to enjoy social support and it be the moral compass for deciding similar cases in the same manner. *Stare decisis* principle protects and guarantees individual and public expectation of the same decisions (i.e. decisions based on the same rule of decision in similar cases). However, it also allows for resignation from or change in the precedent rule if the case in question is significantly different than the precedent case. Consequently, this rule creates opportunities for corrections in the legal order shaped by precedential decisions. What is more, the possibility to overrule the existing precedential rules of judicial decisions in the Anglo-Saxon legal doctrine is extended to include cases regulated directly by acts of statutory law. That is because the court may deem the rule of decision contained in statutory law as unconstitutional and replace it – in the case in question – with their own rule of decision based on justness/fairness as social and moral justification of the ruling.

A characteristic feature of the Anglo-Saxon vision of legal order and its functioning which distinguishes it from the corresponding vision of statutory legal orders is the lack of the assumption of a reasonable lawmaker. Anglo-Saxon legal orders are always *in statu nascendi*, and are being co-created by courts and legislative as well as executive bodies. However, Accountability for social and moral legitimacy of law rests predominantly on courts which have the possibility to institutionally complement and correct the content of the legal order by applying *per rationem decidendi* reasoning.

The doctrine presents a few ways in which precedential decisions can be used. At present, the predominant idea is that the essence of precedent is inextricably linked to its binding character which imposes on courts the obligation to issue rulings based on the rules contained in precedential rulings – even if there are reservations as to the applicability of the precedential rule to the new factual state[21]. This radical position is based on the premise that each subsequent case has only one correct resolution which is aligned with the public morality and socially legitimate. However, it is also possible to assume that the case being decided by the court can have more than one correct resolution, which means that the precedential ruling only delivers a framework for the future decision of the court, and the judge's interpretation of the state of public morality and social justification are decisive for the choice and content of the final ruling. The assumption here is that social progress and transformations of public morality make it impossible to achieve fully repetitive decisions based on the content of the earlier precedent. There are also views that can be branded as "soft" (not binding formally) precedent, whereby it is the similarity between the reasonings and the arguments used (as opposed to the cases themselves) that warrants the application of precedent in the decision-making process[22]. Therefore, the binding character of precedent understood in this "soft" way doesn't result from

21 This position if defined as a "particularly strong version of stare decisis" and contrasted in the doctrine with other, less hardline approaches – see: G. Lamond, op. cit.

22 Ibidem.

legal obligation of binding with a precedential rule but from the conviction that the arguments used and the reasoning applied to analyse the precedential case are correct and adequate.

At least a few applications of precedential rulings in later court proceedings can be distinguished. The first one is directly *following precedent*. This means full application of the rule/ratio contained in the decision, interpreted from the precedential ruling, having taken into account all the significant features of the case in question which are the same is in the description of the precedential ruling. The second mode pertains to a practice which is broadly described by the doctrine, i.e. the practice of *distinguishing*. This second mode pertains to the cases where the factual state of the case in question significantly differs (in some aspects) from the precedential case, which excludes the first mode of direct application of the rule (and with its full content). The practice of distinguishing the status of the case already decided and the case being decided is particularly clearly seen when there is no clarity as to the separation of significant circumstances from accidental circumstances, i.e. the separation of *ratio* from *dictum* (contextual circumstances associated with the case which to not impact the rule of decision. In such a situation, the court has two solutions leading to: (1) upholding the rule of decision – however, with a modification of the content of the rule consisting in a different qualification of some circumstances (as either significant or accidental) or in broadening the scope of circumstances which have been deemed as significant; (2) making an attempt to overrule the precedent by justifying the impossibility of application of the precedent rule to the case in question due to the fact that the factual state of the case in question is not the same as the state of the precedent case. Another mode is the reverse of the practice of distinguishing and consists in narrowing down the scope of circumstances that are significant for the decision (compared with the existing practice of interpreting significant circumstances in similar cases); this leads to accepting the rule of the decision but to a limited extent only, with some circumstances excluded; these circumstances may have been treated as significant before but were not applied by the court in the case in question (the so-called limiting precedent). Both the practice of broadening the scope of significant circumstances and the practice of narrowing them down are attempts at adapting the rules of deciding contained in precedential rulings to a changed social reality, and to the new needs and phenomena within the realm of public morality. It is emphasized in the doctrine that such attempts must not lead to undermining the stability of the existing order (which is the essence of *stare decisis* rule); they are merely fragmentary reactions of courts to the situation of indispensable social change.

The key condition for maintaining the practice of precedent is giving the right shape to the system of legal education, where the case method plays a key role. Analyses of selected precedent cases and rulings by students of law are typically preceded by a doctrinal characteristic of legal reasonings, with special emphasis on *per rationem decidendi* reasoning and other reasonings based on analogy. In precedential reasoning it is particularly important to distinguish the circumstances of the case crucial for the identification of its *ratio* from the case's accidental circumstances (i.e. the case's *dictum* or *obiter dicta*). That differentiation conditions the correctness of the establishment of similarity between the precedential case and the case in question. Legal education based on the case method requires access to precedential rulings. Institutional and technological accessibility has been transforming deeply throughout the centuries. Access to the elite group of judges has required special intellectual predispositions and the skill to apply a dynamically growing body of court rulings. The implementation of electronic forms of recording and dissemination of rulings over the recent decades has radically improved the accessibility of ruling databases. It has also made it far easier to look for precedential rulings or cases for both judges and lawyers. At the same time, this has led to weakening of the previously existing intellectual hurdles hampering access to legal professions and to a dynamic increase in the number of professionally active lawyers across many Anglo-Saxon countries. However, despite all these changes the case method has remained the cornerstone of legal education.

5 Conclusions

The fundamental conclusion is as follows: both analogy and precedential reasoning are based on the discovery of similarities between the compared objects. However, in the case of statutory analogy the comparison is between the contents of the particular norms which form the hypothesis (or the so-called scope of norming). If precedent is applied, the compared objects are the states of things (circumstances) described in the precedential court ruling and in the case being decided in court. That significant difference between the objects of comparison in statutory legal cultures and in the precedent legal cultures leads to the conclusion that a direct transfer of precedential reasoning to statutory legal orders (i.e. with consideration of the specificity of the compared objects and the formally binding power of the precedential rulings) does not seem possible. It must be noted at this point that legislators in statutory legal orders sometimes introduce *sui generis* formal binding of courts by the obligation to interpret the content of provision in a way that clearly refers to some relevant content of other provisions to which the first provision refers. However, there always remains the difference between the statutory culture and the Anglo-Saxon legal culture, i.e. *what* is compared.

Another difference is the binding character of precedent-based rulings which is founded on *stare decisis* principle. The rule is an inherent element of legal practice in Anglo-Saxon legal orders. Precedent-based rulings form the content of the legal order as a "living" organism which shapes the behaviours of legal entities and defines the consequences of their behaviours. By using precedential reasonings, courts co-create the legal order and correct the statutory solutions which are not aligned with the constitutional legal order. In statutory legal orders, the rule of *stare decisis* does not exist. In statutory legal orders the fundamental assumption is the division of legislation and executions, which leads to the recognition of the fact that courts do not have the authority to complement (or modify) or correct statutory legal decisions in a way that could supply binding examples and complement the lawmaker's activities.

Regardless of the differences indicated above, there is one crucial shared feature between the two types of reasoning referred to in the title of this article. They have the same function in their respective legal orders and shape the state of relative homogeneity as regards legal decisions made by courts in similar cases (relative uniformity of adjudication). The uniformity is relative as in statutory legal orders the durability of rulings depends on the decisions made by legislators; changes in legal provisions lead to changes in the consequences of *per analogiam legis* reasoning, while in Anglo-Saxon legal orders the durability of precedential rulings is conditioned by the configuration of significant circumstances (holding), and these circumstances change to much the changes in social reality and public morality. It must be underlined, however, that in precedential legal orders precedential reasonings constitute the basic instrument of achieving a state of legal uniformity, while *analogia legis* is only applied in the sources of statutory law and, consequently, is only of subsidiary importance in the other legal order. In statutory legal orders, *analogia legis* is one of the fundamental topos for legal argumentation and constitutes an important element of striving to uniformity of legal decisions in similar cases. However, *analogia legis* is an intellectual instrument which has no binding force, contrary to the binding force of precedent in Anglo-Saxon legal orders.

Per analogiam legis reasoning combined with the control of court decisions across the instances must be treated as the fundamental instruments which facilitate the achievement of relative uniformity of rulings, based on seeking a common *ratio legis* in the decisions concerning the same or similar cases. It remains open for discussion whether such instruments are effective enough or sufficient to ensure the relative uniformity. I can conclude that the essence of analogy as a comparison of two objects also includes precedential reasonings. *Per analogiam legis* is therefore the basis of precedential reasoning. However, there are significant differences between the compared objects (in analogy the objects are provisions or norms, and in precedential reasoning – factual states), which is why the modes of comparison of such objects are not the same. This pertains also to different assumptions and claims of the European doctrine of interpretation of law compared against the Anglo-Saxon doctrine of precedent. Despite the discrepancies, however, there is a fundamental similarity between the functions of *precedential* reasoning in common law cultures and *per analogiam* reasoning in statutory law cultures. Among legal professionals in continental Europe, the ability (and the ability to recognize the need) to refer to rulings issued by higher courts in similar cases is treated as a sign of judge's professional conduct. However, such reasoning cannot lead to the conclusion that lower courts are formally bound by rulings of higher courts with the exception of the first instance which can be subject to an appeal – if the lawmaker has not intervened to grant courts the authority to create decision-making rules for a particular type of cases.

However, if the constitutional status doctrinal model of the judiciary were changed (in particular regarding common courts) and if courts were granted social legitimacy and competencies to independently look for moral justifications of court decisions, it would be possible to implement a limited reception of the Anglo-Saxon construct of precedent with its inherent rule of *stare decisis* into statutory legal orders. It seems, therefore that a reasonable and compromise formula of precedent in statutory legal orders could be applied in situations where the court discovered a lack of statutory regulation for the case in question and at the same time, recognized a clear and obvious social need to resolve the case in a way that ensured alignment with the social perception of justness/fairness and justice. Such a formula, however, would need to allow for the possibility to control such individual and concrete court decisions by the constitutional legal order, as it is in Anglo-Saxon legal orders. This, in turn, would require further changes in the model of control of the constitutionality of law.

Part Two: Judicial Practice

Ewa Skrzydło-Tefelska

The Precedent in Jurisprudence of the Court of Justice of the European Union (CJEU) – Selected Judgments on Trademarks

Abstract: The article discusses the role of the CJEU and its case law in the structures of the European Union. The CJEU is the only institution authorized to interpret the EU law. By interpretation of the law the Court goes beyond the content of the written legal acts and through its judgments creates its own rules of law which are ranked very high in the system of sources of law of the EU. However, it is difficult to answer the question if the judgment of this Court might be considered as the precedent in the meaning existing in the common law systems. Advocate General Trstenjak expressed the view that the concept of precedent is absent in the system of the EU law. This is due to the fact that European Communities at the first stage were created by the states belonging to the continental system of law. In view of AG Trstenjak, the judgment of the CJEU is not a precedent since if we adopt a different standpoint a deviation from the opinion expressed by the Court in its preliminary ruling interpreting the Treaties would require their revision. The opinion of AG was confirmed by the up to date case law of the CJEU. This conclusion is not confirmed by the recent judgments of the CJEU in trademark matters. In the analysed verdicts the Court quashed appealed judgments of the General Court (GC) on the grounds that the GC did not follow the earlier judgments of the Court rendered in similar matters. The Court assumed that by deviating from former judgments of the Court in similar matters the GC breached the law. In both analysed verdicts, the Court ruled that the GC breached the law by not ruling in line with the earlier judgments of the Court and not because of breach of provisions of the Regulation 207/2009.

Keywords: precedent, trademark, reputation, consumers, functionality

1 Introductory Remarks

CJEU is one of the oldest institutions of the European Union (EU). It was created in 1951 on virtue of the Treaty of European Steal and Coal Community. Almost each consecutive reform of the institutions of the EU affected the Court of Justice and the reforms were not always going into the same direction. As of December 1, 2009 when the treaty of Lisbon entered into force the Court of Justice is composed of thc Court of Justice and the General Court (former Court of I Instance). Currently the Court of Justice of the EU is a uniform judicial institution, acting on behalf of the European Union in the interest of assuring enforcement of the

EU law and providing for uniform interpretation of this law in the procedure of preliminary rulings[1].

Contrary to other international judicial institutions the competence of the CJEU is obligatory and supranational. The member states may be summoned before the CJEU even against their will and they do not need to consent to its competence. Such consent is presumably given by the fact of accession to the EU.

Moreover, the member states can't use other international judicial institutions to resolve the matters which are submitted to the jurisprudence of the CJEU. These matters are permanently excluded from the competence of other judicial institutions both national and international. Judgments of the CJEU are binding for member states and are directly enforceable in these states.

Taking into account the specific role played by the CJEU in the structures of the European integration, and especially its exclusive competence to interpret the EU law it might be assumed that CJEU is a court of precedent. The importance of this particular function of the Court is due to the fact that the language of the Treaties as international agreements is very general and to the great extent abstract.

The composition of the panel of judges within the CJEU is constantly changing. It is composed of judges originating from 28 member states. They are holding their position for 6 years with possibility to be re-elected. Half of the number of judges is replaced every 3 years. These constant changes in the composition of adjudicating panels are influencing the line of jurisprudence regarding various matters falling into the Court competence.

CJEU is rendering judgements, decisions and opinions on compliance of the new international agreements concluded by the EU with the EU law. Judgement of the Court of Justice is in principle final and binding as of the day of its announcement. From that day the judgement is enforceable.

Judgement of the General Court can be appealed to the Court. Appeal may be filed by the party, member states acting as intervening party and EU institutions within two months from its receipt. The appeal has to be limited to the points of law. By accepting the appeal, the Court quashes the judgement and gives its own ruling or sends the matter to the General Court for the second ruling.

---

1 More on procedure of preliminary rulings in: S. Biernat, *Współpraca sądów państw członkowskich z ETS w ramach procedury pytań prawnych*, [w:] *Prawo Unii Europejskiej. Zagadnienia systemowe, prawo materialne i polityki*, ed. J. Barcz, 3rd ed., Warszawa 2006, p. 381 et seq.; M. Szpunar, [w:] *Traktat o funkcjonowaniu Unii Europejskiej. Komentarz*, ed. A. Wróbel, Warszawa 2013.

Taking into account the specific role played by the CJEU in the system of European Integration, and especially the fact that the CJEU gives the binding interpretation of the EU law it might be assumed that it is a court of precedent. By interpretation of the EU law the CJEU is in its specific way going beyond the content of the written legal acts and creates its own rules of law. It can be assumed that the activity of the CJEU related to its function of the court has in a certain way a lawmaking character. Principles of law created by the Court are ranked very high in the system of sources of law of the EU since they are based on the EU law, international law and also on the common principles which may be extracted from the national legal systems of member states. The important task is to establish if the judgements of the Court can be considered as binding rules to the extent that the breach of these rules constitutes grounds for appeal against the verdicts rendered by the court of lower instance. It is the question about the role of precedent in the case law of the CJEU.

2 CJEU as a Court of Precedent

The most important question to answer is what is the meaning of the word "precedent". In the common language the precedent is a decision that for the first time resolves a certain problem[2]. It is important to underline that such a decision may serve as a model to be followed in the future when resolving similar legal issues. The concept of precedent is referring to the Latin word *praecedere*, which means *to* precede or overtake[3]. The concept of precedent has been established in a stable way in the tradition of common law. In the English law this term – understood in a narrow way – means *stare decisis*, in other words it is the part of the former judgement (especially of the courts of the highest instance), which has to be taken into account by the judges giving their rulings in similar cases[4]. In the broader sense the precedent should be understood as a line of jurisprudence elaborated in the judgements of the courts of the highest instance, which must be followed by all the courts adjudicating in similar cases[5].

Taking into account that CJEU is rendering its preliminary ruling when answering the question asked by the national court, it is important to establish

---

2 M. Stępień, *Precedens w orzecznictwie ETS*, "Acta Universitatis Wratislaviensis" 2005, no. 2724, Przegląd Prawa i Administracji, p. 241.

3 More on this in K. Scheuring, *Precedens w orzecznictwie Trybunału Sprawiedliwości Unii Europejskiej*, Warszawa 2010, p. 25 et seq.

4 Ibidem, p. 33.

5 Ibidem, p. 32.

if and to what extent this preliminary ruling is binding for the courts in the other member states adjudicating in similar matters. If such preliminary ruling were binding for the national courts in such sense that deviation from this ruling would result in the legal risk of having such latter verdict overruled by the court of appeal, it could be considered the precedent "de jure". In turn if deviation from the former preliminary ruling does not trigger the risk of the successful appeal based on the error as to the law we would be facing the precedent "de facto".

In the Anglo-Saxon legal system, the norm established by the precedent is binding as a rule and its violation constitutes a breach of law to the same extent as an infringement of legal acts, equally laws and executive acts. It should be noted that the question about the role of precedent in the system of EU courts is valid not only in relations to preliminary rulings, but also in relations to the remaining judgements and decisions rendered by the CJEU.

By giving an answer to the question whether the CJEU is a court of precedent we are addressing the problem if Tribunal's judgements are precedents existing in common law system. This problem has been debated in the legal writings and also in the opinions of advocates general[6]. The problem of the binding force of the earlier judgement of the CJEU may be discussed from various perspectives: the horizontal relationship between the earlier judgement of the Court and the younger judgement issued by the same Court in the similar matter; the vertical relationship between the verdict of the General Court and the earlier judgements of the Court of Justice rendered in the similar matter, and finally – the problem of the binding force of preliminary rulings of the Court for the courts in the member states. CJEU very often refers to its earlier judgements in its current verdicts, but it does not explain for what reason. In most of the judgements it quotes the whole parts of its earlier verdicts. Tribunal evoques its earlier judgements even in cases where for any reason it does not share the view expressed by the panel of judges in the earlier judgement because it may not be applied in the current case. In turn, the predominant position expressed in the legal writings may be summarized as the view that the binding force of the earlier

6 R. Skubisz, E. Skrzydło-Tefelska, *Związanie sądu krajowego wyrokiem Europejskiego Trybunału Sprawiedliwości WE, wydanym na podstawie art. 234 TWE*, [w:] *Prawne problemy członkostwa Polski w Unii Europejskiej*, ed. L. Leszczyński, Lublin 2005, pp. 61–72; M. Szpunar, *Procedura prejudycjalna z perspektywy unormowań kodeksu postępowania cywilnego oraz prawa o postępowaniu przed sądami administracyjnymi*, [w:] *Pytanie prejudycjalne w orzecznictwie ETS. Funkcjonowanie procedury prejudycjalnej w Polsce*, ed. C. Mik, Toruń 2006, p. 185 et seq.

judgement is conditional upon the fact if the national court actually asks for the new preliminary ruling in a similar matter[7].

In the opinion given on March 28, 2007 advocate general Verica Trstenjak expressed her view on the problem if deviation by the Court of Ist Instance from the line of jurisprudence elaborated earlier by the Court may be raised as the only grounds in the appeal[8]. The advocate general did not adopt this standpoint[9]. The advocate general expressed the view that the earlier judgement of the CJEU does not oblige the next panels of judges to give the same interpretation of the EU law. Such opinion is based on the interpretation of art. 220 TWE (currently art. 19 al. 1 of the TUE). This provision reads that EU courts are assuring respect of law in interpretation and application of the Treaty. The advocate general Trstenjak expressed the opinion that this provision is saying that courts of the EU are submitted only to the law. The concept of "law" as applied in this provision, comprises all the codified and non-codified rules of the EU law. The judgements of the courts are not the "law". Despite the efforts of the courts aimed at creating the coherent system, the general structure of the EU law does not allow to assume that Luxembourg courts are bound by their former jurisprudence. The main argument speaking in favour of such conclusion in the opinion of advocate Trstenjak is that the Communities were at the first stage created by the states belonging to the Continental system of civil law. This explains the fact that the precedent is absent in the system of the EU law. Different standpoint would lead – in the view of advocate general – to the situation where deviation from the previous line of jurisprudence in interpretation of the Treaties by the Court would require their revision. Consequently, it is necessary to give the CJEU the chance to modify the previously elaborated line in jurisprudence and create the new solution by solely interpreting the provisions of the EU law in a different way.

The standpoint expressed by advocate general Trstenjak was confirmed by the up-to-date practice of the CJEU. In the need of deviation from the earlier line adopted in interpretation of the provisions of the EU, the Court did not explain the reason for such modification and did not feel bound by its previous preliminary judgements. It was the reason why the jurisprudence of the Luxembourg courts was perceived as autonomous and was obviously different from the practice of common law courts in the member states.

7 Consult K. Scheuring, op. cit. and the literature quoted there.

8 Opinion of the advocate general Verica Trstenjak rendered in the case C-331/05 P, ECLI: EU:C:2007:191.

9 Ibidem, p. 84.

The above standpoint was true not only for the practice of the Court, but also for the General Court. The General Court did not feel bound by its earlier judgements, even those which were confirmed in the instance of appeal by the Court of Justice. Finally, this view was confirmed also in legal writings[10].

The General Court does not feel bound by the judgements rendered by the Court. However, if the appeal is filed and the Court of Justice admits such appeal, it quashes the judgement of the General Court referring to its previous jurisprudence relecting the established line and gives its ruling as to the merits.

More specific question concerns the binding force of preliminary rulings of the CJEU for the national courts. It is undoubtedly that the national court which asked the question on virtue of art. 267 of the Treaty on Functioning of the EU is bound by the preliminary ruling answering the preliminary question. When rendering the judgement on mertis of the case pending in front of the national court it must follow the guidance given to it in the preliminary ruling.

When analysing the binding force of the preliminary ruling for national courts the legal writings distinguished the three categories of national courts which are bound by the preliminary ruling of the Court[11]. The first category comprises all the national courts of higher instance above the court which asked the preliminary question, which have competence to examine the appeal from the verdict of such court. The courts of the first category are bound by the preliminary ruling. The second category of courts which are bound by the preliminary ruling comprises the courts of the same member state which in the later time will be adjudicating in the identical matters where there is need to apply the provisions of the EU law previously interpreted by the Court in the preliminary ruling. The third category of national courts bound by the preliminary ruling comprises the national courts of all instances in all member states which are adjudicating in matters involving the legal problem materially identical to the legal question which was asked by the national court in its preliminary reference. As a justification for such standpoint the reference is made to the rule of the legal certainty and the necessity to assure the uniform interpretation of the EU law[12]. However, it should be noted that the binding force of the preliminary ruling for the national courts described above is not of absolute character. In

10 See among others: A. Arnull, *Owning up to Fallibility. Precedent and the Court of Justice*, "Common Market Law Review" 1993, vol. 30, p. 238; K. Scheuring, op. cit., p. 183.

11 Ibidem, p. 233.

12 More on this: J. Skrzydło, *Doktryna* acte eclairé *w orzecznictwie Trybunału Wspólnoty Europejskiej i sądów krajowych państw członkowskich Unii Europejskiej*, "Studia Prawno-Europejskie" 1998, vol. 2, pp. 143–159; K. Wernicka, *Preliminary ruling of*

accordance with the principle of *acte eclairé* the national court which is of the opinion that the previously given interpretation of the EU law cannot be applied in the current case is authorized to ask the new preliminary question. It will be at the discretion of the CJEU to decide if in this new preliminary ruling it gives a different interpretation of the same provision of the EU law. The national court does not have its own competence to give different interpretation of this provision of the EU law.

3 Selected Judgements of the CJEU Related to Trademarks Comprising Precedential Rules Established by the Court

It would be difficult to overestimate the role of the CJEU in establishing principles governing protection of renowned trademarks. The beginning of the process of harmonization of trademark law in the EU started in 1988 with Directive 89/104[13] and ended with issuance by the EU in the last years of the set of legal acts amending Regulation 207/2009 on the EU trademarks[14] (Regulation 2015/2424[15]) and introducing new Directive 2015/2436[16] (which replaced earlier Directive 2008/95[17]). The last legal act which entered into force on 1 October 2017 was new Regulation on EU trademarks 2017/1001[18]. The CJEU played an important role in the establishment of the rules of protection of trademarks in the market of the EU. Elaboration of such system of rules started usually with issuance of the first verdict which established general rule, and this principle was consecutively strengthened and broadened by the following judgements. In some cases, it was linked with the examination of the ruling of the General Court in the instance of

---

the Court of Justice of the European Union concerning unregistered Community designs, "Prace z Prawa Własności Intelektualnej" 2016, iss. 132, pp. 187–198.

13 The first directive of the Council 89/104/EWG of 21.12.1988 aimed at approximation of law of the member states related to trademarks, O.J. EC L no. 40, p. 1 (non-binding).

14 Regulation of the Council (EC) 207/2009 of 26.02.2009 on the EU trademarks, O.J. EU L no, 78, p. 1.

15 Regulation of the EP and the Council of 16.12.2015 amending Regulation of the Council (EC) no. 207/2009 on the Community trademarks, O.J. EU L no. 431, p. 21 as amended.

16 Directive of the EP and the Council of 16.12.2015 aimed at harmonization of laws of member states related to trademarks, O.J. EU L no. 336, p. 1 as amended.

17 Directive of the EP and the Council of 22.10.2008 aimed at harmonization of laws of member states related to trademarks, O.J. EC L no. 299, p. 25.

18 Regulation of the EP and of the Council (EU) no. 2017/1001 of 14 June 2017, on the trademark of the European Union, ECLI: EU:L:2017:154.

appeal. In such judgements, the Court referred to its earlier case law elaborated during several years.

The verdict of the Court of Justice C-383/12P[19] in the case where the Court quashed the judgement of the General Court in the instance of appeal constitutes the example of such judgement. One of the main grounds for such decision was the fact that the General Court did not follow the established rule of the Court case law. The dispute started before the OHIM (Office for the Harmonization in the Internal market renamed currently as the European Union Intellectual Property Office) and concerned application by Environmental Manufacturing for registration in class 7 of the trademark representing the stylized head of the wolf. Société Elmar Wolf filed opposition against this application relying on its earlier word-graphic trademarks registered for its benefit in France in classes 7 and 8 of the Nice classification. The trademarks of Société Wolf comprised the stylized head of the wolf and words "wolf" and "jardin" in the first case and words "wolf" and "outils" in the second case. Société Elmar Wolf based its objection on art. 8 al. 1 letter b) and art. 8 al. 5 of the Regulation 207/2009. OHIM did not accept the opposition of Société Wolf assuming that there was no risk of confusion among consumers and the objecting party did not provide evidence that registration of the trademark applied for would be detrimental to the reputation of the earlier trademarks and would provide the applicant with undue profits. The Chamber of Appeals of OHIM quashed the decision of the examiner justifying this ruling by the fact that the earlier trademarks enjoyed reputation in the three member states and the earlier and younger trademarks were similar to the extent that the relevant consumers would remark the link existing between the trademarks. Consequently, the younger trademark might dilute the unique image of the earlier trademarks and give the applicant undue profits. Environmental Manufacturing appealed the decision of the Chamber of Appeals of OHIM to the General Court and moved for its invalidation. Among the arguments raised in the appeal, the Environmental Manufacturing argued that in accordance with the earlier judgement of the Court of Justice in the case Intel[20] the fact that the use of the younger trademark is or may be detrimental to the distinctiveness of the earlier trademarks might be proven only by presenting evidence demonstrating change of behaviour of the average consumers of goods for which the earlier trademark is registered.

19 Judgement of 14 November 2013 in the case C-383/12P Environmental Manufacturing v. OHIM and Société Elmar Wolf, ECLI:EU:C:2013:741.

20 Judgement of 27 November 2008 in the case C-252/07 Intel Corporation Inc. v. CPM United Kingdom Ltd., ECLI:EU:C:2008:655.

The General Court referring to the argument of lack of proper evidence confirming the change of behaviour of the relevant consumers ruled that the owner of the earlier trademark has no obligation to demonstrate the factual and continuous infringement of its trademark. In the opinion of the General Court such requirement would oblige the owner of the earlier trademark to prove the actual infringement of its trademark by the registration of the younger trademark. In the opinion of the General Court, the owner of the earlier trademark is obliged to present only the evidence allowing to establish *prima facie* future threat of acting to the detriment of the earlier trademark. In order to establish such threat, the General Court assumed that it would be sufficient to explain the danger through logical deduction based on analysis of similarity of both trademarks taking into account the practices which are characteristic for the given sector of the market and all the relevant circumstances of the given case. The General Court stressed that the owner of the earlier trademark should not be required to demonstrate the influence of the younger trademark on the market behaviour of the average consumers of the goods of the earlier trademark. The General Court indicated that neither art. 8 al. 5 of the Regulation 207/2008 nor the verdict in the Intel case comprised such condition to be met in order to prove the infringement.

In turn the Court of Justice while examining the appeal from the judgement of the General Court quashed the appealed verdict referring to its judgement in the case Intel and rendered its decision in the matter of validity of the earlier decisions of OHIM. Especially the Court underlined that – contrary to the stand point presented by the General Court – demonstration that the use of the younger trademark is detrimental to the distinctiveness of the older trademark (dilution) requires proving change of market behaviour of the relevant consumers of goods of the earlier trademarks, being consequence of the use of the younger trademark or material probability that such change of consumers behaviour will take place in the future. By making this argument the Court pointed specifically at points 77 and 81 of the justification of the judgement in the case Intel and point 6 of this verdict. The Court did not leave open the question how the detriment to the distinctiveness of the trademark may be proven. Referring to the lack of such strict requirement in the art. 8 al. 5 of the Regulation and the case law of the CJEU, the Court ruled that logical deduction as the measure to prove the probability of infringement cannot be based on the mere expectations of market behaviours of relevant consumers but should be based on analysis of rules of probability taking into account the specific sector of the market and other circumstances of the given case. More liberal rules adopted in providing proof of infringement would, in the Court opinion, give the owner of the earlier trademark too broad protection what would be detrimental to the competition on the market. However, the Court did not give any more precise guidance as to how the changement of the market behaviour of the average consumers should be proven.

What is important in the judgement of the Court of Justice in the case C-328/12P Environmental Manufacturing is that the Court assumed that the General Court breached the law by omitting to find out if the condition listed in Intel case was met. This standpoint is in contradiction to the opinion expressed by advocate general Trstenjak in her opinion that the judgements of the Court are not the law. As such the opinion expressed by the Court in this judgement might be perceived as the beginning of the new discussion on the role of precedent in the jurisprudence of the CJEU. This is even more true due to the fact that the new Regulation 1001/2017 does not provide for the standard which should be observed in provision of evidence of infringement.

The following important judgement rendered by the Court of Justice in the appeal proceedings is the judgement in the case C-30/15P Simba Toys GmbH & Co. v. KG/EUIPO[21]. The judgement was issued in the proceedings of appeal against judgement of the General Court T-450/09 Simba Toys GmbH & Co. v. OHIM.[22] The General Court dismissed the appeal against decision of the OHIM refusing to invalidate the trademark right to trademark held by Seven Towns, the British company. The three-dimensional trademark being subject to the dispute represents the cubic form with the walls of the grid structure known as the Rubik's cube. It was registered in the class 28 of the Nice classification for the goods: three-dimensional puzzles. The motion for invalidation of this registration was brought by Simba Toys. The OHIM Division of Invalidation dismissed this motion and the Chamber of Appeals upheld this decision. Simba Toys filed the appeal against this decision to the General Court. Among the provisions indicated as the grounds for the appeal the most important is art. 7 al. 1 letter e) pkt. (ii) of the Regulation 207/2009. This provision provides for the absolute ground of refusal which constitutes the fact that the trademark comprises the form of the good which is necessary to obtain certain technical result. Simba Toys submits that the General Court when making its decision did not take into account that the grid structure of the cubic walls is describing the technical effect. Simba Toys submitted that the General Court did not take into

21 Judgement of 10 November 2016 in the case C-30/15P Simba Toys GmbH & Co. v. KG/ EUIPO, ECLI:EU:C:2016:849.

22 Judgement of 25 November 2014 in the case T-450/09 Simba Toys GmbH & Co. v. OHIM, ECLI:EU:T:2014:983.

account the public interest consisting in the fact that the disputed registration would give its owner the monopoly over the three dimensional puzzles with the rotating capacities.[23] Discussing the argument brought by the OHIM Chamber of Appeals that the technical features of the trademark are not resulting directly from the presentation of the trademark Simba Toys submitted that in the earlier judgements recalled by the Chamber of Appeals namely: Phillips C-299/99[24] and Lego Juris/OHIM (red brick Lego) T-270/06[25] the technical functions of the trademarks which were the reason for invalidation of trademarks did not result directly from the mode of presentation of the disputed trademarks.

When quashing the appealed verdict of the General Court the Court of Justice raised the argument that the aim of the appealing party is to question the criteria and elements resulting from the case law of the Court in order to evaluate the functional character of the disputed mark in the meaning of art. 7 al. 1 letter e) point (ii) of the Regulation 40/94 (currently 1001/2017). The trademark law in turn is aimed at making it impossible for one entrepreneur to obtain monopoly over the technical solutions or useful features of the given goods[26].

The Court of Justice ruled, following the opinion of advocate general M. Szpunar[27], that the stand point expressed by the General Court is the breach of law. The General Court dismissed the arguments of Simba Toys addressing the functionality of the trademark referring to the rotating capacities of the individual elements of the cube reflected by the grid structure of the cubic walls. The General Court ruled that this argument is based on the knowledge which does not result from the sole presentation of the trademark applied for. In other words, the General Court assumed that the presence of grids on the cubic walls does not determine the rotating character of its elements. The mechanism of the rotation may be hidden inside the shape submitted for protection. The General Court assumed that taking into account the elements of the trademark which are

23 This verdict was criticised in the lega writings, see: G.N. Hasselblatt, *Commentary to art. 7 of the Regulation 207/2009*, [in:] *Community Trademark Regulation. A Commentary*, ed. idem, Munich 2015, pp. 118–119.

24 Judgement of 18 June 2002 in the case C-299/99. ECLI:EU:C:2002:377.

25 Judgement of 12 November 2008, in the case T-270/06 Lego Juris/OHIM v. Mega Brands, ECLI:EU:T:2008:483.

26 Judgement of 14 September 2010 in the case C-48/09 Lego Juris v. OHIM, ECLI:EU:C:2010:516, pkt. 68, judgement of 6 March 2014, PI-Design and others v. Yoshida Metal Industry, joined cases C-337/12P to C-340/12P, ECLI:EU:C:2014:129.

27 Opinion of advocate general M. Szpunar of 25 May 2017 in the case C-30/15 Simba Toys Co. & KG v. EUIPO.

not visible when assessing the functionality of the trademark would be in contradiction to the directive that such evaluation should be based only on objective elements and should take into account only the shape of the trademark as it was presented in the application for registration. Consequently, the General Court expressed the opinion that the existence of the grid structure of the cubic walls may not be decisive to determine the technical function of the trademark in question.

In turn the Court of Justice in accordance with the opinion of the advocate general adopted a standpoint that evaluation of the basic properties of the shape of the trademark should be made in light of the technical function of the good in question. The Court relied in this statement on the judgement in the case C-48/09 Lego Juris. Consequently, since in this particular case the shape of the good is not abstract but represents the rotating puzzle the function of rotation should have been taken into account when assessing functionality of the shape. The Court referred as well to the case C-337/12P Pi-Design where it was stated that assessment of the trademark functionality must be made based on detailed examination including graphic representation of the trademark, its potential description and all other relevant elements useful for proper identification of basic features of the trademark. Finally the Court quashed the verdict of the General Court and declared invalid the decision of the OHIM Chamber of Appeals.

It is important to stress that the previous case law of the Court was the point of depart for the assessment of the appealed judgment rendered in Simba Toys case. Art. 7 al. 1 letter e) point (ii) of the Regulation 207/2009 does not provide guidelines how to assess functionality of the trademark. The assessment was based on the earlier case law taking into account the features which were not directly listed in the relevant provision. The grounds of the appeal was the case law of the Court and not the written provision of the Regulation.

4 Conclusions

The judgements discussed above provide arguments to conclude that the line of jurisprudence elaborated by the CJEU is the important element deciding on proper application of the EU law. Especially in the instance of appeal the Court refers to its previous judgements not only as autoreference or illustration of the decision but as the real basis for the judgement. In both cases the fact that the General Court did not give the ruling in accordance with the former case law of the Court of Justice in similar matters was the reason why the appeal turned out to be successful.

Bartosz Liżewski

Few Remarks about the Precedent Qualification of the ECHR Decision

Abstract: The article is a theoretical reflection on the possibility of classifying a judgment of the European Court of Human Rights (ECHR) as a precedent judgment. It is about understanding of the "precedent" term that has been shaped in the continental legal culture. Theoretical considerations on the precedent character of judgments of the Strasbourg Court are justified by their legal character. On a normative level, these judgments create standards, which determine the way of understanding human rights. It can therefore be concluded that the Court has the power to "create" norms (or the way to understand the norms), because it is not possible to understand human rights without those standards. The binding force of ECHR judgements covers two spheres. The first is the binding force of the judgments of the Court for subsequent judgments of this court in similar causes. The second area is the binding force of the Court's judgments for national courts.

Keywords: precedent, continental legal culture, binding force of judgment, source of law

1 Introductory Remarks

The basis for these deliberations consists of the thesis that the decision of the European Court of Human Rights (ECHR or the Court) does not create a precedent in the sense given to that term in common law. However, such a distinction is assigned to ECHR decisions, doubtlessly, in the sense given to the term "precedent" in the culture of continental law. When we read about the precedent-creating potential of decisions made by international courts of human rights in the professional literature[1], about the need to perceive ECHR decisions as precedent judgments, or about the current contents of the Strasburg precedents[2] it seems that their authors try to highlight, in particular, the importance of the Court's decision that decisively goes beyond the dimension of a settlement of *inter partes*. If the wording such as "the precedent nature of the judgment" or "the scope of the precedent nature of the judgment" is used I believe that it is not an attempt at the adaptation of the term designating a specific institution of the

1 M. Balcerzak, *Precedens w prawie międzynarodowym praw człowieka – zagadnienia wybrane*, [in:] *Prawa człowieka w XXI wieku. Wyzwania dla ochrony prawnej*, ed. C. Mik, Toruń 2005, p. 68.

2 Ibidem, nb 20, p. 362.

common law system to the continental system. However, it signifies the need to articulate such a meaning of the judgment that decisively goes beyond its understanding as an individually specific decision to apply the law, which is traditional in the continental legal culture. Even the review of suggested Polish definitions demonstrates a broad meaning of the "precedent" as a term used in the statutory law culture. According to J. Wróblewski, a precedent is each judicial decision *de iure* or *de facto* influencing the making of other decisions[3]. In this dichotomously stated influence, the aspect of the actual impact particularly defines the area for analyses space of the precedential nature of judgments issued in legal systems that do not know the *stare decisis* principle. We can find the essence of that influence in the words of L. Morawski who states, as regards that influence, that it is not about the entire decision of the court but rather about the general standard contained in the sentence or statement of reasons, which constitutes the basis for the settlement of similar cases in the future[4]. This perspective combines the component of the judicial legislation in the form of the court modelling a general standard, i.e. a normative novelty with the simultaneous indication of the function of that standard as a basis for other decisions. However, it is not conclusive whether the standard is supposed to be only a legal basis or whether it can also have an actual impact. The culmination of these general definition formulas can be found in the statement made by M. Zirk-Sadowski who concludes that "...the term »precedent« used in our language has its specific meaning resulting from our law culture. The term exists with different meanings depending not only on the law system where it appears but also depending on a varying theoretical justification of such a decision"[5]. It would be fair to state that, due to the lack of a legal formula of being bound with a judgment, the term "precedent" has a very high meaning potential, especially with regard to a non-Anglo-Saxon systems of law.

The above-mentioned statements also remain current, referring to the specificity of ECHR decisions. The Court stressed many times that it was not bound with its previous decisions. However, it also argued that it adhered to its previous decisions in the judgment process, i.e. "follows and applies its previous

3 J. Wróblewski, *Wartości a decyzja sądowa*, Wrocław 1973, p. 133.

4 L. Morawski, *Czy precedens powinien być źródłem prawa*, [in:] *W kręgu problematyki władzy, państwa i prawa. Księga jubileuszowa w 70-lecie urodzin profesora Henryka Groszyka*, eds. A. Korobowicz, A. Korybski, M. Kuryłowicz, J. Malarczyk, A. Pieniążek, Lublin 1996, p. 187.

5 M. Zirk-Sadowski, *Precedens a tzw. decyzja prawotwórcza*, "Państwo i Prawo" 1980, no. 6, p. 70.

precedents" in the interest of the certainty of the law and the systematic development of the convention case law[6]. It means that the ECHR consciously rejects the construction of a binding precedent in the context of its judgment activity but does not waive the formula of a non-binding precedent.

2 Justification of the ECHR Legislative Competence

The content of the ECHR judgment is commonly characterized in the professional literature with the use of the term "ECHR sentencing standard". Authors writing about specific rights under the European Convention on Human Rights[7] (ECHR or the Convention) give their works titles in which they combine the name of a specific right, e.g. the right to free elections, with the wording: "in the light of standards of the European Court of Human Rights". The judgment aspect is also often combined with standards, e.g. "The impact of judgments of the European Court of Human Rights on standards of protection of the right to...". It is rather axiomatic that protection standards are conditioned on the combination of material provisions of the Convention and ECHR judgments. Therefore, it is not surprising that "...the Convention itself, through its contents, as well as the Court and its judgments play a huge role in the modelling of European standards of human rights..."[8]. The wording of the standard of human rights protection as a product of the legislative judgment activities of the ECHR became so obvious and commonly used that, in principle, it results in its intuitive understanding.

The Court is currently[9] the only agency making decisions concerning violations of the Convention, and competent to examine all cases regarding the interpretation and application of the Convention, pursuant to art. 34 of the Convention. The aspect of the interpretation competence is particularly important here.

---

6 Judgment in the case of Cossey against the United Kingdom of 27 September 1990, complaint no. 10843/84, § 35.

7 Convention for the Protection of Human Rights and Fundamental Freedoms opened for signature in Rome on 4 November 1950. It came into force for Poland on 19 January 1993 (Dz.U. 1993, no. 61, item 284).

8 G. Szyburska-Walczak, *Oddziaływanie europejskiej Konwencji o ochronie praw człowieka i podstawowych wolności na internalizację standardów w dziedzinie demokracji i praw człowieka*, [in:] *Wpływ standardów międzynarodowych na rozwój demokracji i ochronę praw człowieka*, ed. J. Jaskiernia, Warszawa 2013, p. 14.

9 Before the enactment of the Protocol 11 of 11 May 1994, the European Commission of Human Rights was also operating as an agency established to control the obligations under the Convention.

Even its wording in the text of the Convention can by symptomatic of the particularly important nature of the Convention's interpretation, going beyond the traditional understanding of the interpretation done by courts in the law application process. Today, statements such as: "The Convention is a living instrument that should be interpreted in the light of the current conditions", "the interpretation of rights and freedoms under the Convention is supposed to protect and promote ideals and values of the democratic society", "The Court is the creator of human rights protection standards" are undoubtedly axiomatic and do not have to be proven. They belong to the canon of statements regarding the interpretation of the Convention. In essence, the legislative nature of the interpretation of the Convention fully justifies the correlation between the way the material provisions of the Convention are worded and their content and the interpretation competence of the Court established to integrate the European legal area of human rights.

The specificity of material provisions of the Convention is expressed in their wording. It is possible to conclude that Chapter 1, with a catalogue of human rights, is a "collection of normative postulates and slogans". Material regulations of the Convention have not only remained unchanged since its establishment (they have not been novelized or derogated) but are also very general. However, their conciseness or succinctness is characteristic for the way that human rights are regulated in international law. They require creative development and detailing. In fact, this is the reason why their understanding is determined by the ECHR that thus creates human rights protection standards in a legislative manner and the long-term judgment practice of the Court leaves no doubt regarding the legislative nature of such standards. The Court creates the law in a secondary manner, i.e. on the basis of regulations of the Convention expressing human rights and freedoms. In principle, it lacks the power to construct the meaning of rights not expressed in the Convention. Without the ECHR judgment standards, regulations of the Convention would have been normatively handicapped.

3 Building Formula in a Normative Novelty Judgment

The specific nature of the Convention's general regulations is the reason why sentencing standards involve the formulation of a normative novelty by the ECHR. This nature has its foundation in the structure of the right protected by the Convention. A normative novelty cannot by synonymized with a general standard, which is a definition of a right, freedom or ban formulated in the Convention. The Court, in its judgment process, refers to definitions formulated in international agreements on issues to which the Convention devotes only one article. It is so, e.g. in the case of the ban on slavery from art. 4[10]. It means that the establishment of a protection standard is not limited only to the definition aspect but also covers a range of detailed aspects of the conventionally guaranteed right. They include: the determination of the scope of a right or freedom as regards the parties concerned and the subject matter[11] and, in the case of bans, the formulation of premises allowing for the differentiation and qualification of prohibited activities, if multiple bans are mentioned in a single regulation of the Convention (e.g. art. 3 of the Convention)[12]. The principle of the decision resulting from a judgment (i.e. normative novelty) does not create a disposition of the standard but rather its fragment only. A single judgment of the Court related to a specific right sometimes articulates a few detailed aspects of the same protection standard while in other ones, the ECHR refers to a few protection standards. It means that building a sentencing standard of the protection is based on the formulation of fragmentary behavior patterns that are modelled according to a context of a specific aspect of a right, freedom or ban. It is only their collection frequently consisting of a few, a dozen or even a few dozen (e.g. regarding the freedom of speech) "parts of the protection standard" that comprises the whole complex standard. This is why the ECHR precedent concept should be understood as a thesis contained in a decision, modelling a fragment of the standard of protection the Court invokes when making a decision in another case. For sure, it is not the understanding of a precedent adopted in the common law.

---

10 M.A. Nowicki, *Wokół Konwencji Europejskiej. Komentarz do Europejskiej Konwencji Praw Człowieka*, 6th ed., Warszawa 2013, p. 442.

11 While analysing the freedom of speech, I.C. Kamiński (*Swoboda wypowiedzi w orzeczeniach Europejskiego Trybunału Praw Człowieka w Strasburgu*, 2nd ed., Kraków 2003, p. 660) distinguishes, among other things, the freedom of speech in a political debate in the context of the protection of public figures and private individuals, freedom of speech vs. preservation of the authority and impartiality of the system of justice and countering the commission of an offence, freedom of speech in the context of the protection of confidential messages, freedom of artistic speech, freedom of speech in connection with the protection of morality and religion, freedom of commercial speech, freedom of speech from the public service employment area, freedom of speech in the army and in the police as well as the freedom of speech in the context of the broadcasting activity, rights to receive the information and the protection of journalistic sources of information.

12 Art. 3 of the Convention provides: "No one shall be subjected to torture or to inhumane or degrading treatment or punishment".

4 Binding Power of an ECHR Judgment

Two conditions have to be met in order to classify a judgment as a *de iure* binding precedent. The first condition is the general standard or the normative novelty resulting from the legislative activity of the court, while the second condition consists of the consideration that such a decision binds other courts in similar cases, which results from the *stare decisis* principle. Such a judgment is a source of the law. Such a distinction cannot be assigned to ECHR judgments from the formal perspective. As E. Łętowska writes: "The establishment of human rights infringement by the state has a specific and situational dimension: it applies only to that infringement, that state and that specific victim"[13]. This statement is closely related to the obligation articulated in art. 46 section 2 of the Convention for the state to comply with final judgments of the Court in all cases where the state is a party. Such wording limits the binding power of the judgment exclusively to the effectiveness between the parties (*inter partes*). And, even though the binding effect of a judgment is subjectively limited, it is justified to make an attempt at offering arguments enabling the qualification of that judgment as a source of the law, a carrier of standards of the protection of human rights whose violation causes specific consequences. Three arguments seem particularly important. The first one is related to the unique nature of the Convention and the Court judgments based on it. H. Klebes classifies these two sources as the "constitutional block" of the Council of Europe, whose standards have the nature of *ius cogens* and, therefore, binds all member states. However, the author of that thesis states clearly in the context of ECHR judgments that not all sentencing standards can acquire the status of mandatory ones[14]. One has to agree with the presented opinion and also to express the belief that it is difficult to unambiguously determine the binding effect of ECHR judgments in the common effectiveness area. The opinion established in the doctrine states that the Convention combined with the case law mechanism of the development and determination of specific standards of human rights protection comprise communicating vessels. Such a connection is necessary and inseparable. Therefore, as the Convention is a source of the law in force, the judgments shaping the sentencing standards should also

---

13 E. Łętowska, *Zapewnienie skuteczności orzeczeniom sądów międzynarodowych*, [in:] *Zapewnienie efektywności orzeczeń sądów międzynarodowych w polskim porządku prawnym*, ed. A. Wróbel, Warszawa 2011, p. 45.

14 H. Klebes, *Rola Zgromadzenia Parlamentarnego Rady Europy w upowszechnianiu standardów demokratycznych w Europie*, [in:] *Polska w Radzie Europy. 10 lat członkostwa. Wybrane zagadnienia*, ed. H. Machińska, Warszawa 2002, p. 31.

be classified in the same manner as they determine the understanding of its material regulations. The statement that "...obligations resulting for the states under the Convention are developed and updated in the judgments of the Court and that the state and its agencies are bound with the content of a regulation of the Convention in the meaning assigned to it in the current judgment practice"[15] is current in full.

The second argument refers to the procedural aspect that determines the connection between the violation of protection standards specified in a judgment and consequences for a state resulting from that violation. The source of such a procedure and such consequences is in art. 28. 1 b of the Convention. It constructs the competence a Committee of three judges to admit the permissibility of an individual complaint with the simultaneous issue of a judgment without hearing if a state infringes on the established case law of the Court. It entails a close relationship between the infringement on the established judgment standard and a judgment against a state. If such a decision is made as a result of an infringement of a protection standard that standard has to bind the state. It means that we can examine its binding effect as a source of the law and also in the context of a precedent as the standard is contained in a judgment. An interesting theoretical issue emerges on this occasion as on the one hand, a judgment on an international court is considered an auxiliary source of the international law in the international public law (art. 38. 1 d of the statute of the International Court of Justice) while, on the other hand, the *stare decisis* principle denoting the legal binding effect of a precedent judgment of other courts in similar cases does not apply. However, if an infringement on the established case law of the ECHR by national agencies is the reason for the issue of a judgment by a committee of three judges without a hearing (art. 28. 1 b of the Convention) and judgments of the Court (the ECHR interpretation monopolist) have to be complied with and executed in the national law system (art. 46 clauses 1 and 2 of the Convention) a natural question about the scope of their precedent nature for agencies applying the law in the national system appears.

The third and final argument involves the recognition of the binding effect of judgment standards by states of the Council of Europe, which is necessary to guarantee the projected effectiveness level of the Convention's system. One has to agree with the opinion that, despite the limited binding effect, a national

15 I. Kondak, [in:] L. Garlicki, op. cit., art. 32, nb 9, p. 103.

court cannot ignore the interpretation adopted in the statement of reasons for an ECHR decision irrespectively of the state to which that decision applied[16].

5 The ECHR Sentencing Standard as an Argument Justifying the Decision to Apply the Law

When issuing sentences against a state, the ECHR treats its prior sentences as arguments included in the statement of reasons; however, it happens only if it considers that, due to the nature of the case, the use of the sentencing standard is not only possible but also recommended. Therefore, the case in which the Court issues a sentence and a case already settled have to be identical (or at least relative identical). The reference to a standard in the statement of reasons for the judgment and not in its sentence shows that the judgment is not a source of the law with a legally binding effect. It is a very important argument of a formal nature, in particular, when an attempt is made to perceive an ECHR judgment as a precedent. The fact that the ECHR searches for a proper (identical) judgment in order to refer to its arguments and uses them for the needs of the settlement means that the law created in the protection standard generates a standard that constitutes the legislative development of a provision of the Convention, which is the basis for the decision to apply the law.

The method of referral by the Court to its previous judgments mostly depends on the specificity of the conventionally guaranteed law. In the freedom articles providing for limiting clauses in their contents, the ECHR constructs the statement of reasons by applying the top-down thinking. In this manner, the Court starts from the general specificity of the protected law and, after that, gradually links detailed components of the standard with it reaching that aspect to which the case refers. Such argumentation is contained, e.g. in the award in the case of Błaja News Sp. z o.o. against Poland[17]. The Court starts with the statement that the freedom of speech is one of the most important foundations of the democratic society and basic conditions of its development and self-development of each individual[18]. After that, it tackles the problem of guarantees given to the press[19] as a public supervisor[20] and limits that the press cannot exceed. The issue

---

16 P. Grzegorczyk, *Skutki wyroków Europejskiego Trybunału Praw Człowieka w krajowym porządku prawnym*, "Przegląd Sądowy" 2006, no. 6, p. 15.

17 Judgment in the case of Błaja News Sp. z o.o. against Poland of 26 November 2013, complaint no. 59545/10.

18 Ibidem, § 49.

19 Ibidem, § 50.

20 Ibidem.

of the precision and reliability of expression and its compliance with the rules of the ethics of journalists[21] as well as the issue of the diversification of expression distinguishing the statement of facts and evaluating judgments are also tackled.

In its judgments against a specific state, the ECHR tries to invoke standards (usually their fragments) contained in previous judgments against the same state. Obviously, the statement of reasons also invokes arguments – standards formulated in judgments against other states, which is the proof of their versatility. Standards are created for the European legal system and constitute the law for that area to the extent that is possible and does not go beyond the specificity of local conditions of individual states. If the ECHR invokes a judgment against another state in a Polish case it shall stress clearly that the standard is also applicable to solutions found in the Polish law even if procedures, e.g. lustration proceedings differ somewhat in two different countries (e.g. the equality of arms principle in the case of the access to files).

In each of its judgments, the ECHR invokes protection standards or their fragments established in its previous judgments many times. They are arguments contained in the statement of reasons. The wording: "The Court has been reiterating many times" or "The Court continues to stress"[22] is characteristic. As a rule, it is followed by the citation of the purpose of the regulation and detailed standards with a reference to judgments where they have been formulated or reiterated. The fact that a reference is made in a case to an argument of the prior multiple references to the identically formulated standard or its thesis is a clear suggestion that such a standard is established. It suggests its acceptance in the entire European legal area. One can say that such a standard is indisputable.

When referring to its prior judgments, the Court also indicates their specific § and uses the reference term such as "see" or "see, for example". It is a very frequent practice. Such a method of referral means that the entire thesis covered in the indicated editorial unit applies to the analyzed case[23]. The ECHR sometimes indicates two judgments in which the same standard is contained in one reference[24]. This formula is very often used a few times in the same judgment, which is a sign of both the multi-faceted nature of sentencing standards and of the continuation and consolidation of the Court's own jurisprudence. The "see, among

21 Ibidem.

22 E.g. Judgment in the case of Grabowski against Poland of 30 June 2015, complaint no. 57722/12, § 42.

23 E.g. judgment in the case of Kalicki against Poland of 8 December 2015, complaint no. 46797/08, § 49, 50, 51, 52.

24 Ibidem, § 50.

other things" formula applied by the ECHR is very similar[25]. That wording shows that the standard to which the Court refers by indicating a specific judgment was also invoked in other judgments and, therefore, it is a standard commonly used in the judging practice.

The Court sometimes uses the term *mutatis mutandis* or once the necessary changes have been made[26]. In such a situation, one can talk about an appropriate application of the protection standard. The Court considers it important but takes it into account in the examined case with appropriate modifications resulting from the specificity of the case.

As stressed before, the ECHR is not formally bound with its previous judgments; however, it invokes them and this practice is immanently linked to the judgments of that court without which ECHR judgments would be difficult to imagine. It is deeply ingrained in the model of the law application by the Court in Strasburg. The ECHR creates human rights protection standards but in a manner adequate to the current level of social axiology. The liquidity of their evolution is determined by social changes potentially leading to a modification of standards. A normative novelty is created then, different than the existing one and reflected in the judgments of the Court; it should be taken into account in the national decision-making processes.

In the context of the decision-making level of national courts, it is worth noting that the ECHR as a source of the national law plays the role of a validation argument of the normative basis for a decision. The subsidiary nature of the European human rights protection system implies the identical nature of the Convention in the law application process taking place on the level of a state because the legislator that has a particular obligation to establish normative guarantees protecting the rights of an individual. This is why the ECHR regulations perform the function of the necessary or auxiliary detailing of statutory legal bases for the decision to apply the law[27].

To sum up these deliberations, I suggest summarizing the arguments that weaken and strengthen the precedent nature of ECHR judgments in the conclusion. Weakening arguments include the lack of the *stare decisis* principle because of which

---

25 E.g. judgment in the case of Mehmet Sentürk and Bekis Sentürk against Turkey of 9 April 2013, complaint no. 13423/09, § 79.

26 E.g. judgment in the case of Tysiąc against Poland of 20 March 2007, complaint no. 5410/03, § 107.

27 For more on this topic see: B. Liżewski, *Operacjonalizacja ochrony praw człowieka w porządku Europejskiej Konwencji Praw Człowieka (studium teoretycznoprawne)*, Lublin 2015, p. 398–403.

ECHR judgements are not a formal source of the law and are not legally binding for the national agencies (mostly courts) applying the law. Additionally, the position taken by the ECHR itself that decisively rejects the construction of a binding precedent has to be taken into account. Another argument refers to the context of the national ruling and weakening of the universalism of a standard in all states of the Council of Europe. This fact is related to the doctrine of the evaluation margin enforcing the consideration of local conditions that has been developed to such a degree that it currently occupies the central position in the ECHR jurisprudence[28]. As a consequence, there are a number of cases in which the settlement contained in the judgement has to be subjectivized as it was made strictly in connection with the specific conditions of a country. It is not in each case that such a settlement can be adapted for the needs of the settlement of a similar case in another European state. The last argument refers to the number of judgments passed. The Court whose assumption was to be the creator of human rights protection standards and to settle disputes as the super-arbitrator in cases between the state and citizens became the "super-producer" of judgments. Most of them are decisions regarding the application of the law rather than a source of human rights protection standards.

Arguments strengthening the precedent nature of judgments are varied. There is no doubt that the creation of human rights protection standards by the ECHR has to be perceived from the legislative and axiological perspective. They constitute the necessary detailing of the Convention, have to build the community of the law and unify the European legal area. Regulations of the Convention create the formal dimension that indirectly indicates the binding power of a judgement, i.e. the protection standard, by considering an infringement of the established ECHR case law as the basis for the issue of a judgement against a state without a hearing by a committee of three judges (art. 28 clause 1b of the Convention) and also by the obligation of a state to comply with it in the national system (art. 46 clause 1 of the Convention). The combination of these arguments strengthens the importance of the Court's judgment to such a degree that it can be considered a *quasi de iure* binding precedent. The use of the "*quasi de iure*" term is supposed to stress that the importance of the ECHR judgment should not be limited to the actual impact only. However, as the *stare decisis* principle does not apply, we can only talk about the generation of an effect similar to the one that classifies a judgment as a legally binding one.

---

28 O. Gross, F. Ni Aoláin, From Discretion to Scrutiny. *Revisiting the Application Doctrine in the Context of Article 15 of the European Convention on Human Rights*, "Human Rights Quarterly" 2001, vol. 23, p. 625.

Marzena Myślińska

Precedent-Setting Argumentation in the Rulings of the Polish Constitutional Tribunal

Abstract: The subject of this article is the analysis of the scope of use by the Polish Constitutional Court (Constitutional Tribunal) of judicial decision (both own and issued by other courts). The analysis was carried out according to research criteria: the method of their appointment, their role in the process of law interpretation, their use at individual stages of the law application process and the nature of their use in decision-making. The analysis of the research material (case law of the Constitutional Tribunal from three selected periods) allows to draw conclusions concerning the actual role played by the argumentation referring to the contents of earlier individual and concrete decisions in the process of applying the law by the Polish Constitutional Court in the perspective of the legal system of continental law culture.

Keywords: Constitutional Tribunal, precedent, precedent argumentation

1 Precedent-Setting Argumentation in the Rulings of the Constitutional Tribunal

Precedent as a term characteristic of the legal culture of *common law* is defined as a general norm derived from a judgement given for a specific fact, which has binding force (*de iure*). The essence of the principle of *stare decisis*, typical of this legal culture, is to issue rulings in similar cases which are the same as earlier decisions for a given factually similar controversy[1]. Rulings issued in conflict with a general precedent-based norm are considered to be in conflict with the binding law. In principle, such a precedent is binding for the courts of the same or higher instance[2]. The Polish legal nomenclature does not use the term of precedent/precedent-setting decision; this term is widely used in the legal doctrine and practice[3]. The connotation of the term relates to its function, which is to have impact on other law-enforcing decisions (including mainly court rulings)[4].

1 See more i.a.: M. Koszowski, *Anglosaska doktryna precedensu. Porównanie z polską praktyką orzeczniczą*, Warszawa 2009, p. 21.

2 See more: A. Orłowska, *Precedens w systemach prawnych różnych krajów europejskiej kultury prawnej*, "Radca Prawny" 2000, no. 5, pp. 14–17.

3 See more: J. Wróblewski, *Sądowe stosowanie prawa*, Warszawa 1972, pp. 304–305.

4 Cf. ibidem, pp. 72–73. At the same time it should be stressed that the distinction mentioned could be identified with the guidelines of the judiciary and court practice

The factors implying greater significance of precedent-setting decisions are, i.e. development of IT techniques and consequently access to the contents of rulings, flexibility of legal practice and first of all uniformity of decisions related to equal treatment of decision addressees before the law[5].

2 Decision-Making by the Constitutional Tribunal - General Characteristics

The fundamental role of the Constitutional Tribunal (hereinafter: the CT), as per the provisions of art. 175 of the Constitution of the Republic of Poland[6], is to control conformity to the Constitution which, as the literature shows, does not fit either in making or enforcing the law[7]. The purpose of operation of the CT is to adjudicate upon the conformity of a legal system to the Constitution in the manner which ensures consistency and effectiveness of the requirements of the Basic Law and protection of constitutional axiology[8]. Judgements of the CT shall be of universally binding application (as per the provisions of art. 190 of the Constitution). Public authorities are obliged to adhere to and enforce such judgements[9]. In addition, the effects include influence on the law-making process if a judgement on the non-conformity to the Constitution of a given normative act (legal norm) has been issued[10], reproduction of the constitutional principles which have not been directly verbalised in the Constitution[11] (in this respect, the potential of precedent-setting argumentation can be most clearly seen).

---

issued by the Supreme Court, as well as rulings of the Constitutional Tribunal issued before 1997.

5 A. Orłowska, op. cit., p. 23. More on the impact of uniform rulings on the principle of equality before the law in: L. Gardocki, *Jednolita interpretacja prawa a niezawisłość sędziowska*, "Rzeczpospolita" z dnia 23 października 2000 r., no 248; J. Wróblewski, *Precedens i jednolitość sądowego stosowania prawa*, "Państwo i Prawo" 1971, iss. 10, pp. 523–526.

6 Constitution of the Republic of Poland of 2 April 1997 (Dz.U. 1997, no. 78, item 483).

7 Cf. J. Trzciński, *Orzeczenia interpretacyjne Trybunału Konstytucyjnego*, "Państwo i Prawo" 2002, no. 1, p. 9; D. Czoik, *Kompetencje Trybunału Konstytucyjnego do wydawania orzeczeń interpretacyjnych*, "Jurysta" 2003, no. 12, p. 27.

8 Z. Czeszejko-Nowacki, *Orzeczenia Trybunału Konstytucyjnego. Pojęcie, klasyfikacja i skutki prawne*, "Państwo i Prawo" 2000, iss. 12, p. 25.

9 See more: ibidem, p. 28.

10 Ibidem, p. 16.

11 So-called *implicite* principles, see more: L. Morawski, *Zasady wykładni prawa*, Toruń 2006, p. 116.

The application of the law by the CT comes down to "comparing two legal norms which are always given some specific meaning, when adjudicating on the control of conformity of the law to the Constitution"[12]. It is different from the law enforcement by courts in the lack of classification of the actual state (to the extent typical of enforcing the law by courts), the effect of which is issuing an individual and specific decision[13]. What is essential is the impact of the interpretation made by the CT on the process of law interpretation by the law-enforcing bodies (particularly in court). Following a different interpretation may result in losing legal force by a currently binding law (e.g. if consequently, a court comes forward to the CT with a question of law or a constitutional appeal is filed)[14]. The Polish constitutional court does not use the notion of precedent. Further in the article, I will use the notion of precedent alternatively with either precedent-setting argumentation or an earlier/another decision.

While pointing to selected detailed conclusions drawn from the analysis of the CT rulings, it should be clarified that the research material comprises the analysis of grounds for the judgements and decisions issued by the CT in the following three periods: I) 1998, II) 2005 and III) 2015–2016, with the reservation that the psychological examination concerning the motives of the judges for using specific earlier decisions and reasons for using such decisions, has not been performed. Focusing on the structure of the CT judgement, it should be noted that CT makes use of the precedent-setting argumentation in the statement of reasons for a particular decision, referring to the arguments stated in the justifications of earlier decisions more often. Argumentation from the reasoning (understood as determination of the decision) has not been found.

3 The Manner of Binding by an Earlier Decision of Applying the Law

The analysis of the manner of referring to earlier decisions allows for a conclusion that the CT feels bound by its own judgements issued. In the overwhelming majority of cases, the CT relies on its own earlier decisions. In the context of referring to the national law-enforcing bodies, the CT makes use of the decisions issued by the Supreme Court (hereinafter the SC); in the periods analysed no referrals can be found to the decisions of first and second instance courts (except for the decisions issued in cases subject to control or a question of law). Referring

12 See more: J. Trzciński, op. cit., p. 10.

13 Cf. i.a.: J. Nowacki, Z. Tobor, *Wstęp do prawoznawstwa*, Warszawa 1993, p. 175.

14 D. Czoik, op. cit., p. 26.

to the decisions of other courts (either national or foreign) is occasional. More often, the CT refers in this respect to the decisions of the German constitutional court (particularly in the 1st period analysed), as well as to the European Court of Justice (2nd and 3rd period). A frequent procedure is also using the standards of protection of the European Court of Human Rights in Strasbourg which, from the perspective of the contents of the Polish Constitution (particularly chapter II which regulates fundamental human rights), is a natural consequence (with the growing trend in the 2nd and 3rd period analysed).

When specifying the role which the CT attributes to the use of precedent-setting argumentation derived from its own decisions (similarly, from the decisions of the European Court of Human Rights, hereinafter the ECHR), it can be defined as following an earlier decision (within the meaning of the term defined by J. Wróblewski). The connotation of the term (unlike taking into consideration)[15] assumes a greater degree of binding by the decisions issued and their stronger influence on the decision issued in a specific case[16]. Although it has been pointed out, that classification of a given manner of decision-making (this also applies to the CT) requires psychological examination, i.e. as regards the knowledge of earlier decisions[17]: however the analysis of justifications for the judgements of the CT is intuitively in favour of adopting such a thesis. This is reflected, i.e. in: 1) numerous statements made by the CT that "this issue does not need any explanations because it has been presented in detail in the judgement", 2) the purpose of controlling conformity to the Constitution (and by that of the rulings) performed by the CT, which is to ensure cohesion of the legal system with the primary norms resulting from the constitution, 3) expertise of the judges composing the CT, including primarily legal expertise and professional experience exceeding the requirements for performing the duties of a judge in lower instance common courts.

Specifying the issue of the manner of using external decisions here, we should note the tendency to take into consideration the rulings of the SC, ECJ, as well as other constitutional courts (mostly German). This is particularly observed in the middle and final period of the research material analysed, which seems natural in the context of accessing to and functioning of the Polish legal order in

---

15 As J. Wróblewski (*Precedens…*, op. cit., p. 529) points out, taking into consideration assumes using previous decisions issued in the context of the additional argumentation in the justifications of judgments.

16 Ibidem, p. 530.

17 Ibidem.

international structures (in particular of the European Union) and the binding force (and by that the obligation to ensure conformity) of the Polish law and the EU law. Despite relative occasionality of using external decisions, it seems justified to state that the CT is aware of the necessity to implement the ruling function in multi-centric legal orders: however, it does not determine changing the manner of using own decisions.

The justification style does not seem to demonstrate the features of a discourse; the CT does not argue or evaluate previous decisions. When following its own earlier decisions, the CT treats the statements included therein as facts which do not need any additional clarification in the currently adjudicated case (which is demonstrated by the following expressions used in the rulings: "the issue clarified in the judgement/decision remains valid in this case", "this issue has already been clarified in judgement"). Considering decisions of other bodies' takes place in the context of confirming own argumentation.

Clear identification of the manner of quoting earlier decisions as adopted by the CT is not possible. The analysis of the rulings has revealed inconsistency in this respect, as well as lack of differentiation with regard to such factors as, e.g. number of ruling judges, trends with regard to individual years analysed. However, what draws our attention is the fact that when quoting individual fragments of justifications for its previous decisions, the CT refers to complete data of the ruling (i.e. type of ruling, date of issue, ref. No.); in turn when relying on the "ruling practice" or a "view expressed in previous rulings", the CT provides at least several refs. Nos of its previous decisions after the argument presented in brackets.

The reasoning using other law-enforcing decisions resembles applying the *per analogiam* principle by the CT. Referring to the principle expressed in other decisions (mainly their own decisions) takes place in particular when: 1) the CT concludes that a previous and current case are similar, 2) a referral is made to own principles defined with the indication that there are no fundamental differences between the facts. The research material does not allow for expressing a clear conclusion whether such similarity resembles reasoning *per analogiam legis* or maybe *per analogiam iuris*. However, taking into consideration the part of the rulings where the CT follows the established rules defining the contents of constitutional principles, the reasoning seems to be closer to *analogiam iuris*. The point of reference here is not the principles and common features of a branch of the law or a legal system, but the values and principles expressed in the constitution. The reasoning conducted by the CT is aimed at ensuring cohesion of the legal system with the norms expressed in a normative act having the highest legal force.

The analysis of using other decisions by the CT in the context of the stages of the law enforcement process, irrespective of the analysed period, leads to the conclusion that referring to decisions (first of all their own decisions) takes place at the validation[18] and derivation stages. In stage 1, the CT makes use of previous decisions, in particular in cases where it follows its own decisions which relate to legal principles derived directly from a constitutional provision (e.g. the rule of the good tax legislation derived from art. 2 of the Constitution or clarification of the proportionality test from art. 31 of the Constitution). A similar trend can be observed in using ruling standards by the CT which have been formulated in the judgments of the ECHR, whereas "binding" by the argument seems to be less intensive than by their own decision (in particular in further periods analysed).

4 Using Previous Decisions to Apply the Law in the Interpretation Process

Limiting the derivation stage to interpretation, the analysis of the research material has shown that the CT makes use of (mainly its own) decision both with regard to the principle of language, system as well as the principle of purpose and function. In the context of the first rule mentioned, the CT is driven by another decision in clarifying expressions, stating that "the meaning of a given term used in a provision subject to interpretation has already been established in the rulings of the CT" (referring to the ruling practice or ref. Nos of individual judgements). In addition, we should note the tendency to limit the use of other decisions in the context of the principle of language in criminal law cases, which is obviously connected with the interpretation typical of this field of law[19].

The purpose of the operation of the CT (examining conformity of legal provisions to the Constitution) naturally translates into the application of a systemic principle in the process of interpreting the law. The essence of this interpretative directive is demonstrated in the fact that it is not acceptable to state non-conformity of a norm or a normative act to the Constitution if it is possible to interpret the same in line with the constitution[20]. In addition, the obligation

18 Here, it should be noted that due to the obligation existing in the statute law culture to found the decision on legal provisions, another precedent-setting decision/ruling may not in principle be an independent ground for a decision.

19 See more on interpretative judgements: T. Woś, *Wyroki interpretacyjne i zakresowe w orzecznictwie Trybunału Konstytucyjnego*, "Studia Iuridica Lublinensia" 2016, no. 3, pp. 986–994.

20 See more: L. Morawski, op. cit., p. 112.

to interpret in line with the legal principles (including these interpreted by the constitutional court itself) naturally goes hand in hand with the directive which requires that the hierarchy of normative acts is observed in the interpretation[21]. The analysis of the research material has shown that in relying on other (mostly its own) decisions, the CT consistently implemented these principles, whereas in the 2nd period in its decisions the constitutional court implemented another directive on the principle of systemic interpretation of the domestic law in line with the EU law (based on art. 91 par. 3 of the Constitution). The principle, recognised as binding, justifies making use of the decisions issued by the European Court of Justice, which refer to the interpretation of Community law. In addition, the role of the CT should be stressed in following its earlier decisions in the context of the conflict of principles or the conflict of principles with the legal provisions whose conformity to the Constitution is questioned. In this respect, the analysis of the justifications of CT judgements has shown that the constitutional court relies on the established ruling practice which formulates the conditions for observing the principle of proportionality from art. 31 of the Constitution (particularly in the rulings from the later of the analysed periods).

Pointing to the principle of purpose and function and its application by the CT in the context of using earlier law-enforcing decisions it should be stressed that the CT (particularly in earlier periods) makes use of this principle in the context of referring to the purpose of the operation of the legislator mentioned in its own decisions, as well as legislative materials accompanying the process of drawing up a given normative act. In the 2nd and 3rd period, the CT relies on its own law-enforcing decision (and also decisions issued by the SC or the ECJ) with reference to the purpose or the function of a legal institution defined in earlier decisions. It seems to be an obvious conclusion that the CT follows its earlier decisions in determining connotations of general clauses and indefinite terms which, due to the axiological openness of the constitution, can be frequently found therein.

5 Conclusions

Summing up the discourse presented in this article, some general remarks should be noticed in the context of using precedent-setting argumentation by the CT. First of all, it should be noted that in relying on its own, earlier decisions the CT treats such decisions as binding; a deviation from its own, established

21 See more: ibidem, pp. 114–116.

ruling practice entails referring the case to the ruling of the full panel of the CT (horizontal effect of the precedent). The reasons for this include, i.e.: 1) powers of the CT and direct influence on creating constitutional rule, 2) binding force of judgements issued by the CT, 3) awareness of the consequences for settled cases (possible reopening of the proceedings) and impact on the process of law enforcement by domestic courts. In the last context it should be pointed that it is projective in nature for the law-enforcing practice of the courts. Frequent stressing that the applied principle is reflected in the established ruling practice or at least several previous decisions of the CT (this approach is used irrespective of the period analysed) implies the importance for the Polish constitutional court of uniformity of decisions in the context of legal certainty and creating the constitutional rule which sets out the framework of the legal system. As regards the last respect, the influence of the CT on the process of interpretation made not only when settling cases by the CT itself but also by domestic courts should be noticed, because in its previous decisions the constitutional court formed detailed interpretative directives which are consistently implemented both by the CT itself and also by the law-enforcing bodies, treating them as binding.

Adam Szot

Precedential Argumentation in the Application of Public Law in a *Civil Law* Culture

Abstract: The subject of this paper is the issue of reaching in the process of applying public law to "precedents" in civil law countries. The precedent-based argumentation is the use of arguments expressed in earlier legal decisions in the reasoning of the entity applying the law. The aim of the conducted analyzes is to present the presence of said arguments – the frequency and schematicity of calling an argument from the precedent in the application of law in the civil law culture and showing the manner in which the entities applying the law reach for such arguments.

Keywords: precedential argumentation, public law application, civil law culture

1 Introductory Remarks

In the contemporary state of law, it is unacceptable to pass law enforcement acts which regulate the rights and obligations of their target and which are not established in the sources of law acknowledged in the given legal order. In countries rooted in the *civil law* culture, this primarily means that the acts are founded on the legal provisions in force. At the same time, upon a general observation of the decisional practice of entities which make particular legal decisions, it is possible to formulate a hypothesis that such decisions are often grounded on precedents, despite the lack of similar principles to the *common law* culture, whereby precedents are used as binding sources of law. This does not mean, however, that such decisions are taken without any legal basis or in breach of law. It is the very concept of a source of law that is ambiguous. In the dynamic approach, it is possible to recognize and analyze the impact, in particular the actual impact of earlier law enforcement decisions (precedents) on the subsequent decisions. Adopting this perspective opens a new field of research and affects a number of potential sources of law to be selected and used by a law enforcement authority in the ruling process. In this perspective, every factor which affects the content of a legal decision may be considered a source of law[1]. This assumption refers

1 This is called the decision-making approach to the sources of law. Cf. L. Leszczyński, *Podstawa decyzji stosowania prawa administracyjnego. Ustalenia walidacyjne*, [in:] *Wykładnia w prawie administracyjnym*, eds. R. Hauser, Z. Niewiadomski, A. Wróbel, Warszawa 2012, pp. 57–58, series: System Prawa Administracyjnego, vol. 4.

to "expanded doctrine of the sources of law"[2] whereby the legal system should include not only legal provisions, but also political justifications, customs, and precedents, interpretative rules and inference rules, as well as rules for norm conflict resolution in the system.

The decision-making[3] approach to the sources of law makes it possible to move away (to a certain degree) from purely juridical categories. In the culture of statutory law, adopting the expanded doctrine of the sources of law allows for reaching beyond the system of legal provisions and for employing other normative facts. These, along with the former, create an environment (legal order) in which the decision-making entity passes decisions.

The subject of this paper is the use of precedents in the process of public law enforcement (i.e. the process leading to a regulatory legal ruling in a particular case). The employment of arguments from precedent referred to in the title denotes the use of arguments expressed in past law enforcement decisions in the reasoning of a decision-making entity. It therefore involves the use of earlier decisions for the purposes of the ongoing proceedings, to be concluded with an individual legal decision. At this point, it is possible to distinguish between three situations: the first one, where a decision-making entity uses precedents during the law enforcement process, but does not invoke them in the judgment rationale; the second one, where a decision-making entity uses previous rulings and expresses it (in various ways) in the content of the final decision; the third one, where precedents are not used in the law enforcement process, but are still invoked (on various grounds) in the judgment rationale. An analysis of each of these situations requires the adoption of different methodological assumptions.

The aim of the analyses presented in this paper was to demonstrate arguments from precedents, as well as the frequency and patterns of their use in law enforcement in the *civil law* culture, as well as to present the manner in which law enforcement entities employ those arguments. The latter two situations are thus going to be the prime concern of the analysis. Individual legal decisions in public law comprise the subject of the study. The analysis encompassed the

---

2 Cf. S. Wronkowska, Z Ziembiński, *Zarys teorii prawa*, Poznań 1997, pp. 141–146. Cf. J. Wróblewski, *Decyzja sądowa a koncepcja systemu prawa,* "Acta Universitatis Lodziensis, Zeszyty Naukowe Uniwersytetu Łódzkiego, Nauki Humanistyczno-Społeczne" 1978, vol. 28, pp. 7–8 and Wróblewski's concept of a "broad legal system".

3 Cf. i.a. A. Korybski, L. Leszczynski, *Decision-Making Approach in a Study of the Enactment and Application of Law. A Pragmatic Context of Legal Theory,* [in:] *Legal Theory and Philosophy of Law. Towards Contemporary Challenges*, eds. A. Bator, Z. Pulka, Warszawa 2013, pp. 156–181.

official reasoning for the decisions issued by public administration organs (if available), as well as statements of courts supervising those decisions. In terms of this analysis, there is therefore no significant difference between the second and the third group of the above-mentioned situations. This is because the argument from precedent is present in the reasoning of a legal decision regardless of whether the law employment entity has in fact invoked a previous decision or not.

The starting point of this research was public law enforcement, primarily because of the diversity of decision-making entities. On the one hand, these are public administration bodies related to each other by way of organization and (frequently) dependent on the current political situation. Their aim is to achieve the tasks assigned to them. On the other hand, there are independent courts, entrusted with exercising control over the administration. This research was carried out with regard to the Polish legal order, since these were the initial assumptions of the scientific grant under which it was conducted. At the same time, however, the theses presented in this publication are of a largely universal nature (taking into account specific legal solutions), and may be used in the legal order employed in other countries belonging to the continental legal culture.

At the end of the introductory remarks, it is valuable to point out that employment of precedents may refer to the use of (a) previous administrative decisions, i.e. decisions of the given authority (especially issued in similar matters) or other entities (especially superior to the given decision-making authority), or (b) court rulings (particularly in respect to judgments relating to the activities of a decision-making administration authority, principally in similar matters) in the law enforcement process.

2 Precedent as a Binding Source of Law in the Activities of Public Administration

The impact of precedents (established both by the administration and the judiciary) on the process of issuing administrative decisions can be analyzed from the perspective of the decision-making authority being formally bound by legal arrangements or factual findings in a given case. The other perspective is focused on the informal (non-formal) influence on the organ.

The first approach covers all the situations in which an administrative authority is legally obliged not only to employ, but also take into account (or at least consider) the arguments expressed in other administrative decisions or court rulings. This therefore involves all the cases in which legal standards impose such an obligation of a given authority. At the extreme, this obligation may imply adopting the findings of another decision or judgment. In such a situation, the authority does not have any discretionary power to decide whether to take these findings into account or not. Formal influence encompasses all cases of a direct impact on the decision-making authority, i.e. where another administrative authority or a court may affect the process of issuing a single administrative decision regarding a case by means of its decision or arguments used in the reasoning in a given case. In practice, this pertains to any situation where a decision issued by a body of public administration is repealed due to an appeal or a complaint lodged, without being replaced with a decision of an inspection authority or a court. The procedural outcomes involve remitting the case for reconsideration. With the application of the standard pertinent in the legal order whereby the findings made by the inspection authority are to be taken into consideration, the precedent becomes *de facto* legally binding.

The obligation to ground a decision on a precedent in a given case does not imply it should be binding by analogy in other cases, however similar they may be. Should an authority receive a case with similar facts, it invokes the said precedent nevertheless, in order to verify its suitability in the given case as well. This might happen inadvertently, since the occurrence of such action is unrelated to the fact whether it is actually deliberate or not. Familiarity with previous rulings is just a part of the decision-maker's proficiency, similarly to the knowledge of the legislation and the expertise necessary to regulate an area of social reality. Moreover, such precedents become a part of the legal order in the broader sense. Thus, the administration authority (the decision-maker) is not able to "switch off" and refrain from considerations in this area. At the same time, there are two reasons why an authority may invoke and consider the arguments expressed in prior administrative or judicial decisions, without being legally bound to do so.

The first reason is of a pragmatic nature. By respecting the assessment and arguments expressed in previous administrative decisions or court rulings, in particular in similar matters, the administration authority precludes the possibility of its actions being challenged. Another factor is rooted in the process of economics, whereby disregarding previously presented assessments and interpretation, as well as the views expressed by the inspection bodies, which results in severe consequences the authority wishes to avoid, and the administrative decision being repealed as a result of an appellate or a court review of the proceedings. It is of particular importance in cases where those assessments are a part of a '"fixed" jurisprudence in respect of judgements or decisions.

The other reason is of an axiological nature. These arguments pertain both to the axiology of the law enforcement authority, i.e. its objective to maintain the integrity (coherence) of the legal order, and the axiology of the legal system.

The latter is expressed in more or less general principles of the law, including the principles aimed at building trust in a citizen to the state and its bodies, legal certainty and predictability of law and its application, or the state of law in a wider sense. The Voivodship Administrative Court in Krakow[4], e.g., stated in its judgment of 21.09.2009[5] that "the Polish law does not apply the principle of precedent; it is, however, an obligation of a decision-making authority, if it has previously taken a different decision in an almost identical factual situation, to explain why it has changed its position or why the previous position may not apply in the present case, in particular due to this point being raised in the appeal".

The non-formal impact therefore entails all cases where an authority is not legally bound by the findings of other authorities or the court, but invokes them independently and voluntarily. It is not, of course, formally required to take account of them, and may make different findings in another case, even in a very similar one.

A different point of view allows for the claim that it is the informal impact that is the actual impact, while the formal impact denotes both the actual and legal impact at the same time. The legal impact encompasses all cases in which an authority is obliged by law to invoke or (in a more compelling manner) to take into account the findings, assessments, and arguments expressed in the precedent. The actual impact is visible in any case where the authority invokes earlier (administrative or judicial) decisions and uses them even to the slightest extent (in the decision-making or argumentation), in relation to the entire process, its individual stages, or its decision-making policy in a wider sense. The actual impact in this meaning also includes all cases of legal impact, with the exception, however, of situations where an authority invokes a court ruling, but in fact does not use it to any extent. There is, namely, no impact on administration at all, regardless of the difficulty of noticing such situations.

The issue of the administrative decision-making process bound by a precedent may be considered from a *micro* and *macro* perspective. The former focuses on an individual administration case and its effect in the form of a final law enforcement decision. The *micro* perspective allows for adopting the analysis perspective, which presents the impact of precedents on the reasoning

4 The Polish model of judicial control of public administration is based on a two-instance administrative judiciary as a separate division of the judiciary. Judgments of the first instance are made by voivodship administrative courts, whereas the court of the second instance is the Supreme Administrative Court.

5 Judgment of the Voivodship Administrative Court in Krakow of 21 September 2009. II SA/Kr 1247/09, CBOSA.

of an administration body in respect of factual and legal findings and their qualifications, as well as of the content of the administrative decision, in particular when the authority has a discretionary power to determine the direction and/or a scale of the decision (e.g. if the decision is based on administrative discretion). The *macro* perspective, in turn, allows for the analysis of the relationship between the previous decisions and the jurisdiction (especially a fixed and stable jurisprudence) and the development of an administration policy in the form of a fixed procedure employed in specific matters, or as the protection of human rights and freedoms in a wider sense. This impact is visible both in the decision-making process of a particular administrative body and in various bodies operating in a task-oriented or hierarchical relationship.

Analyses of the impact of the precedent on the decision-making process in public administration, under consideration of the variable of instance (1st or 2nd instance) of the body taking an administrative decision, have demonstrated several correlations. Firstly, if an authority is legally bound to use findings of another authority or court, the impact is always valid, regardless of the rank of the authority in the structure of public administration. Secondly, taking into account the organizational and political links between public administration authorities, the decision-making process is subjected to a much stronger impact of administrative precedents (previous law enforcement decisions) than of court rulings. Decisions of superior bodies in the hierarchy may often be a source of influence which strongly determines the decision taken by a lower-level body, thus limiting its discretionary power. This phenomenon may be called a "reverse hierarchy of sources of law", which refers to the situation where acts issued by higher-level authorities in practice have often a stronger impact on the operation of lower-level authorities than a statutory act[6]. Thirdly, in the case of informal impact, court rulings exert a more significant influence on higher-level authorities, which are to verify the correctness of decisions taken by subordinate bodies. It is the effectiveness of the verification system of the second instance authorities that determines whether the court repeals a decision or not. Finally, the force of any informal impact of court rulings on subordinate entities depends on the "approach" of the second instance authority to the findings and an assessment of the administrative court, including their compliance with the administration policy. This is a consequence of the "reverse hierarchy of sources of law": if a higher-level authority adopts the arguments of a court, it becomes a control model for decisions issued by the first instance bodies, and thus it indirectly

6 Cf. J. Zimmermann, *Prawo administracyjne*, Kraków 2005, p. 362.

affects the reasoning of a lower-level authority ("top-down" relationship). From a pragmatic point of view, the latter acknowledges and takes into account the assessment of the court as if it were rooted in the administration itself. Otherwise, the lower-level authority would not seek to issue a decision, accepting a court reasoning which is not acknowledged by the review authority and may therefore be repealed during later proceedings.

3 Argument from Precedent in the Jurisdiction of Administrative Courts

The results of research (with regard to the Polish legal order) clearly indicate that the precedent and the precedent reasoning are indeed present in the administrative court jurisdiction, both in first instance courts and the Supreme Administrative Court. There are, however, significant differences as to the understanding, usage, and the presence of precedents in justification. These are not related to the position of the court in the hierarchy, or type of the case at hand, but are rather a consequence of the lack of coherent assumptions underpinning this type of court activity.

In terms of semantics, the very term "precedent" is not rare in the jurisdiction of Polish administrative courts. It is used in various contexts and in different parts of the justification. There are two major manners of employing the term:

1) In relation to a court ruling (administrative or a different court) or an administrative decision, where a precedent means a previous law enforcement decision[7],
2) In relation to the assessment of certain circumstances which could arise and be considered a precedent (as in "the first", which "gives rise to something") upon adopting specific findings or issuing a judgment or decision of a specific content, where a precedent denotes a precedent factual situation[8].

---

7 E.g. the following judgments: SAC of 30.08.2017, II FSK 1703/15, CBOSA; VAC in Warsaw of 14.06.2017, II SA/Wa 141/17, CBOSA; VAC in Krakow of 20.04.2017, II SA/Kr 80/17, CBOSA; VAC in Lublin of 15.03.2017, III SA/Lu 849/16, CBOSA; VAC in Krakow of 7.06.2016, II SA/Kr 379/16, CBOSA; VAC in Krakow of 22.09.2016, II SA/Kr 624/16, CBOSA; decision of the SAC of 16.02.2017, II OSK 1442/15, CBOSA.

8 E.g. the following judgments: SAC of 16.05.2017, II OSK 2340/15, CBOSA; VAC in Kielce of 29.12.2016, SA/Ke 577/16, CBOSA; VAC in Poznan of 14.10.2016, II SA/Po 404/16, CBOSA; VAC in Lodz of 20.09.2016, II SAB/Łd 178/16, CBOSA; VAC in Gliwice of 20.07.2016, II SA/Gl 304/16, CBOSA. This occurs relatively frequently in the matters of spatial planning – cf. i.a. judgment of the SAC of 22.04.2017, II OSK

Statistically, cases where the second definition is applied are much more frequent. Courts avoid using the concept of a precedent in its first meaning and strongly emphasize the fact of not being bound by previous decisions, as well as their independent status[9]. The term is mostly used by a party which has invoked another decision for the purposes of their case, and in order to derive particular consequences from it (usually regarding the termination of proceedings in cases of a similar factual situation, or the understanding of the standard used as the grounds for judgement)[10]. In such situations, generally, the court clearly underlines that the precedent is not binding and impossible to consider as a (formal) source of law. This disclaimer applies, therefore, mostly to the content of the previous judgment, and not the arguments used in the reasons for judgment.

At the same time, it would be stressed that precedents are present in the majority of the decisions analyzed within this study, although the term itself is not used. The practice of invoking and citing an argument from a precedent takes many forms. Most common cases (often found in one judgment) include: (1) reference to one or more previous judgments[11], (2) reference to the "jurisprudence" ("fixed", "stable", or "well-established", if necessary) or the "jurisdiction of administrative courts"[12]. In both cases, these are cited in one of the following manners: as a general reference to the past jurisdiction (jurisprudence, court jurisdiction) without clarifying its extent; a reference to a specific judgment(s), including a paraphrase or a summary of the arising arguments; a reference to a specific judgment(s) including a citation of the reference.

2092/15, CBOSA; VAC in Poznan of 14.10.2016, II SA/Po 404/16, CBOSA; VAC in Olsztyn of 27.10.2015, II SA/Ol 834/15, CBOSA.

9 E.g. the VAC judgment in Lublin of 15.03.2017, III SA/Lu 849/16, CBOSA – "A method of resolving a similar legal matter adopted by a specified court does not oblige another court to apply the same solution, especially when the other court does not accept the interpretation adopted by the first court".

10 E.g. decision of the SAC of 24.11.2016, II FZ 777/16, CBOSA.

11 E.g. decision of the SAC of 31.10.2017, I FZ 191/17, CBOSA; judgment of the SAC of 20.10.2017, II FSK 2672/15, CBOSA; judgment of the SAC of 16.03.2017, FSK 1201/14, CBOSA.

12 Similarly A. Jakubowski, S. Gajewski, *Argument z linii orzeczniczej w orzecznictwie sądów administracyjnych*, Warszawa 2015, pp. 15–17. Cf. e.g. the following judgments: VAC in Lodz of 23.11.2017, I SA/Sc 689/17, CBOSA; SAC of 20.10.2017, II OSK 1457/17, CBOSA; SAC of 18.10.2017, II FSK 1092/16, CBOSA; SAC of 14.06.2017, I OSK 2920/16, CBOSA.

A specific judgment is most often referred to by invoking its fragment (arguments used in the reasons for judgment) along with the case number. This may be performed in two forms, i.e. either by presenting the argument directly, as resulting from an earlier judgment, or indirectly, as an argument of a given court, also used in another (earlier) judgment. In most cases, more than one judgment is invoked, but usually one (less frequently two or more) is used with regard to a single claim. It is also worth noting that there are often situations in which a court directly cites the whole thesis formulated in another judgment, yet without referring to its source[13].

Reference to a precedent (an earlier judgment) is usually used in favor of a selected claim made in the judgment rationale (far more seldom to challenge it). Such a reference is made in order to convince consumers that the reasoning of the court complies with the legal order, whereas the presented standpoint is not an isolated view. There is, however, almost no dispute found with claims formulated in other judgments. Courts in general do not present a contrasting line of argumentation, nor do they debate the invoked arguments.

Reference to a precedent is used to form an argument and not to issue a final decision. Although not bound by previous rulings, courts are willing to invoke them, often citing their entire fragments. It is therefore not the judgment as a whole nor the final decision of a court that forms a precedent, but the argumentation. If the reasoning (of the claim) of the court is approved of, it has an opportunity to become a beginning of a new "line of argumentation" which includes a reference to the particular claim(s) made in the original judgment. The above-mentioned "reluctance" of administrative courts to use precedents stems from the fact that these are often associated with the rationale for the decision (*ratio decidendi*), which is precisely the decision-making approach to a precedent, and not an argumentative one, although the former is almost a non-existent in practice. At this point, on the basis of these considerations, it is necessary to invoke the issue of judicial independence, which courts emphasize so often. It is imperative that they remain not bound by previous judgments or other non-legal factors all the more. Taking into account arguments from precedent may prove very advantageous and, in practice, contribute to the implementation of such values of law enforcement as certainty or coherence.

---

13 The claim that the term "public tasks" is broader than the term "tasks of public authority" was used in, e.g. II SAB/Lu 62/17 – Judgment of the VAC in Lublin of 1.08.2017, as well as I OSK 3119/15 – Judgment of the SAC of 23.08.2017.

4 Conclusions

This study has shown that precedents (previous law enforcement decisions) are used in the decision-making process in public administration, as well as in rulings of the courts which supervise this administration. This phenomenon is a result of an increasingly more frequent and bolder practice of invoking elements of a legal order which are not a part of the system of the sources of the *sensu stricto* law. The acknowledgment of arguments expressed in previous administrative or judicial decisions as essential elements of the legal basis of a judgment creates an entirely new field of discourse. This phenomenon is undoubtedly reinforced through the convergence of legal cultures and multi-centered legal systems in the dynamically changing social realities.

Although earlier legal decisions or the *stare decisis* principle are not binding (in *civil law* countries), administrative authorities and courts often make use of past decisions, yet seldom in an explicit manner. Apart from situations where a decision or a court ruling is legally binding (strictly defined in the respective legal system), it is primarily pragmatic considerations that support the use of the argument from precedent. A pragmatic approach to established assessments, principles, as well as interpretive assumptions precludes a deficiency of proceedings and resulting decisions. By complying with the views rooted in a well-established jurisprudence or decision-making practice, a public law enforcement authority (an administration body or a court) may avoid sanctions applied in the form of a repeal of the defective decision (judgment), in particular if the factual situation is similar. Re-shaping an existing interpretation may be therefore compared to "reinventing the wheel". If there is a pattern for interpretation at hand, it seems obvious to use past proceedings and create a base of administrative decisions. It is also clear that one wishes to avoid obvious undesirable severity which may be imposed by a review authority (authority of the second instance or a court). At the same time, the principles of legal certainty and predictability of judgment may be implemented to a greater extent. The party to proceedings which is familiar not only with the legal standards in force, but also with the actual decision-making practice or jurisprudence (in particular if these are, in fact, well-established) may be more successful in predicting the decision. This does not, however, affect the possibility to leave the precedent out of account for the purposes of a given case, where unique factual circumstances justify such a step. This is not to prompt *contra legem* decisions, regardless of the impact of a precedent on the reasoning of the public law enforcement authority and on the content of the decision which is both grounded on and at the same time limited by the legal standards in force in the given system, and inscribed in the sources of law acknowledged by the legislator.

The analyses conducted have also allowed for capturing the correlation between administrative courts and the public administration bodies they control. The process of verifying their compliance with the law is not limited to "simply" stating whether this condition, fundamental for the state of law, is fulfilled or not, but rather set against legal and non-legal axiology. Precedents may exert various (i.e. in terms of depth, breadth, and intensity) impact both on individual decision-making processes in the administration and on the development of decision-making practice (administrative policies) understood as patterns (customs) of activities adopted in specific cases. A court may influence an administrative decision with a force which depends primarily on the extent to which the administration body is bound by the content of a judgment, i.e. by the reason for the decision or the argumentation expressed in the judgment rationale. The system of judicial control over the discretionary power of decision-making, exercised by administration bodies, is on the one hand an absolute limit to administration activity, and on the other hand it is one of the factors determining the manner of decision-making, influencing both the discretionary power (as it may raise its limitations) and the reasoning of the decision-maker.

Public law enforcement authorities ought to pursue rationalized decisions on the law application, which denotes issuing not the best decision in general, but rather the best possible decision in the given circumstances. The circumstances encompass a specific factual status of the case, the condition of the legal system at the decision time as well as its fundamental values, the performance conditions for the functioning of administration, and social and political values preferable at the time. A decision should fulfil the compliance requirement if taken under consideration of these circumstances and if developed as a result of a discourse among various "participants" of processes constituting the law application discourse in a broad sense. Thus the argument from precedent becomes an element of legal and factual circumstances (conditions) of public law decision-making on the one hand, and a part of the discourse among various actors in the law application process on the other hand.

Paweł Sadowski

Judicial Judgment as a Decision-Making Determinant of the Second Instance Administration Bodies

Abstract: In the contemporary functioning of public administration, it is impossible not to see the role of judicial decisions in shaping the acts of applying the law coming from administrative bodies. It determines the content of the justifications of administrative bodies in a clear and often direct way. A practice is noticeable, according to which in the case of conflict of standards, it is noticeable to use judicial decisions in order to eliminate doubts of interpretation. The use of jurisprudence consists in the broad borrowing of interpretation arguments and helps in solving legal problems resulting from difficulties in the interpretation of unclear and constantly changing legal provisions. The publication aims to bring this issue to the fore in the perspective of the operation of self-government boards of appeal, present in the Polish political system.

Keywords: judicial judgment, administrative decision, administration bodies, self-government boards of appeal, control of administration

1 Introductory Remarks

The Polish government system in the nineties, along with the development of the local self-government practice, introduced self-government boards of appeal as control bodies of a local self-government. Their responsibilities were adapted to new structure of local government administration introduced in 1998[1].Within the range of their activities there were both their own competences as well as the commissioned ones, implemented at the level of the community, county and self-government voivodship. In the following years, the role and tasks of the local self-government grew steadily, as successive cabinets of different political provinces undertook efforts to decentralize the functioning of the state, increasing the scope of tasks that local governments at all levels had to manage.

The Constitution of the Republic of Poland of 2 April 1997 indicates that the principle of territorial self-government results not only from its preamble, but also from the principles of solidarity and subsidiarity adopted in its provisions.

---

1 The Act of 18 December 1998 amending the Act on Local Self-Government Board of Appeal, Dz.U. 1998, no. 162, item 1124, hereafter as a.s.b.a.

Many of the constitutional provisions express an idea to decentralize decision-making process at different levels of government. At the same time, the functioning of territorial self-government results is associated with the assumption that it performs many public tasks, which the Constitution or special laws do not explicitly reserve for administration bodies.

It should also be noted that public administration reforms have been introduced in Poland in order to establish democratic model of state, i.e. to implement the establishment of the appropriate shape of the structure and competence of administrative bodies and entrusting them with various functions. Certain assumptions of the model, following the existing one in other European countries, have been developed and improved in the subsequent stages of the process of implementing legal solutions and adapting them also to European Community regulations. That was done by frequently seeking compromise solutions, optimal from the point of view of the impossibility of violating basic constitutional assumptions, while maintaining legal values relevant to the assessment of public administration. The result was the introduction of structural and functional solutions that could reconcile the pursuit of the foundations of a civil society with the values of the rule of law. From the point of view of the need to introduce pro-European changes, appeal boards were to achieve the goal of compliance with the broadly understood right to good administration in the Polish legal system. At the same time, it can be said that in some aspects it was ahead of later European solutions, e.g. implemented in the Code of Good Administrative Behavior.

The activities of appeal boards, a kind of quasi-judicial bodies, within the self-government structure have implemented and developed the rule of two-instance administrative proceedings expressed in the Constitution of the Republic of Poland prior to bring a case to the administrative court. Art. 78 of the Constitution establishes the right to appeal against decisions issued in the first administrative instance, which is also expressed in the procedural provisions[2]. In this regard, Polish administrative courts have repeatedly expressed their opinion that it is always necessary to comply with the principle of two substantive proceedings. When an administrative act is issued without respect of the principle of two instances, it violates the fundamental rights and procedural guarantees of the citizen, and must be assessed as a gross violation of the law[3]. The doctrine has

2 The Act of 14 June 1960, Code of Administrative Procedure, Dz.U. 2017, item 1257.

3 See: judgment of the Supreme Administrative Court of 10 April 1998, II SA 1198/88, ONSA 1989, no. 1, item 36 or from 12 November 1992, reference number act V SA 721/92, ONSA 1992, no. 3–4, item 95.

also stressed that appeal boards play the role of a guardian of independence of local government units, verifying their administrative decisions in an impartial and lawful manner, before the formal introduction of judicial control of public administration[4].

It should be stressed that under the provisions of art. 184 and art. 175 of the Constitution, the administrative judiciary tasks are carried out, inter alia, by controlling the activities of public administration bodies covering the activities of administrative bodies. The bodies include the appeal boards as self-government appeal bodies. Their system and status are regulated by the Act of 12 October 1994 on Local Self-government Boards of Appeal[5]. In accordance with the regulation of art.1 point 1 of Act on Local Self-government, Boards of Appeal are higher-level bodies within the meaning of the provisions of the Code of Administrative Procedure and Tax Ordinance in individual matters in the field of public administration that belong to the territorial self-government units, unless specific provisions provide otherwise. In the light of art. 1 point 2 a.a.b. on the terms set out in separate laws, the appeal boards rule/decide on matters other than those mentioned in paragraph 1. The act mentioned constitutes in art. 2 par. 1, that in matters referred to in art. 1 point 1, the appeal boards are competent in particular to review appeals against decisions, complaints about orders, warnings, requests to resume proceedings or cancel the decision.

2 The Reasons for the Development of a New Judicial Role in Local Self-Government Boards of Appeal Ruling

With the accession of Poland to the European Union, the tendency for state bodies to accept and introduce the rules characteristic in the common law system is natural. This process is manifested by the increasingly frequent use of judicial decisions as the basis for creating the content of administrative decisions. As a result, the current practice observed in the case of judicial authorities, consisting in building decisions based on previously presented views, begins to be taken over by public administration bodies in the administrative type of application of the law. The reason for this state of affairs is to be found in the impact of the Community acquis and in the constant increase in the role of judicial decisions in the process of applying the law.

---

4 See: M. Bąkiewicz, *Self-Government Boards of Appeal. Evolution, Current Status and Perspectives of the Institution*, “Local Self-Government” 2008, no. 9, p. 53.

5 The Act of 12 October 1994 on Local Self-government Boards of Appeal, Dz.U. 2015, item 1659, hereafter as a.a.b.

From the point of view of the activities of administrative bodies at the basic level and second instance bodies, it is important to determine to what extent judicial decisions may influence the content of administrative decisions. Therefore they create individual acts based on judicial interpretation of generally applicable legal norms.

At the same time, the application of the imperious and individual form of operation of the authorities, which is an administrative decision, cannot be presumed, and the basis for its application must result from the applicable substantive law provision[6].

Formally, there are insufficient grounds to assume that administrative bodies are entitled to assess independently the compliance of the applicable law with the provisions regulating the principles and procedure of law making and to refuse to apply a provision considered incompatible with a higher-level normative act. It should be emphasized that public administration bodies, while acting under the principle of legalism, cannot refuse to apply the applicable provisions, based on binding legal acts even if they perceive their non-compliance with the statutes or the Constitution. The administrative units unlike courts do not enjoy the status of independence. However, due to the increasing authority of judicial practice, it is more and more often referred to in a situation when it would be necessary to issue a decision based on the provisions in an obvious manner (as stated in a court ruling, e.g.) contrary to the Constitution.

The essence of the law application process under the administrative procedure is the implementation of norms of procedural law and substantive law through their concretization and subsumption to a specific, individual factual state. The correctness of this process determines not only the correctness of the proceedings carried out, but also its effect in the form of a final decision as to the substance of the case or otherwise closing the proceedings. Therefore, any irregularities in the applied procedure and the interpretation of the applicable provisions will in essence determine the final effect of the decision-making process of the public administration bodies. As part of the application of the law, the administrative authority aims to establish and reconstruct the normative basis of the decision, which will be primarily the competence standard, followed by procedural and substantive law norms. It is obvious that from the perspective of the legal culture of law, this process will be based on the applicable legal provisions. However, it will also be noticeable that the authority reaches other normative facts, including the so-called well-established practice and jurisprudence. Therefore, there is no

6 This is clearly the case with art. 6 c.a.p.

doubt that a modern, contemporary approach to the legal system interpretation will determine the inclusion of not only strictly legal provisions, but also customs, interpretative and collisional rules, as well as views resulting from judicial case law. As a consequence, in the decision-making process, it will be possible to refer to earlier manifestations of the law (specific case law precedents) or to access to non-legal criteria for the assessment of given facts, which will affect (directly or indirectly) the final effect of the process.

Achieving the goal of issuing a correct act of applying the law depends on several factors, which in particular will foster the implementation of the principle of legalism. They will include an appropriate level of knowledge related to applicable law, as well as the ability to interpret them correctly, which will lead to proper subsumption of legal norms to a given factual state. They will therefore have a significant impact on building the legal bases for administrative acts and their appropriate interpretation.

In the process of interpreting the regulations and decoding the standards from them, an indispensable and valuable element influencing the formation of interpretations made by public administration bodies in the administrative type of application of the law is the administrative judiciary.

According to art. 1 § 1 of the Act on the system of administrative courts[7], these courts exercise the administration of justice by controlling the activities of public administration. This provision, interpreted in conjunction with the provisions of art. 184 of the Constitution of the Republic of Poland, which requires this control to be understood as adjudicating on compliance with the bills adopted by local self-government boards of appeal and normative acts of local government administration bodies, defines the basic function of these courts and the proceedings before them, which is the exercise of justice through control over the performance of public administration. In turn, art. 1 § 2 s.a.c. defines the basic principle of the administrative courts control function. Unless specific statutory provisions provide otherwise, this control is performed by the courts "in respect of legality". This means that the administration of justice exercised by the administrative courts is a judicial review of the legality of public administration activities.

The doctrine indicates that the core of the judiciary is to issue a judgment stating what norm of administrative law (constitutional, material or procedural) is applicable in the given case under consideration and determining, specifying

7 Act of 25 July 2002 on the System of Administrative Courts, Dz.U. 2016, item 1066, hereafter as s.a.c.

the disposition of this norm[8]. This ruling on legality binds both the parties to the dispute and – sometimes – other entities, and its enforcement is secured by means of legal enforcement. These measures create a sanction on the legal norm.

Judicial control of public administration activities, limited to the control of the legality of its decision-making process, is only one of many legal tools, but nonetheless, it constitutes a basic mean of control in the public administration system. At the same time, it involves examining the behavior of specific entities from the point of view of compliance of these activities with the models established by law, identification and indication of possible discrepancies and their causes, as well as formulating conclusions and recommendations aimed at their elimination. In the case of compliance monitoring (legality), this examination is carried out by administrative courts with regard to compliance of the behavior of controlled entities with applicable law. Thus, the subject of the control of legality is compliance with the provisions of the act by public administration bodies, i.e. the protection of the right in question, and the effect of this control – if the administrative court finds its violation, the court applies the law of the measures envisaged, e.g. cancel the contested decision, repeal a supervisory act or an administrative body's obligation to issue a decision within a specified period. Thus, the control of public administration includes: a control of reconstruction of procedural norms constituting the basis for the assessment of the implementation of the requirements for fact-finding by the legal administration; control of the legal way of qualifying these facts, which refers to the substantive legal basis of the administrative decision, including as regards the control of the interpretation of the law carried out by the legal entitle; through the prism of the provisions of procedural laws defining the legal requirements regarding the justification of the administrative decision (resolution), the control of a specific way of determining the actual and legal basis of the decision in a given case[9]. For the most part, however, the protection of substantive law combines with the protection of the subjective rights of citizens, which result from the norms of subject law, and have been violated by unlawful activities of public administration bodies. The protection of these rights is the primary goal of establishing the institution of judicial control over the legality of administrative activities, in particular in the form of administrative decisions. As part of its jurisdiction, the court examines whether there was no breach of substantive law and administrative proceedings when

8 T. Woś, *Law on Proceedings Before Administrative Courts. Commentary*, Warszawa 2016.

9 See: judgment of the Supreme Administrative Court in Warsaw of 25 November 2014, II GSK 1684/13, CBOSA.

the contested act was issued, without being bound by a complaint[10]. At the same time, the control from the point of view of the legality of the contested act should be understood as an assessment of the correct application of the provisions of the applicable law, international agreement or Community law and the correctness of their interpretation[11].

It should be noted that the subject of administrative court proceedings is not only an administrative act being the subject of appeal, but it is also a set of activities and actions taken by the administrative body in the case of this completed act. The jurisdiction of the administrative court delimited by the administrative court imposes an obligation to assess the entire course of the administrative procedure, all acts and actions issued in the proceedings, including the assessment of the contested decision and issuing a decision creating such a situation that there is no legal circulation there was no act or act of a public administration body illegal. Only such scope of operation of the administrative court meets the one specified in art. 1 point 2 s.a.c. or in art. 3 of the law on proceedings before administrative courts[12], the requirement to control the activities of administrative bodies in terms of compliance with the law[13].

The basic goal and effect of judicial control is to eliminate from the current legal order the acts and activities of public administration bodies that are incompatible with it and to restitution of the state in accordance with the law. In this way, the repressive function of judicial control is drawn, which is – naturally – important both from the point of view of the complainant and the entire state administrative apparatus. The whole administration should be interested in eliminating illegal acts and actions of state officials from legal transactions. The correctness and legality of activity of public administration bodies is, at the same time, an extremely important element of effectiveness and the premise of the existence of social acceptance of the entire administrative system of the state. The degree of acceptance of the operation of this apparatus directly affects the overall and detailed assessment of the functioning of the whole government.

10 See: judgment of the Provincial Administrative Court in Krakow of 20 April 2012, II SA/Kr 214/12 or from 16 May 2012, II SA/Kr 1877/11, CBOSA.

11 See: judgment of the Provincial Administrative Court in Warsaw of 5 August 2010, VIII SA/Wa 268/10, CBOSA.

12 Act of 30 August 2002 Law on Proceedings Before Administrative Courts, Dz.U. 2016, item 718, hereafter as p.b.a.c.

13 See: judgment of the Supreme Administrative Court in Warsaw of 20 January 2010, I GSK 982/08, CBOSA.

In addition to the repressive function, the preventive role of judicial control is equally important. Its purpose is to prevent law enforcement bodies from infringing the law in the future. This goal can be achieved in two ways. First of all, there may be measures exercised and aimed directly at preventing similar violations of law in the future, e.g. the institution of judicial signaling, used in addition to a substantive decision (referred to in art. 155 p.b.a.c.). Secondly, similarly but though indirectly, the judicial control affects the administrative awareness of the existence of an independent and repressive control body. The result of the joint impact of both these functions is the unification of the interpretation and application of the norms of administrative law by public administration bodies, in accordance with the position of the courts.

It should be further pointed out that the subject of administrative court proceedings isn't an "administrative matter", but examining the lawfulness of the contested act or the decision-making process. The administrative court is not an appeal body on decision merit and the court-administrative proceedings are not a continuation of the administrative proceedings. The essence of public administration control is the settlement of a court-administrative case understood as a dispute between an individual (addressed to a public administration authority) and a public administration authority (author of a decision addressed to an individual), the object of which is allegation of violation of law by a public administration authority. The resolution of this dispute by an administrative court boils down to a statement in the zero-one category, i.e. compliance or non-compliance with the law, which results in maintaining it or eliminating it from legal transactions. In effect, the result of a judicial decision is not limited to the specification of a legal norm, but to the control of the interpretation made by the administrative body, taking into account the criterion of compliance with the law. As a result of the control process, the administrative court is to apply the measures provided by the law[14].

The binding legal regulations and the teaching of constitutional law in a way that is unquestionable, quite rigorously assume that the activity of administrative courts should be limited to the control of administration, and thus the substantive adjudication of administrative matters should be ruled out, because then they would assume the role of administrative bodies, which is unacceptable from the point of view of the principle of the separation of powers[15]. Adjudication as

14 See: T. Woś, H. Knysiak-Molczyk, M. Romańska, *Law on Proceedings Before Administrative Courts. Commentary*, Warsaw 2005, p. 17.

15 For more see: L. Garlicki, *Polish Constitutional Law. Outline of the Lecture*, Warsaw 2016; J. Drachal, P. Gołaszewski, J. Jagielski, [in:] *Law on Proceedings before Administrative Courts. Commentary*, eds. R. Hauser, M. Wierzbowski, Warsaw 2011; P. Czarny,

a result of court-administrative proceedings should therefore be limited only to the assessment of the legality of public administration activities, and in the case of a lack of or a violation of legality – their cassation. With this assumption, the concretization of rights and obligations of individuals would still be made again by the public administration body, whose operation was effectively contested in court proceedings. Nevertheless, this body would be obliged to comply with the findings and indications contained in the court judgement. From this point of view, it would be doubtful to extend the jurisdiction of administrative courts to matters outside the scope of public administration control by means of ordinary legislation, as this is not fully consistent with the regulation of art. 184 of the Constitution. In fact, there is no doubt that the jurisdiction of the administrative appeal bodies, referring to the control of the instances of self-government public administration activities, in accordance with the patterns of modern administration, should be determined by views arising from the current administrative judiciary. It is important and in principle unquestionable that the theses presented in the case law affect directly and indirectly, in a visible manner, the content of administrative decisions of these bodies. The consequences of interpretations expressed in court judgments are visible in the decisions of first instance bodies. Thus, the transfer of judicial interpretation to the public administration is often quite broad. This effect is due to several reasons.

Firstly, as a result of legislative changes, administrative courts exercised a significant influence on the content of later administrative decisions issued after the control of the conducted proceedings by administrative bodies of both instances. This is the effect of the validity of art. 153 p.b.a.c., which states that the legal assessment and indications as to the further proceedings expressed in the court's judgment shall be binding in the case bodies whose action, inaction or lengthy proceedings were subject to appeal, as well as the courts, unless the law has changed.

Secondly, the causative factor is a kind of pragmatism in the scope of application to a specific factual situation that was subject to judicial review, but also to other analogous situations, interpretations and theses presented in court judgments, even loosely related to them.

Thirdly, one should not forget about the process economics understood as the desire to avoid severity in the form of revoking the administrative decision as a result of judgment and extending the proceedings only because the authority has

---

A. Kulig, B. Naleziński, P. Sarnecki, P. Tuleja, K. Wojtyczek, *Constitutional Law of the Republic of Poland*, Warsaw 2013.

not survived to the previously presented assessments, interpretations and views stemming from the so-called well-established judicial practice.

3 Judicial Jurisprudence and the Principle of Instance of Administrative Proceedings

It is necessary to notice that the introduction of provisions allowing the administrative courts to adjudicate in a reforming way, in essence, that court's judgments may replace decisions of public administration authorities or determine them sufficiently and imperiously. Thus, these authorities leave no room for maneuver when re-adjudicating in a given administrative case or decree clearance. As a consequence, the court-administrative proceedings implemented in the Polish model do not correspond to the classical solutions applicable to cassation proceedings, because the administrative body to which the case was referred for re-examination is not fully free to re-examine the case. The competence of the administrative court allowing it to formulate legal assessment of the case and indications as to the further proceedings binds this court as well as the authority to such a large extent that the administrative courts directly influence the content of the decisions taken in the administrative proceedings. This influence should be aimed more at explaining the content of the legal provision constituting the basis of the disputed resolution then not, at the same time, going beyond the scope of the public administration's control exercised by the courts. Thus, the court in its ruling should express guidelines as to the interpretation of a specific provision of law, and not impose on the authority that it will re-examine the matter a specific understanding of the given regulation in the context of the facts of the case. In this practice, this would mean that the administrative courts would replace and assume an important part of the administrative task of applying the law[16]. However, it does not raise any doubt that, due to the mandatory nature of Art. 153 p.b.a.c. neither the public administration body nor the court, re-stating in the same matter, cannot avoid to take into account the legal assessment and indications expressed earlier in the court decision, because they are legally related to them. Failure to comply with this provision would in fact undermine the principle of judicial control over the acts and activities of administrative bodies in a democratic state ruled by law and led to incoherence in the operation of the public authority system. Binding the legal assessment

16 Compare the judgment of the Provincial Administrative Court in Lublin of 21 March 2013, III SA/Lu 498/12, CBOSA.

expressed in the judgment and the resulting indications regarding further proceedings means that the formulation of the new legal assessments contained in the judgment is excluded by the administrative body whose decision was subject to judgment. This body is obliged to comply fully with it and to respond consistently in the event of a failure to comply with the indications regarding further proceedings before the public administration authority[17]. Therefore, art. 153 p.b.a.c. defines such a relationship between the administrative body and the court, which consists in binding the body to legal assessment and indications for further proceedings. Therefore, there is no room for polemics of the body with legal assessment and indications for that further proceedings[18]. The case law of the Supreme Administrative Court emphasizes that the obligation to comply with the legal assessment expressed in the administrative court ruling of the body and the court may be excluded only in the event of a significant change in legal or facts making the legal view obsolete and also in case of a judgment being passed in the mode provided for by law[19].

The legal assessment indicated above means a specific interpretation of substantive and procedural law and aims to clarify the important content of legal provisions and the manner of their application in a specific case in relation to the case being examined. Indications regarding further proceedings are usually the consequences of the legal assessment and concern the way of acting in the course of re-examining the case. In addition, they are designed to avoid errors already committed and to indicate the direction in which future proceedings should be aimed at avoiding further or other defects or procedural defects. Therefore, when a given matter will be the subject of a diagnosis, the authorities will be bound by the legal assessment made by the court, until the decision expressing it will not be repealed or the applicable provisions will not change significantly[20].

---

17 Such judgments of the Supreme Administrative Court of 30 July 2009, II FSK 451/08; of 23 September 2009, I FSK 494/09, CBOSA; of 13 July 2010, I GSK 940/09 and of the Provincial Administrative Court in Wrocław of 14 January 2010, I SA/Wr 1591/09, CBOSA.

18 Compare judgment of the Provincial Administrative Court in Poznań of 27 November 2013, IV SA/Po 537/13, CBOSA.

19 Compare judgment of the Supreme Administrative Court of 26 June 26 2000, I SA/Ka 2408/98, CBOSA; judgment of the Provincial Administrative Court in Opole of 3 July 2012, II SA/Op 239/12, CBOSA.

20 Such judgment of the Supreme Administrative Court in Warsaw of 6 February 2013, II GSK 2101/11, CBOSA.

It should also be noted that the provisions of Art. 153 p.b.a.c. mean that the court's decision covers the future administrative proceedings in this case[21].

The legal assessment expressed in the court's judgment is the manifestation of the so-called judge-made-law, which is created by the jurisprudence of administrative courts, interpreting the norms of administrative law, as well as showing what standards and how to be applied in a specific case. Although courts are not generally authorized to issue substantive decisions, in practice they do so for the purpose of monitoring the decisions appealed to them. Thus, they formulate secondary standards of the second level, and with their help they shape future case law and the way in which public administration bodies handle cases. On this basis, one can simplify the thesis that, through their case law, administrative courts in a sense also "administer" and even act as "legislators", somewhat violating the principle of the separation of powers – appropriating the functions of the executive and the legislature.

It cannot be omitted that the second of the regulated institutions is also covered by art. 153 p.b.a.c., i.e. indications as to the further course of action, which is usually a consequence of the legal assessment included in the court's cassation ruling. Such indications relate to the way in which the case is re-examined; their purpose is to avoid and eliminate errors previously committed and to outline the direction in which future proceedings should proceed in order to avoid defects consisting of deficiencies in the procedural material or deficiencies in the scope of procedural regulations.

The opinions expressed in court rulings as to the interpretation of the law, but also the proceedings, become the basic instrument for shaping the decisions of public administration bodies. Binding to judicial interpretation does not refer only to the court and public administration authority, whose action or inaction was the subject of court proceedings, but also includes any other body that participated in the proceedings conducted within the given case, if the judgment was covered acts or activities preceding the act or act complained of. This means that the administrative court's decision exceeds beyond the scope of the court-administrative proceedings. A pragmatic approach to the rules and interpretative rules formulated in the jurisprudence allows the authority to avoid defects in administrative proceedings and administrative acts issued as a result of it. It is obvious that since the administrative body already received a ruling in which the opinion was expressed in the matter of interest to it, the use of theses contained

21 See: judgment of the Supreme Administrative Court in Warsaw of 14 March 2013, I GSK 1591/11, CBOSA.

in it is highly probable in analogous as to the assessed facts and cases examined. The application of an opposite rule of conduct seems not only senseless but also pointless. At the same time, if the judicial decision is based on the interpretation (courts of the same and higher instance) already existing in the judiciary, it is more likely that it would be replicate in analogous matters. Since the court's opinion is known, it can be expected that it will be used and disseminated by other courts. One cannot resist the impression that even by its very nature the court will use its jurisprudence as much as the administrative body. Of course, it is not excluded to move away from the well-established case law, but this situation is quite unique.

Adherence by the authority to views and opinions arising from well-established case law also allows the avoidance of the possibility of applying sanctions in the form of repealing an administrative decision made in a similar factual state. It seems pointless to re-balance the specific "open doors" and to shape a new interpretation of the provisions for which a binding interpretation has already been made. Therefore, in the situation of having a ready interpretation pattern, it is obvious that using the judicial achievements and creating administrative achievements is obvious. It also determines the willingness to avoid the obvious severity of the courts in the sphere of questioning administrative decisions themselves, as well as generating court costs as a result. Statistics on the elimination of administrative acts from legal transactions as a result of judicial opinion also shape the assessment of effectiveness, efficiency of administration and affect the development of the rule of law and general social approval of the public administration.

It follows from the case law of administrative bodies that such action of administrative bodies is a common phenomenon. E.g., it is possible to indicate the practice of applying an administrative fine after repealing the provisions of the Nature Conservation Act by a judgment of the Constitutional Tribunal[22], in which despite the actual postponement of the entry into force of a constitutional court ruling until the amendment of art. 88 of the Act on Nature Conservation, administrative courts and then public administration bodies of both instances applied to the opinion expressed in it. The practice was shaped by judicial decisions, as a result of which the administrative authorities not only did not apply the sanctions contained in the said regulation, but also due to the fact that the administration was bound by judicial interpretation, recognizing the case

22 See: judgment of the Constitutional Tribunal of 1 July 2014 in case SK 6/12, OTK-A 2014/7/68, Dz.U. 2014, item 926.

again and bearing in mind the judgment of the Constitutional Tribunal and the legislation works aimed at changing the rules for administering administrative penalties for the removal, without the required permit, of trees or shrubs, considered suspending administrative proceedings in accordance with art. 97 par. 1 point 4 c.a.p., while examining the subject matter, they took into account the interpretation of art. 88 § 1 point 2, art. 89 paragraph acts presented in case law[23]. Although the judgment of the Tribunal was not yet effective, as the Tribunal decided to postpone the loss of binding force of unconstitutional provisions, it is the position of the Tribunal and administrative courts adjudicating on its issuance and the assessment in it confirming the non-compliance with the Constitution of the legal provisions that are the basis for issuing of the contested decision, determined the elimination of the legal turnover of decisions issued on the basis of provisions incompatible with the indicated provisions of the Constitution. The above example clearly indicates the development of the practice of administrative bodies based on judicial decisions they followed and this is not a one-off case. Similar cases occurred in the application of provisions relating to the applicability of sanctions in the form of a levy for the use of the environment, which in specific factual situations would be difficult to reconcile with the constitutional principles of the rule of law, including the principle of justice[24] and would lead to the exclusion of this sanction in the case of non-culpable the lack of a permit or until a constitutive decision confirming the expiration of such a permit has been issued[25].

At present, the case law practice, especially in higher-level administrative bodies such as appeal boards, does not consist in examining a given case in the course of appeal proceedings in isolation of the administrative court case law.

---

23 Compare judgment of the Provincial Administrative Court in Lublin of 30 September 2014, II SA/Lu 717/14, CBOSA; judgment of the Supreme Administrative Court in Warsaw of 4 December 2014, II OSK 2697/14, CBOSA.

24 See: judgment of the Provincial Administrative Court in Warsaw of 8 July 2005, IV SA/Wa 714/05, CBOSA; resolution of the Supreme Administrative Court of 21 December 1998, OPS 13/98, CBOSA and views expressed in the doctrine of A. Lipiński, OSP 1996, no. 6, item 107; W. Radecki, OSP 1999, no. 6, item 107; P. Sadowski, *The fee increased as a consequence of the lack of a water permit*, "CASSUS" 2009, no. 4 or later in the resolution of the Supreme Administrative Court of 12 December 2011, II OPS 2/11, CBOSA.

25 See: judgments: of the Provincial Administrative Court in Białystok of 19 April 2007, II SA/Bk 832/06, CBOSA; Provincial Administrative Court in Krakow of 18 March 2009, II SA/Kr 1224/08, CBOSA; of the Provincial Administrative Court in Wrocław of 21 December 2010, II SA/Wr 462/10, CBOSA; of the Provincial Administrative Court in Lublin of 11 April 2013, II SA/Lu 1095/12, CBOSA.

An important element of the proceedings by the adjudicating panels of these bodies is the prior search for court decisions issued in similar facts. It allows to build both the decision support and its justification based on current theses and views created by the courts. In this way, principle of persuasion resulting from art. 11 c.a.p., as well as the principle of deepening the citizens' trust toward the state from art. 8 § 1 c.a.p. are enforced. It cannot be ignored that the current regulation of the administrative procedure code also indicates in art. 8 § 2, that public administration bodies without a justified reason should not deviate from the consolidated practice of settling cases in the same facts and legal state of affairs. Therefore, based on the established court practice, the decision identity of the appeal bodies themselves is built.

4 Conclusions

Several conclusions follow from the above considerations. First of all, one may observe an increasing role of judiciary and well-established case law in activity of public administration in shaping their opinions and decision expressed in the acts of applying the law of administrative bodies. It determines in a clear and often direct way the content of the justification of administrative bodies of both instances. It is also noteworthy that in the case of a conflict of norms or judicial argumentation and preliminary interpretation by the authority in the majority of cases (which results from the analysis of the judicial practice of appeal boards), priority is given to the first one, which was associated primarily with the pragmatism and economy of legal proceedings indicated above as well as the willingness of the authority to avoid a possible sanction in the form of a court decision issued with additional financial severity. The use of jurisprudence has the advantage of fairly wide borrowing of interpretative argumentation and helps in solving legal problems resulting from difficulties in the interpretation of often vague (even almost enigmatic) legal provisions. The use of judicial decisions in the manner described above begins to resemble using them as a sort of precedent, on the basis of which the content of issued administrative acts is created. This phenomenon should be considered as desirable in all respects. The previously observed practice in the case of judicial authorities based on building decisions on the grounds of the previously presented view begins to be taken over by public administration bodies. This is one of the important elements of building the principle of legal certainty and the citizen's trust in state, recognized as a legitimate right to be expected by a citizen as far as a given state action, predictability and consequences of actions of its bodies are concerned.

Andrzej Jakubecki

A Precedent as a Doctrinal and Jurisdictional Category of Civil Law

Abstract: The concept of a precedent in the Polish civil law science is most frequently analysed from the perspective of sources of the civil law. The topic of interest is whether judicial decisions and, formerly, also decisions of the State Economic Arbitration can be considered the source of civil law standards. The position of the contemporary Polish civil law science regarding the legislative role of judicial decisions and the judicial precedent are summed up well in the statement that, in the Polish legal system, decisions made by courts, including the highest courts, are not officially binding for lower courts. As for the judicature's approach to this issue, it is common to negate the thesis that precedent decisions create commonly applicable legal principles. However, that approach does not mean that the doctrine and the court decisions do not appreciate or diminish the importance of the activity of courts in the modelling and directing of the interpretation and application of the law. On the contrary, the doctrine highlights the role of the judicature but does not usually place it among sources of the law.

Keywords: civil proceedings, precedent, judicial decision, sources of law

1 The Concept of Precedent in the Civil Law Doctrine

The concept of a precedent in the Polish civil law science is most frequently analysed from the perspective of sources of the civil law[1]. The topic of interest is whether judicial decisions and, formerly, also decisions of the State Economic Arbitration can be considered the source of civil law standards. If the concept of a precedent[2] appears in such deliberations it is referred to sources of the law in the common law system. According to M. Safjan, a precedent modelled by decisions of higher courts is binding for all lower courts and creates "a rule of a more general value whose significance goes beyond a specific case"[3].

1 See, e.g.: S. Grzybowski, [in:] *System prawa cywilnego*, vol. 1: *Część ogólna*, ed. idem, Wrocław 1985, p. 69 et seq.; M. Safjan, [in:] *System prawa prywatnego*, vol. 1: *Prawo cywilne – część ogólna*, ed. idem, Warszawa 2012, p. 236 et seq.; A. Wolter, J. Ignatowicz, K. Stefaniuk, *Prawo cywilne. Zarys części ogólnej*, Warszawa 1996, p. 63 et seq.

2 See: M. Safjan, [in:] *System...*, op. cit., p. 237.

3 Ibidem, p. 238, invoking the work by Cross, *On Precedent*, Oxford 1990.

It is characteristic for the approach presented in the Polish science that even if the legislation component is perceived in the activity of the judicature, the concept of a precedent will not be used in that area. However, the prevailing belief is that the activity of judicial agencies is not the source of the law but rather involves the application of existing legal standards.

The work by S. Grzybowski from the mid-1980s[4] is a summary of achievements of the Polish doctrine referring to the legislative role of judicial decisions from the mid-1980s. S. Grzybowski states there that the legislative activity of the judicature is disappearing in developed statutory law systems. The same author also states that opinions about the legislative role of the judiciary (A. Stelmachowski[5] and S. Włodyka[6]) were isolated in the Polish science.

According to A. Stelmachowski, if one talks about the legislation in the activity of courts, it involves the creation of such general standards that do not result from the statutory regulations but rather operate as if they were based on the statutory authority. According to the same author, the difference between the judicial decisions and legislative acts of the statutory nature is in the fact that a legal standard operates for the future, regulating a certain social relation in line with an abstractly assumed hypothesis while decisions refer to historical facts that occurred in the past. However, it sometimes happens that a legal principle is created on the basis of such facts and, according to the common practice, it should be applicable in each similar case[7]. As the cited author observes, the latter type is usually negative in the continental doctrine and the view prevalent in the Polish doctrine is that courts do not create the law. According to A. Stelmachowski, that approach to the legislative role of judicial decisions is based on the hypostasis that courts have no legislative competence. When justifying his opinion about the legislative role of judicial decisions, A. Stelmachowski stated that art. 87 of the Constitution in which judicial decisions are not mentioned among the sources of the law refer to the "codified" law only, which does not rule out the existence of other sources of the law[8].

---

4 S. Grzybowski, op. cit., p. 89 et seq.

5 A. Stelmachowski, *Wstęp do teorii prawa cywilnego*, 2nd ed., amended, Warszawa 1984, p. 434. See also: idem, *Prawotwórcza działalność arbitrażu*, "Przegląd Ustawodawstwa Gospodarczego" 1959, no. 11, p. 369; idem, *Klauzule generalne w kodeksie cywilnym*, "Państwo i Prawo" 1966, no. 3, p. 480 et seq.

6 S. Włodyka, *Prawotwórcza działalność Sądu Najwyższego*, "Zeszyty Naukowe Uniwersytetu Jagiellońskiego" 1967, no. 31, p. 157 et seq.

7 A. Stelmachowski, *Wstęp…*, p. 435.

8 Idem, *Zarys teorii prawa cywilnego*, Warszawa 1998, p. 295 et seq.

A. Stelmachowski assumed that art. 87 of the Constitution does not refer to non-statutory sources of the law[9].

A. Stelmachowski perceives symptoms of the legislative role of judicial decisions even in the case of the *secundum legem* interpretation and even more so in the case of the *praeter legem* interpretation. In the former case, those legal standards that, while using ambiguous terms, create a freedom for the judge to choose a decision as well as general clauses, in particular, the clause of the principles of social co-existence, offer ample room for the legislation[10]. As for the *praeter legem* decisions, the author stresses that the analogy is only an excuse, one of numerous fictions we use to save the value of certain rules that are practically unsustainable[11]. The views of A. Stelmachowski remain isolated.

The position of the contemporary Polish civil law science regarding the legislative role of judicial decisions and the judicial precedent are summed up well in the statement of M. Safjan, who states that in the Polish legal system, decisions made by courts, including the highest courts, are not officially binding for lower courts. Therefore, there are no obstacles, theoretically, for the court examining a case to change the interpretation in comparison with the previously adopted jurisprudence and take a different position than what has been considered accurate in the judicature so far[12]. However, the author also observes the symptoms of a *quasi*-normative function of court decisions in the creative case law, i.e. the one that introduces new normative contents to the system going beyond the conclusions drawn from the semantic and logical interpretation[13]. M. Safjan stresses that it has been possible to observe many fundamental breakthroughs and judicature directions in the Polish private law for the last decades; in fact, they have been creating legal principles not based on the wording of applicable regulations. Examples mentioned by the author[14] include: modelling, in the judicature of the Supreme Court, of the liability of the State Treasury pursuant to art. 417 of the Civil Code as the autonomous liability detached from other bases of the liability in tort, based on the risk principle and the presumption of

9 Ibidem, p. 297 et seq.

10 Ibidem, p. 299 et seq.

11 Ibidem, p. 301. A. Stelmachowski invokes an example from art. 1 of the Swiss Civil Code, which states that in specific conditions where there are no legislative indications, a judge should settle a case as if the judge was a legislator. However, he notes that the regulation has been applied in practice extremely rarely.

12 M. Safjan, [in:] *System...*, op. cit., p. 239 et seq.

13 Idem, p. 241.

14 Idem, p. 241 et seq.

culpability of the direct perpetrator of a loss[15]; the gradual development in the judicature of the *ex delicto* responsibility for a dangerous product, which led to the creation of a separate type of the responsibility based on the producer's risk principle[16]; development of the liability for losses caused to the *nasciturus* in court decisions[17], introduced to the Civil Code in 1993; the Supreme Court accepting the admissibility of the transfer of title to a property for security purposes, which has been considered inadmissible until 1990[18].

While noticing the existence of a *quasi*-normative activity of judicial decisions, M. Safjan observes that its source is in general clauses as well as gaps in the legal system. The creative interpretation performs the adaptation function involving the adaptation of legal institutions to existing social relations and effectively anticipates future normative solutions, thus preparing the ground for the legislative intervention[19].

2 The Meaning of "Precedent" in the Code of Civil Procedures

In 1996, the term "precedent" appeared in the provision of the Code of Civil Procedures and, therefore, became a statutory term. According to art. 47 § 4 of the Code of Civil Procedures, the court president can order the cognisance of a case by three professional judges if the president considers it useful due to the particular complexity or the "precedent nature of the case"[20]. The term "precedent" was used with a wrong, common meaning[21]. It is because the essence is not in the creation of a binding judicial decision but rather in the case where the emerging legal issue has not been fully explained in the literature and in judicial decisions yet or its settlement "will create a precedent for similar cases"[22].

15 Decision of the Supreme Court of 15 February 1971, III CZP 33/70, OSN 1971, no. 4, item 59.
16 Decision of the Supreme Court of 30 December 1988, III CZP 48/88, OSN 1989, no. 3, item 36.
17 See, e.g. the judgment of the Supreme Court of 3 May 1967, III PR 120/67, OSN 1967, no. 10, item 89. More about this topic in: M. Safjan, *Prawo wobec ingerencji w naturę ludzkiej prokreacji*, Warszawa 1990, passim.
18 Judgment of the Supreme Court of 29 May 2000, III CKN 46/00, OSN 2000, no. 11, item 213.
19 M. Safjan, [in:] *System...*, op. cit., p. 245 et seq.
20 The precedent nature of the case as of 1989 was mentioned in art. 479[5] of the Code of Civil Procedures in the proceedings in commercial cases.
21 A. Harla, *Precedensowy charakter sprawy cywilnej w rozumieniu kodeksu postępowania cywilnego. Uwagi* de lege lata *i* de lege ferenda, "Przegląd Sądowy" 2001, no. 4, p. 26.
22 J. Pietrzykowski, *Sądownictwo gospodarcze. Komentarz*, Warszawa 1990, p. 21.

Therefore, the said provision does not contribute to the understanding of a precedent in the Polish civil law system.

3 The Judicature's Approach

As for the judicature's approach to this issue, the term "precedent" is rarely used in court decisions relating to civil law cases and it is usually used in the common sense of the word. In relatively infrequent cases where statements of reasons for the court decision use the term "precedent", the word is usually supposed to mean an event that will be repeated many times in the future or a certain example of behaviour for the future. A precedent may also happen to be used with the meaning of something exceptional (unique) that did not occur in the past. In particular, the wording such as "the interpretation creates a dangerous precedent" is characteristic for the above-mentioned understanding of a precedent.

However, it is worth noting that the term "precedent" in above-mentioned meanings appears nearly exclusively in the historical part of statements of reasons for decisions (i.e. factual justification), in the description of demands of a party (the complainant). In fact, it means that not the court but rather that party uses the term. Examples include the following citations: "(The Complainant) expressed an opinion that the adoption of the legal opinion being the basis for the decision of the court of the second instance would equal the actual lack of sanctions for such behaviour and could become a precedent precluding the application of control procedures by the Respondent to protect the property"[23] or "An improper interpretation of the said regulation creates a very dangerous precedent for the future"[24]. The above-mentioned use of the term "precedent" in court decisions is not addressed in this work.

As for the exact meaning of the "precedent", judicial decisions very rarely use it in civil law cases. It seems that, due to the negation of the importance of a precedent in the system of sources of the law in Poland, courts intentionally avoid using that term even when referring to cases involving the court settlement modelling the practice in other, similar cases.

The statement that appeared in the award issued by the District Court in Białystok of 27 January 2014 can be considered symptomatic[25]; it contains the

---

23 Supreme Court Proceedings of 24 June 2002, I PKN 562/01, Lex 1169631.

24 Judgment of the Supreme Court of 2 June 1953, I C 464/53, OSNCK 1954, no. 1, item 23.

25 VU 2016/13, Lex 1722285. See also: judgment of the Court of Appeal in Poznań of 30 April 2013, III AUa 61/13, Lex 466555.

opinion that: "According to art. 390 § 2 of the Code of Civil Procedures, an award of the Supreme Court settling a legal issue binds the court exclusively in that case in which the legal issue emerged. The Constitution of the Republic of Poland does not mention awards issued by the Supreme Court among sources of the law. In this situation, there is no way to consider the resolution of 2 July 2013 a precedent". The case involved a decision of the Supreme Court defining the period of the unemployment benefit collection made in another case covering the same subject matter. The complainant claimed in an appeal from the decision made by ZUS that the decision made by ZUS was contrary to that decision of the Supreme Court.

The clear reference to a precedent as a decision modelling the practice of the system of justice appears in those decisions in which the concept of a material point of law is analysed. The "material point of law" is a term that occurs in art. 398^9 § 1 (initially art. 393 § 1 section 1 the Code of Civil Procedures) the Code of Civil Procedures among the circumstances justifying the acceptance of the cassation complaint for consideration (i.e. pre-trial proceedings). In its decision of 7 January 2005[26], the Supreme Court stated that "the point of law is material, as understood in art. 393 § 1 section 1 of the Code of Civil Procedures if it is of the fundamental importance for law development or a precedent for the settlement of other civil law cases". The discrepancy between the opinion expressed in the contested decision and the opinion presented in the case by the party (the complainant) by itself is not a point of law. The Supreme Court expressed the same legal opinion in the decision of 29 November 2012[27] stating that "a material point of law is such a juridical issue that is of importance for law development or constitutes a precedent for the settlement of cases".

Even though the judicature avoids using the term "precedent" in civil law cases, the analysis of decisions of the Supreme Court, courts of appeal and also (to a limited degree) district courts makes it possible to formulate the following conclusions as regards the perception of the importance of prior court decisions for the practice of the system of justice.

1) In those cases that truly involve the issue of an impact of prior decisions on the modelling of the practice of the system of justice, statements of reasons for decisions mention the "settled case law" rather than a precedent.

26 I CZ 183/04, Lex 1503135.
27 IV CSK 466/12, Lex 1288724.

2) The judicature decisively negates the legislative role of judicial decisions. Prior court decisions are perceived as indications regarding the interpretation of regulations rather than a source of legal standards.
3) It is a common practice that justifications of court decisions refer to prior settlements relating to opinions expressed in the justification. In most cases, we have to do with a full indication of a decision (date, signature and, potentially, the place of publication). However, general references not indicating any specific decision also happen.

As for the reference to the ruling practice, the prevailing approach is to indicate court decisions comprising that practice irrespectively of the form of individual decisions and whether they have been published[28]. However, a reference to an established ruling practice may be accompanied only by one decision with a note "see, among others"[29] or even the lack of any decision representing that ruling practice[30]. It does not mean that the ruling practice is non-existent; it is just that the court made no effort to mention decisions illustrating the line.

A reference to a ruling practice is not usually accompanied by the citation of the argumentation or rationale presented in previous decisions. While referring to a certain ruling practice, the court making a decision regarding the case feels relieved of the need to explain why a specific legal opinion is considered right in it. What is more, the reference to a ruling practice by itself is frequently considered the sufficient argument for the validity of the opinion adopted in the case[31].

The following example can be mentioned. In the chronologically oldest decision of 20 September 2007[32], the Supreme Court expressed the opinion that the introduction of a manifestly ungrounded legal measure by a representative established by the court does not justify the assignment of costs of legal aid to such a representative from the State Treasury. This thought was expressed in the thesis of the decision. In the justification, the Supreme Court claimed, indicating two previous decisions, that the opinion that activities violating professional principles pursued by an attorney nominated by the court do not justify the assignment

28 Judgement of the Court of Appeal in Warsaw of 30 April 2015, VI ACa 861/14, Lex 1747538; decision of the Supreme Court of 14 November 2013, III CNP 33/12, Lex 1422015.

29 Decision of the Supreme Court of 24 February 2004, III CK 322/02, Lex 1129110.

30 Judgment of the Court of Appeal in Łódź of 23 April 2015, I ACa 1565/14, Lex 1711502.

31 See, e.g. the decision of the Supreme Court of 14 November 2013, III CNP 33/13, Lex 1422015; decision of the Supreme Court of 16 January 2015, III CSK 308/14, Lex 1628928.

32 II CZ 69/07, OSNC 2008, no. 3, item 41.

of unpaid legal aid costs to such an attorney has to be considered established. It also observed that, as a rule, it is the case when a legal measure prepared by a professional helper is subject to rejection due to its structural defects. After that, the Supreme Court states that the compilation of a complaint that will be rejected as manifestly ungrounded is not the legal service. The thesis of another decision made by the Supreme Court on 18 December 2007[33] states that the rejection of a cassation complaint due to its material deficiencies is not the legal service the costs of which should be borne by the State Treasury. The mention of the lack of legal service appears in the thesis of the decision but the Supreme Court only stresses that it is not the legal service whose costs should be borne by the State Treasury (rather than no legal service at all). Even though the thread seems to be taken from the justification of the decision of 20 September 2007, it is not mentioned here. However, in the decision of 16 January 2015[34], the Supreme Court states that the submission of an inadmissible cassation action "is not the legal service" and does not justify the award of a fee from the State Treasury to the attorney established by the court. The justification mentions dates and signatures of both the previous decisions with no additional argumentation or reference to the motives of these decisions.

However, there are examples of judicial decisions where *prima facie* the court does not limit itself to mentioning a specific ruling practice and indicating the settlement illustrating it but also cites the content of the settlement and certain components of the justification. In the justification of the award of 4 April 2008[35], the Supreme Court refers to the ruling practice in cases for benefits due to police officers indicating, in particular, the decision of 7 judges of the Supreme Court of 21 October 1997[36]. The Supreme Court cites the opinion expressed in a previous decision but, in fact, it is nothing more than a summary of the contents of that decision.

Observations made regarding decisions in which courts refer to a specific ruling practice or established case law as regards the reference to previous decisions also apply to those court decisions in which there is no *expressis verbis* reference to the ruling practice. Such decisions comprise the most numerous group in the judicial practice of the Supreme Court.

The most typical way of referring to previous decisions involves the inclusion of the term "see" in brackets and citing dates and signatures of decisions with the

33 III CSK 336/07, Lex 795782.
34 III CSK 308/14, Lex 1628928.
35 I CSK 456/07, Lex 393853.
36 III CZP 34/97, OSNC 1998, no. 2, item 19.

place of publication or a note that they are not published. There is no indication whether an opinion is formulated in the thesis of the cited decision or a fragment of the justification. This method is applied both in decisions issued by the Supreme Court and by common courts. It is a rare thing for the justification to cite the argumentation contained in previous settlements.

4 The Practical Importance of Prior Court Decisions – The Binding Precedents?

Even though the review of court decisions shows that the situation in which it is possible to refer to opinions previously expressed in the judicature is doubtlessly comfortable for the court settling a case, discrepancies between opinions of the Supreme Court in similar points of law are a frequent occurrence. Of course, it sometimes happens that the Supreme Court renounces opinions expressed in prior decisions.

The question of the court being bound with the grounds for the suspension of proceedings in the civil law proceedings can serve as an example. The Supreme Court initially assumed that such an obligation did not apply. In its decision of 14 April 1983[37], the Supreme Court assumed that, while examining the case pursuant to art. 182 § 1 of the Code of Civil Procedures (dismissal of the suspended proceedings), the court was not bound with the grounds for the suspension indicated in the decision concerning the suspension of proceedings if the evidence demonstrates that the actual cause of the suspension was different. The Supreme Court expressed a similar opinion in the decision of 25 February 1985[38], where it stated that, in the case of the suspension of proceedings despite the lack of grounds, the court shall decide upon the reinstatement of the suspended proceedings at any time, also when considering the premises of suspension of proceedings. The change of opinion occurred in the decision 7 of the Supreme Court judges of 17 December 1998[39]. In the statement of reasons for that decision, motives of previous settlements briefly cited in the content of the statement of reasons were undermined by stating that the Supreme Court examining the case "does not share these opinions". Juridical argumentation in favour of a different position was also presented. Additionally, it was mentioned that the existing interpretation would be even more ungrounded as it would go in the direction

37 IV PRN 4/83, OSNC 1983, no. 10, item 167.
38 III CZP 86/84, OSNC 1985, no. 11, item 168.
39 II CKN 713/98, OSP 1999, no. 10, item 176.

opposite to changes introduced in 1996 that strengthened the dispositive principle in the civil law proceedings.

The evaluation of the practical importance of court rulings on points of law giving rise to doubts or divergences is not clear. The negation of the thesis that precedent decisions create commonly applicable legal principles creates a relatively wide area for adjudicating panels to make decisions in which opinions previously expressed in the judicature are either accepted or renounced from time to time. Even decisions made by the Supreme Court to standardise the judicature do not always guarantee the attainment of such an effect.

The above-mentioned brief review of the position taken by the doctrine and court decisions offers grounds for the statement that the judicial precedent is not considered a source of the law except in statements of very few scientists. Even the term "precedent" by itself is rarely used in science and judicature referring to the Polish legal system. However, that approach does not mean that the doctrine and, even more so, the court decisions do not appreciate or diminish the importance of the activity of courts in the modelling and directing of the interpretation and application of the law. On the contrary, the doctrine highlights the role of the judicature but does not usually place it among sources of the law. An interesting thing though is that the creativity of court decisions going beyond the area of the semantic or logical interpretation of the law is observed in the literature. Calling these cases the *quasi*-normative activity of courts seems to reflect well the "legislative" component of the judicial application of the law. However, as the practice of the system of justice demonstrates in civil law cases, the lack of the common binding force of rules of law created in this manner speaks against the consideration that such cases are created legal norms in the strict sense. Except for special cases regulated in the law[40], courts are not and, importantly, do not feel bound with previous individual decisions or even established jurisprudence. They do not treat previous decisions as binding precedents.

40 E.g., art. 398^{17} § 2 and art. 398^{20} of the Code of Civil Procedures, art. 62 § 1 of the act of 23 November 2002 on the Supreme Court (consolidated text: Dz.U. 2016, item 1254 as amended).

Ireneusz Nowikowski

The Problem of Precedents in the Criminal Judgements of the Polish Supreme Court

Abstract: This study is the result of research on the criminal case law of the Polish Supreme Court. At the beginning, the position of the literature on the notion of "precedent decision" and "law-making decisions" is presented and the views of the doctrine of criminal procedural law concerning the issue of admissibility of a precedent are quoted. The subject of the research are judgments from different periods of the Polish judicial system development (1972–1973, 2002–2003, 2012–2013). The aim of the research is to answer the question whether the concept of precedent is used in the justification of criminal law judgments of the Supreme Court and for what reasons the Supreme Court referred to earlier decisions.

Keywords: precedent, criminal procedural law, Polish criminal process, the judgements of the Criminal and Military Chamber of the Supreme Court

1 Precedents in the Doctrine of Polish Criminal Process (Selected Issues)

The following reflections result from research on the judgements of the Criminal and Military Chamber of the Supreme Court referring to the use of the term "precedent" in the judgements of that court and the practice of quoting earlier judgements by the Supreme Court. Before the results of the research are presented, it should be discussed whether a precedent is treated as a source of law in the criminal law in its broad meaning.

Analysing the importance of court judgements in the light of the above presented question two situations should be first indicated. The first would be connected with distinguishing "precedent decisions", the second with the concept of "law creating decisions". By a precedent decision one should understand such a decision which normatively or effectively influences the taking of other decisions[1]. According to L. Morawski, a precedent is constituted not by the whole

---

1 See: L. Morawski, *Czy precedens powinien być źródłem prawa*, [in:] *W kręgu problematyki władzy, państwa i prawa. Księga jubileuszowa w 70-lecie urodzin Profesora Henryka Groszyka*, eds. A. Korobowicz, A. Korybski, M. Kuryłowicz, J. Malarczyk, A. Pieniążek, Lublin 1996, p. 187; L. Morawski, *Precedens a wykładnia*, "Państwo i Prawo" 1996, iss. 10, p. 3; J. Wróblewski, *Precedens i jednolitość sądowego stosowania prawa*, "Państwo i Prawo" 1971, iss. 10, p. 525.

decision of the court but by the general norm, contained in the sentence or its statement of reasons, which becomes the basis or a model for deciding similar cases in the future[2]. In the opinion of M. Zirk-Sadowski, the term "precedent" is applied to characterise a court decision as far as its relationship to other court decisions is concerned[3]. In the case of "law creating decisions", the main issue is the relationship between the decision and the legal norm on whose basis the decision was formulated[4].

Analysing the statements made by criminal procedural law scholars referring to the possibility of treating precedents as the source of law, the following groups of opinions should be mentioned.

The first group comprises the statements of those authors who, when discussing the sources of criminal procedural law, mention only the normative sources and omit the issue of judgements[5] or leave the solution of the problem of the extent to which court judgements can be the source of law to the general theory, assuming that this problem does not constitute a specific issue in the field of criminal procedural law[6].

The second group is constituted by the statements of those authors who express a clear opinion about the admissibility of precedents, saying that court judgements are not the source of law[7].

---

2 L. Morawski, *Czy precedens…*, p. 187.

3 M. Zirk-Sadowski, *Precedens a tzw. decyzja prawotwórcza*, "Państwo i Prawo" 1980, iss. 6, pp. 71, 72–73.

4 Ibidem, p. 73. On the law making role of courts, see further: B. Wojciechowski, *Dyskrecjonalność sędziowska. Studium teoretycznoprawne*, Toruń 2004, pp. 213–217 and the literature quated there.

5 See: K.T. Boratyńska, [in:] K.T. Boratyńska, Ł. Chojniak, W. Jasiński, *Postępowanie karne*, 2nd ed., Warszawa 2016, pp. 25–26; R. Kmiecik, [in:] R. Kmiecik, E. Skrętowicz, *Proces karny. Część ogólna*, Warszawa 2009, 7th ed., pp. 37–40; P. Kruszyński, [in:] B. Bieńkowska, P. Kruszyński, C. Kulesza, P. Piszczek, *Wykład prawa karnego procesowego*, 2nd ed., amended and supplemented, Białystok 2003, pp. 13–17; Z. Świda, [in:] Z. Świda, R. Ponikowski, W. Posnow, *Postępowanie karne. Część ogólna*, Warszawa 2008, pp. 17, 18.

6 So states W. Daszkiewicz, *Proces karny. Część ogólna*, 3rd ed., amended and supplemented, Poznań 1996, p. 25.

7 M. Cieślak, *Polska procedura karna*, Warszawa 1984, pp. 141–142; K. Dudka, [in:] K. Dudka, H. Paluszkiewicz, *Postępowanie karne*, Warszawa 2015, p. 23; S. Kalinowski, *Polski proces karny*, Warszawa 1971, p. 16; M. Lipczyńska, [in:] M. Lipczyńska, A. Kordik, Z. Kegel, Z. Świda-Łagiewska, *Polski proces karny*, 2nd ed., Warszawa–Wrocław 1975, p. 41; K. Marszał, *Proces karny. Zagadnienia ogólne*, 3rd ed., Katowice 2013, p. 41; Z. Sobolewski, M. Rogalski, [in:] G. Artymiak, M. Klejnowska, Cz. Kłak, M. Rogalski,

According to S. Waltoś and P. Hofmański, the following arguments are against granting the courts the right to law creating activity: Firstly, such an activity may create the danger of infringing the principle of *lex retro non agit*[8]. Secondly, the law creating activity of courts always results in the danger of infringing on the hierarchy of legal norms as a result of introducing exceptions from the norms issued on the basis of a statute[9]. Thirdly, there might arise the danger of constructing abstract legal norms, stemming from the specific circumstances of a given case, whose application to the broader category of similar cases would have to cause very serious difficulties in practice[10]. The acceptance of the thesis that court interpretation, including the one performed by the Supreme Court, cannot be treated as the source of law is accompanied, however, by the mentioning of art. 190 section 1 of the Constitution, according to which the judgements of the Constitutional Tribunal are universally binding[11].

It is also accepted in the substantial criminal law literature that a court precedent in its strict meaning is of no normative importance[12]. The law creating role

---

Z. Sobolewski, P.K. Sowiński, *Proces karny. Część ogólna,* Warszawa 2007, p. 26: R.A. Stefański, *Instytucja pytań prawnych do Sądu Najwyższego w sprawach karnych*, Kraków 2001, p. 385; L. Schaff, *Proces karny Polski Ludowej. Wykład zasad ogólnych,* Warszawa 1953, pp. 37, 42; S. Steinborn, [in:] J. Grajewski, K. Papke-Olszauskas, S. Steinborn, K. Woźniewski, *Prawo karne procesowe – część ogólna,* Warszawa 2007, p. 13; T. Taras, [in:] T. Taras, E. Skrętowicz, R. Kmiecik, *Proces karny. Część ogólna*, Lublin 1971, p. 26; J. Tylman, [in:] T. Grzegorczyk, J. Tylman, *Polskie postępowanie karne*, 9th ed., Warszawa 2014, p. 64; S. Śliwiński, *Polski proces karny przed sądem powszechnym. Zasady ogólne,* Warszawa 1948, pp. 67–68; idem; *Polski proces karny przed sądem powszechnym*, Warszawa 1959, pp. 47–48; S. Waltoś, *Proces karny. Zarys systemu*, 10th ed., Warszawa 2009, pp. 144–145; S. Waltoś, P. Hofmański, *Proces karny. Zarys systemu,* 12th ed., Warszawa 2016, pp. 140–142.

8 S. Waltoś, P. Hofmański, p. 141.

9 Ibidem, pp. 141–142.

10 Ibidem, p. 142.

11 S. Waltoś, *Proces…*, p. 145; S. Waltoś, P. Hofmański, op. cit., p. 142; M. Żak, [in:] *System Prawa Karnego Procesowego*, t. 1: *Zagadnienia ogólne*, cz. 1, ed. P. Hofmański, Warszawa 2013, pp. 472–476. See also the remarks of K. Marszał, op. cit., p. 41.

12 M Cieślak, *Dzieła wybrane*, t. 3: *Polskie prawo karne. Zarys systemowego ujęcia*, ed. S. Waltoś with the cooperation of M. Rusinek and S. Steinborn, Kraków 2011, p. 61. See also: A. Marek, *Prawo karne*, 3rd ed., amended and supplemented, Warszawa 2001, p. 60; J. Warylewski, *Prawo karne. Część ogólna*, 6th ed., amended and supplemented, Warszawa 2015, p. 114; W. Wróbel, A. Zoll, *Polskie prawo karne. Część ogólna, Kraków 2010*, p. 99. The opinion that court judgements are not the source of binding criminal law is also expressed by other authors – see, e.g.: K. Buchała, *Prawo karne materialne*, Warszawa 1980, p. 102; L. Gardocki, *Prawo karne*, 7th ed., amended, Warszawa 2001,

of court judgements is being denied[13]. It is indicated that law creating interpretation is contradictory to the *nullum crimen sine lege* principle[14]. This principle is expressed in art. 42 section 1 sentence 1 of the Constitution[15]. It is also expressed in art. 1 § 1 of the Criminal Code[16]. The principle of the statute's exclusivity in criminal law stems from it[17]. It is emphasised in literature that this principle in reference to criminal law requires that all legal norms referring to the application of criminal sanctions should be inferred exclusively from acts of law making which have the status of statutes[18]. It has been stated that the necessary and unquestionable consequence of accepting the principle of the statute's exclusivity is the interdiction to introduce criminal law norms into the system otherwise than by lawmaking acts. The postulate of excluding judgements (precedents) from criminal law sources is inferred from that. Furthermore, accepting the thesis about the law creating role of judgements infringes on the principle of separation of the three powers since a court making such an interpretation assumes in fact the competences of the lawmaking power[19]. In W. Wróbel's opinion, the taking over

---

p. 31; M. Kulik, [in:] M. Budyn-Kulik, P. Kozłowska-Kalisz, M. Kulik, M. Mozgawa, *Prawo karne. Część ogólna*, 2nd ed., Warszawa 2009, p. 82; Ł. Pohl, *Prawo karne. Wykład części ogólnej*, Warszawa 2015, p. 45; P. Wiatrowski, *Dyrektywy wykładni prawa karnego materialnego w judykaturze Sądu Najwyższego*, Warszawa 2013, p. 276.

13 A. Zoll, *"Pozaustawowe" okoliczności wyłączające odpowiedzialność karną w świetle konstytucyjnej zasady podziału władzy*, [in:] *W kręgu teorii i praktyki prawa karnego. Księga poświęcona pamięci Profesora Andrzeja Wąska*, eds. L. Leszczyński, E. Skrętowicz, Z. Hołda, Lublin 2005, p. 426; P. Kardas, *Glosa do postanowienia SN z 9 stycznia 1996 r., II KRN 159/95*, "Palestra" 1997, no. 1–2, pp. 255–256. See also: P. Gensikowski, *O wykładni prawa karnego*, [in:] *Wykładnia prawa i inne problemy filozofii prawa*, ed. L. Morawski, Toruń 2005, p. 121; R.A. Stefański, [in:] *System prawa karnego*, ed. A. Marek, vol. 2: *Źródła prawa karnego*, ed. T. Bojarski, Warszawa 2011, p. 513; P. Wiatrowski, op. cit., p. 276.

14 See: R.A. Stefański, [in:] *System prawa karnego…*, op. cit., p. 513; W. Wróbel, *Prawotwórcze tendencje w orzecznictwie Sądu Najwyższego w sprawach karnych. Mity czy rzeczywistość?*, [in:] *W kręgu teorii i praktyki…*, op. cit., p. 383.

15 See: Ł. Pohl, op. cit., p. 37. According to W. Wróbel, the requirement of a statute form of criminal law making can be inferred from the general principle of a statute's exclusivity in the sphere of restricting the rights and freedoms which is expressed in art. 31 section 3 of the Constitution – see: W. Wróbel, *Zmiana normatywna i zasady intertemporalne w prawie karnym*, Kraków 2003, p. 109 and the literature and judgements quoted there.

16 Ł. Pohl, op. cit., pp. 37–38.

17 W. Wróbel, A. Zoll, op. cit., p. 97.

18 W. Wróbel, *Zmiana normatywna…*, op. cit., pp. 101–102.

19 See: R.A. Stefański, [in:] *System prawa karnego…*, op. cit., p. 513; P. Wiatrowski, op. cit., p. 276.

of the lawmaking function by the courts, even if restricted to "correcting" the lawmaker, inevitably entangles them in political arguments since it means choosing one of many possible solutions representing one of many interest groups or axiological options present in the society[20]. The Supreme Court has also expressed its opinion on the law creating role of judgements. In the statement of reasons to the resolution of the full Criminal Chamber of the Supreme Court from 11.01.1999, I KZP 15/98 it has been declared that no court, the Supreme Court included, cannot infringe on the competences of the lawmaking power and – under the pretence of interpreting a given provision of law or interpreting the mutual relationship of legal provisions – create in fact a totally new content of the analysed provisions or contradict their mutual relationship which stems clearly from the content of the statute[21].

In the literature of criminal procedural law, the judgements of the Constitutional Tribunal are treated as a source of criminal procedural law[22]. In the substantial criminal law doctrine, it is assumed that the acceptance of the exclusivity of the statute as a source of law is not contrary to accepting the judgements of the Constitutional Tribunal as a source of law. It is assumed that the judgements of the Constitutional Tribunal which state the incompatibility of a normative act with the Constitution can constitute the source of criminal law[23]. It is indicated that while the judgements of the Constitutional Tribunal may deprive certain provisions from a statute of their binding force because of their incompatibility with the Constitution, the same judgements may not determine any orders and interdictions and punishments for not obeying them. In this respect, they are not the source of criminal law[24].

The legal character of the guidelines of the Supreme Court was a problematic issue in the literature[25]. A revision of the statute on the Supreme Court of

---

20 See: W. Wróbel, *Prawotwórcze…*, op. cit., p. 384.

21 OSNKW 1999, iss. 1–2, poz. 1. See also: sentence of the Supreme Court of 20 April 2000 r., WKN 4/00, Lex 535089; the Supreme Court Decision of 16 March 2010 r., WO 3/10, OSNwSK 2010, iss. 1, position 566; sentence of the Appellate Court in Wrocław of 6 May 2003 r., II AKa 130/03, OSA 2003, iss. 10, position 98.

22 See more about this issue: M. Żak, op. cit., p. 472–476.

23 W. Wróbel, *Zmiana normatywna…*, op. cit., pp. 166–167.

24 A. Marek, *Prawo karne*, 10th ed., amended and supplemented, Warszawa 2011, pp. 57–58.

25 See, e.g.: M. Cieślak, *Polski proces…*, p. 141; S. Śliwiński, op. cit., p. 48; S. Frankowski, *Wytyczne Sądu Najwyższego w zakresie prawa karnego materialnego – problem otwarty*, "Państwo i Prawo" 1971, iss. 10, pp. 623–624. See more on the issue of the legal character of the guidelines: R.A. Stefański, op. cit., pp. 55–73 and the literature quoted there.

20.12.1989[26] abolished the institution of the guidelines referring to law and court practice established by the Supreme Court and in the resolution of the full Supreme Court of 5.05.1992 (Kw Pr 5/92) it was stated that all earlier resolutions containing guidelines referring to the interpretation of law and court practice do not have the force of legal principles[27].

Accepting the thesis according to which judgements are not the source of law does not mean that the Supreme Court does not issue judgements which are a manifestation of the law creating by the court. Such cases are observed in the literature[28]. These are, e.g., the judgements which correct the content of the legal statute by restricting the scope of criminal responsibility[29], which supplement the legal gaps and inconsistencies in the statutory law[30], and some even make interpretation contra legem, i.e. contrary to the statute[31]. It is also noticed in the criminal procedural law doctrine that there are judgements which can hardly be considered as acts of law interpretation. Such a situation occurs when the Supreme Court supplements a legal gap in a creative way in so that even with the best intentions it cannot be considered law interpretation, even when applying the concept of creative interpretation[32].

It is worth quoting the opinion of M. Cieślak here, who, accepting the thesis that on the ground of our criminal law precedents have no normative power, stated that, taking into account the psychologically understandable phenomenon of the tendency to do a task in the same way, a way at least once tested

---

26 See: art. 3 point 9 of the statute of 20.12.1989 on the change of the statute – The law on the system of common courts, on the Supreme Court, on the Supreme Administrative Court, on the Constitutional Tribunal, on the system of military courts and the Law on notaries, Dz.U. 1989, no. 73, item 436.

27 OSNKW 1993, iss. 1, position 1. See also: *Jednolitość orzecznictwa w sprawach karnych*, ed. S. Waltoś, Kraków 1998, p. 10.

28 See: S. Majcher, *W kwestii tzw. prawotwórstwa sądowego (na przykładzie orzecznictwa SN w sprawach karnych)*, "Państwo i Prawo" 2004, iss. 2, pp. 69–81; W. Wróbel, *Prawotwórcze tendencje…*, op. cit., p. 383–396.

29 See: resolution of 18 November 1998 r., KZP 16/98, OSNKW 1998, iss. 11–12, position 48 quoted by Z. Majcher (op. cit., p. 72); See: M. Królikowski, *Problemy wykładni w prawie karnym*, "Edukacja Prawnicza" 2007, no. 12, p. 7 and the literature quoted there.

30 See: resolution of 25 October 2000 r., I KZP 28/2000, OSNKW 2000, iss. 11–12, position 91 quoted by Z. Majcher (op. cit., p. 76).

31 See: resolution of 11 August 2000 r., I KZP 17/2000, OSP 2001, no. 1, p. 18 and the following quoted by Z. Majcher (op. cit., pp. 73–74).

32 S. Steinborn, op. cit., p. 13; S. Waltoś, P. Hofmański, op. cit., p. 141; S. Majcher, op. cit., pp. 70–80; M. Żak, op. cit., pp. 496–500.

earlier and the concept of routine connected with this tendency, there are no reasons to suppose that precedents have no importance indeed – at least in the activity of the same judge[33]. Making the same decisions according to the same rules connected with the presence of the same premises serves the uniformity of court application of law[34]. It is accepted in the literature that the uniformity of law application is important for the fulfilment of the principle of equality before the law, the principle of the stability of law and legal safety of citizens[35]. One should fully approve of the thesis that whether some decision is in fact a precedent can be stated taking into account the subsequent practice[36]. The conducted research was to establish to what extent earlier procedural decisions are being used in the judgements of the Criminal and Military Chamber of the Supreme Court.

2 General Characteristics of the Analysed Judgements

Before presenting the results of the research covering the judgements of the Criminal and Military Chamber of the Supreme Court, it should be stressed that the aim of the research was to establish the ways in which the term "precedent" is being used in judgements as well as the reasons for using earlier judgements or a line of judgement in preparing the statement of reasons of procedural decisions.

With this aim, using the programme LEX, the database of criminal court judgements of Polish courts was searched in order to find out whether the term "precedent" is expressly used in the statements of reasons of judgements. Fourteen such judgements were found. A closer analysis of these expressions leads to the conclusion that not in every case in which the word "precedent" was used, its meaning referred to a decision, which would become the basis of decision-making in future similar cases.

On the basis of the judgements found, it can be stated that the concept of precedent was used in the following meanings. Firstly, it should be noted that it was understood as the appearance of a case (situation), which has not appeared before.

---

33 M. Cieślak, *Dzieła wybrane*, t. 3: *Polskie prawo karne*…, op. cit., p. 61.

34 See: R.A. Stefański, op. cit., p. 138 and the literature quoted there.

35 S. Waltoś, *Wprowadzenie i próba podsumowania*, [in:] *Jednolitość orzecznictwa w sprawach karnych*,ed. idem, Zakamycze 1998, p. 7. See more on this issue: R.A. Stefański, op. cit., pp. 138, 139–141 and the literature quoted there; B. Wojciechowski, op. cit., pp. 222–226 and the literature quoted there.

36 J. Wróblewski, op. cit., p. 528.

In further judgements, the use of the term "precedent" was to counteract the use of a given norm in the future; therefore it was to stop it from fulfilling the role of a precedent.

The term "precedent" was also applied by the Supreme Court in its judgement of 18.01.1928[37], which referred to the issue of criminal responsibility on the basis of the press law of 10.05.1927. The analysis of the content of that judgement leads to the conclusion that also in this judgement the concept of precedent did not mean a court decision which was to be applied in future similar cases.

A different situation appears in the statement of reasons of the resolution of 25.03.2003[38]. The Supreme Court stated that it decided to adopt the resolution mainly because of its precedent character since the problem might lead to disputes and controversies in judicial practice. It is difficult however to accept that the decision has the qualities of a precedent. It seems that it can more justly be considered as an example of a law creating decision.

Secondly, the analysis covered judgements issued by the Criminal and Military Chamber of the Supreme Court in the following time spans: 1972–1973, 2002–2003, 2012–2016. Altogether 1115 judgements were analysed, including 377 from the period 1972–1973, 223 from the period 2002–2003 and 515 from the period 2012–2006. First of all, the judgements placed in the official collection of judgements of the Supreme Court were the object of analysis. The selection of different years was to answer the question whether there were any specific features of the use of earlier judgements in the selected periods. The table below illustrates the number of analysed judgements in the selected years and the percentage of those judgements in the selected periods in which there appeared references to earlier judgements.

Analysing the data one should observe the increase of the percentage of judgements making references to judgements issued earlier in the period covered by the research in comparison with the results of the research referring to judgements of the Criminal and Military Chamber of the Supreme Court in the years 1972 and 1973.

3 Conclusion

The research on the judgements from the years 1972–1973, 2002–2003, 2012–2016 leads to the following conclusions:

---

37 KR 407/27, Lex 1631102.

38 I KZP 50/02, OSNKW 2003, iss. 3–4, position 28.

Tab. 1: Judgements in which there appeared references to earlier judgements

Year	*Number of analysed judgements*	*Number of judgements in which there appeared references to judgements issued earlier*	*The percentage of the judgements in which there appeared references to judgements issued earlier*
1972	*202*	*59*	*29,21 %*
1973	*175*	*40*	*22,86 %*
2002	*113*	*59*	*52,21 %*
2003	*110*	*64*	*58,18 %*
2012	*136*	*117*	*86,03 %*
2013	*107*	*88*	*82,24 %*
2014	*92*	*82*	*89,13 %*
2015	*105*	*90*	*85,71 %*
2016	*85*	*65*	*76,47 %*

Referring to earlier judgements, the court would indicate the file reference, place of publication and would quote the thesis expressed earlier. Rarely did the Supreme Court refer generally to its earlier judgements without indicating concrete decisions. In the sentence of the Supreme Court of 14.09.1972[39] a reference was made to the judgements of the Supreme Court. The same solution was used in the sentence of the Supreme Court of 6.02.1973[40]. In the resolution of the Supreme Court of 23.04.2002[41] the court, interpreting the term of "gross disproportion of punishment" indicated in art. 438 point 4 sentence 1 of the Code on Criminal Proceedings, referred to the judicial practice without indicating, however, any concrete judgements.

Analysing judgements from the years 1972–1973, 2002–2003, 2012–2016, it is possible to state that in the majority of judgements the court, while referring to earlier judgements, did not explain why it was quoting the judgement issued earlier. In the statement of reasons it was only pointed out that a given issue had already been the object of a decision. The standard expression was "see" or "compare" and the proper judgement was indicated which contained the opinion quoted by the Supreme Court in the statement of reasons of an individual

39 III KR 156/72, OSNKW 1974, iss. 4, position 45.
40 V KRN 516/73, OSNKW 1973, iss. 9. position 112.
41 I KZP 12/02, OSNKW 2002, iss. 7–8, position 50.

judgement. One might say that such a method of referring to earlier judgements has become a sort of paradigm for making statements of reasons.

Referring to earlier judgements was to serve the aim of justifying a given thesis. Quoting earlier judgements was to present certain continuity and stability of an opinion of the Supreme Court on a given issue. It happened when the discussed problem has already been solved by the Supreme Court or some other court (the Constitutional Tribunal or an appellate court). It was stated that the opinion represented by the Supreme Court in the case was the continuation of an opinion already existing in the judicature, a manifestation of the existence of a consistent judicial line. The reference to earlier judgements also served the purpose of presenting a specific judicial interpretation line, it expressed the will to preserve the unity of judgements, the consistent acceptance of a given thesis in the judicature. The reference to earlier judgements was justified by the fact that the Supreme Court had many times expressed its opinion on a given issue, by the approval for the existing opinion of the judicature, by a given understanding of a provision at present and in the past. Sometimes the quoting of earlier judgements was justified by the continued relevancy of an opinion expressed earlier.

Referring to an earlier opinion of the Supreme Court was to illustrate the way a given term was understood. Sometimes it was added that the opinion expressed in the quoted judgement was approved in literature. Indicating earlier judgements was to justify the thesis that a given opinion is contrary to an opinion adopted earlier in the judicature. Referring to earlier judgements in the statement of reasons took place when the Supreme Court renounced a given opinion, which was justified by the loss of validity of the opinion expressed earlier as a result of law modification.

Another group comprises those cases in which earlier judgements were quoted to state that the opinion expressed in the judgement issued earlier was of no reference for the analysed case.

Referring to judgements issued earlier also took place when the Supreme Court stated that there were contrary opinions on a given issue. Analysing the judgements of the Supreme Court one may also make one more remark. It should be stressed that in each of the analysed periods the court issued judgements which could be treated as examples of "law creating judgements". They referred to issues which could be interpreted ambiguously.

Part Three: Comparisons and Optimizations

John McClellan Marshall

The Utility of *Stare Decisis* in American Common Law Jurisprudence

Abstract: The paper focuses on the *stare decisis* principle and its influence on the formation of precedent and later judgements in the United States constitutional order. The precedent practice of American courts is being analyzed in relation to various branches of law in a complex system of state and federal courts. It also discovers how *stare decisis* influence the practical aspects of legal practices of attorneys.

Keywords: *stare decisis*, common law, precedent

"The life of the law has not been logic; it has been experience… The law embodies the story of a nation's development through many centuries, and it cannot be dealt with as if it contained only the axioms and corollaries of a book of mathematics". This statement by Justice Oliver Wendell Holmes, Jr.[1] sums up not only the underlying philosophy of the common law system. It also posits the reason behind the principle of *stare decisis* and emphasizes its importance in that system. While it is a commonplace that the principal distinction between the civil law and common law systems is that the latter is more flexible in its ability to evolve with society, it is not totally accurate. The civil law system, while it is less flexible as to the discretion vested in the judiciary, has the ability to evolve with the times through the ability to evolve through the political action of the legislative branch of government. The distinction, therefore, is rooted in the fundamental polity that governs the relationship between the judiciary and the legislative functions of government. Historically, the more independent the judiciary, the more discretion is vested in the judges to interpret legislative enactments, and that is why *stare decisis* as a limitation on that discretion is a key to the consistency of, yet allowing evolution of the law through, judicial decisions in jurisdictions such as the United States.

It is important to understand that the "common law" of the United States is itself derived from several sources, primarily court decisions that become precedents for judicial decision-making. That viewpoint, however, ignores the reality of The Constitution of The United States itself and its role in the

1 L.W. Holmes, *The Common Law*, Boston 1881, at 1.

common law process. Simply put, the Constitution was a popular reaction to the ineffectiveness of the Articles of Confederation to provide an adequate post-Revolutionary government. At the same time, the first seven Articles of the Constitution were designed to be the framework of a government that, being tripartite in structure, would do two things: first, it would function as a government in the usual tasks that government does, such as national defense and taxation; second, be capable of protecting the rights of the citizenry that had been fought for in the Revolutionary War. That this was part of the intent of the Framers is clear from the fact that the Bill of Rights was promulgated as the first act of the new Congress in 1791. The passage of the Bill of Rights was, of course, part of the original compromise that brought the Constitution into being, so it is proper to regard them as part of the original document. Indeed, the focus of the combined seven Articles and the first ten Amendments is clear from the language that they begin with "We, the People" and conclude with "to the people". Because these were created by elected representatives of the people of the original states and not by the government then in power, it can be asserted that the Constitution is part of the common law of the United States and therefore conditions the juridical process that implements it.

In the United States, the three-branch structure of the government established by the Constitution does two things that are at the heart of the decision-making process: first, it defines the powers of the respective branches in such a way that they can balance each other in the overall exercise of the governmental function; second, the judicial branch is co-equal in dignity and power with the executive and legislative branches of the government. The federal judiciary, as represented by the Supreme Court of the United States in the tripartite structure of American government, makes public policy on a co-equal level with Congress or the Executive branch of government through the mechanism of the opinion that determines the outcome of the case before the court. "It is emphatically the province and duty of the judicial department to say what the law is" in the familiar words of *Marbury v. Madison*[2]. This is called "judicial review", and it establishes the authority of the Court to declare a law passed by Congress to be un-Constitutional, that is, not in accordance with the powers given to Congress under the Constitution. In this process, the Court reviews both the circumstances of the case and the phraseology of the statute to reach its decision. Of necessity such a review embraces the content and intent of administrative regulations and congressional enactments, as measured against the requirements

2 1 Cranch 137, 5 U.S. 137 (1803).

of the Constitution. This is generally referred to as "due process," and it depends in large part on *stare decisis* for its orderly evolution. Generally, the doctrine of *stare decisis* requires that once the Supreme Court has announced a proposition of law, the decision is considered binding precedent, but the doctrine is not absolute[3]. Of course, if the issue is one of Constitutionality, then it is absolute, but if the decision deals with statutory interpretation, then there may be some room for the precedent still to be applied in a different context.

In the United States, the relationship between the state court systems and the federal court system is a component of the federal Constitutional structure. In part because of the Tenth Amendment to the Constitution, the state courts have authority to declare acts of the U.S. Congress un-Constitutional, just as a federal court could. Similarly, the federal courts can declare acts of state legislatures to be un-Constitutional. In effect, there are fifty-one court systems in the United States that are in simultaneous operation, each of which employs *stare decisis* as a component of its decision-making process. This seemingly simple relationship is made much more complex with the legislative capability to define jurisdiction of the federal and state courts. E.g., federal courts have jurisdiction to hear cases involving citizens of different states by virtue of acts of Congress. They also have exclusive jurisdiction of certain types of cases, such as bankruptcy, as provided in Article III of the Constitution. State courts generally can hear cases involving citizens of different states, but in such a situation, the case might be taken away from the state court (a process called "removal") and sent to a federal court. In such a situation, the decision of the federal court would become useful as precedent in state courts in later, similar cases.

With such an overlap in authority, there would be ample opportunity for confusion in the judicial system, but that generally does not happen because of *stare decisis*. Within this system, the decisions of the state courts of appeal or the state Supreme Court normally are the rules of decision for all of the trial courts of the state. That said, it is not uncommon for the courts of one state to refer to the decisions of another state or the federal courts if the case has not been previously ruled upon. In the case of the federal courts, the decisions of the trial courts are not considered binding precedent even on other federal trial courts. Any conflict would be resolved by the federal circuit courts of appeal or by the Supreme Court of the United States. Of course, the decision of the Supreme Court would be binding on all the courts in the United States, both state and federal, pursuant

3 See: *Southwestern Bell Telephone v. Mitchell,* 276 S.W.3d 443 (Tex. 2008) for an example of this aspect of *stare decisis* in the evolutionary process of legal development.

to the Supremacy Clause of Article VI of the Constitution. Though they are not obligated to do so, federal courts from time to time will review the decisions of state courts for guidance on a particular issue. E.g., the Fifth United States Circuit Court of Appeals from time to time will ask the Supreme Court of Texas for an advisory opinion dealing with a point of Texas law to help them decide a case involving Texas parties. Though such an opinion is advisory and not formally binding on lower courts in Texas, it does provide some evidence as to how the Supreme Court of Texas will rule if such a case comes before it. Even though it is a somewhat indirect statement of the law, it does tend to become precedent. In this way *stare decisis* as a principle of judicial decision-making promotes efficiency, fairness, and legitimacy through consistency[4].

In the jurisprudence of the American common law system, there are two principal sources of authority that serve to guide decisions of the trial and appellate courts so as to create both consistency and finality. These are legislative actions, whether by state legislatures or by Congress, and judicial precedent, sometimes referred to as "legislating from the bench" or, more accurately, *stare decisis*. The principle of *stare decisis*, or precedent from prior legal decisions that binds the lower court in the case at bar, is so well-established in Anglo-American jurisprudence that it can be considered fundamental to any discussion of procedural or substantive law in the common law system.

That said, however, it should be noted that normally the longer a precedent has been in place, the less likely it is to be overturned and the higher the court that is likely to be required to overturn it. The failure of the judicial process to overturn a precedent that has in fact outlived its usefulness creates a situation in which one of the other branches of government must act. At the state level, it would normally be the state legislature that would pass a law that would address the issue. On the federal level, if the decision were one rendered by the Supreme Court, an amendment to the U.S. Constitution might be required. In such a situation, political considerations very likely would play a part in that process of adjustment of public policy.

If political considerations should be removed from the judicial process, the authority of the courts to overturn prior decisions is significant. Seen in the proper perspective, this authority derives from a combination of the principles enunciated by Holmes that the common law is an expression of "experience" and the well-established Roman tradition that invests the court with the power of *parens patriae*, the ability to do what is right. To that extent, courts may appear to

4 See: *Weiner v. Wasson*, 900 S.W.2d 316 (Tex. 1995).

many to "legislate from the bench", when in fact they have merely assisted the law in moving with the times to meet the needs of society. This "evolutionary" capability of the common law makes the principle of *stare decisis* much more flexible than it might initially appear. To that extent, though, there is no question that the ability of the courts to overturn prior precedent relieves the legislative branch of government from having to be highly reactive to current events.

Stare decisis as a principle of judicial decision-making, at both the state and federal levels, promotes efficiency, fairness, and legitimacy through consistency[5]. As such, it enhances both consistency and finality internally within the judicial system because it requires that in a given case the lower court must take notice of the decisions of a higher court that have been made on the same or similar matters. Precedent in the common law system can, however, be overruled by the court at any level if the public policy factors for doing so are sufficiently weighty. Among these factors are: 1) the original rule or decision was flawed; 2) the application of the prior rule can lead to and has led to inconsistent results, thus belying one of the underlying justifications for *stare decisis* in the first place; 3) the rule conflicts with other precedent in some respect, especially if there is a newer and better reasoned case; 4) the rule regularly produces an unjust result unanticipated by the original decision or places an unnecessary burden on the system; or 5) the reasons that supported the precedent in its original form no longer exist because of the passage of time[6]. It can also be that in the event that the legal basis of the rule has been changed or abolished, the precedential value of the prior decision has been undermined and may be overruled. E.g., the ratification in 1865 of the Thirteenth Amendment to the Constitution abolishing slavery had the effect of overruling *sub silentio* the *Dred Scott Decision* of 1857 that had been a factor in precipitating the War Between the States. At the Constitutional level, the overruling of precedent can occur either in the amendment process or by legislation. Either way, the independence of the judiciary is not impacted, but is in fact reinforced by having the opportunity to create afresh precedents that will serve as *stare decisis* in the new legal context.

Stare decisis as a principle of decision-making at all levels of the judicial system, particularly at the state level, is strongest in cases involving statutory construction because the legislature then has the opportunity to correct perceived construction errors through statutory amendment[7]. An example of this occurred

5 See: ibidem.
6 *Ex parte Lewis*, 219 S.W.3d 335 (Tex.Crim.App. 2007).
7 See: *Fiess v. State Farm Lloyds*, 202 S.W.3d 744 (Tex. 2006).

as recently as 1999 when the Texas Legislature recodified a statute with no substantive change in the statutory language. In such a case, it can be presumed that the Legislature simply chose to agree with the court and was reaffirming its decision as correct[8]. Of course, the fact that the Legislature has not changed the statute in response to a ruling does not justify continuing to apply a holding that is simply incorrect[9]. In this context, it is an important characteristic of the doctrine that *stare decisis* governs only the determination of questions of law and its observance does not depend upon identity of parties to the lawsuit[10]. This has the important public policy effect of extending the reach of a particular decision through many cases, sometimes many years, and aids in the overall consistency and stability of the judicial process.

Perhaps the most negative aspect of *stare decisis* is the tendency of some in the judiciary to follow precedent slavishly and unimaginatively. It has been said that "Often it is better to be consistent than right"[11]. This attitude is in part a function of human nature in that it is simply easier to follow the established case law than it is to examine why that case law should be followed or discarded in a given case because times have changed. In the case of trial judges, this tendency is reinforced by the desire not to be the subject of reversal by appellate courts, and following precedent is the best, though not flawless, way to avoid reversal. Such an attitude can, and often does, lead to a mechanical jurisprudence that fails to evolve.

Ultimately, such a body of jurisprudence withers into an irrelevancy that, ironically, may set the stage for a change in public policy at a higher level of the judicial system or by one of the other branches of government. When adherence to a judicially created rule of law no longer furthers the interests that it had served, regardless of the length of time that it was in place, and the general interest will suffer less by a departure from it than strict adherence, the Supreme Court should not hesitate to depart from a prior holding[12]. Put somewhat more pragmatically, when the reason for a rule ceases to exist, the rule should cease to exist, and the application of *stare decisis* to a factual context that is radically different from what has existed is simply inappropriate.

8 *Grimes County Bail Bond Board v. Ellen*, 267 S.W.3d 310 (Tex.App. – Houston [14th] 2008, no pet.).

9 See: *Tooke v. City of Mexia*, 197 S.W.3d 325, 342 (Tex. 2006).

10 *Swilley v. McCain*, 374 S.W.2d 871 (Tex. 1964).

11 *Malik v. State*, 953 S.W.2d 234 (Tex.Crim.App. 1997).

12 *Lehmann v. Har-Con Corporation*, 39 S.W.3d 191 (Tex. 2001).

In a common law system or one in which some component of *stare decisis* exists, if the case should reach the Supreme Court [or other court of last resort], the parties to the case may well find themselves in a legal environment in which the primary consideration is one of defining "public policy". The definition of public policy by the Supreme Court is generally considered a legitimate exercise of the judicial function. That is in part because of the heritage of the tripartite division of governmental power that exists in the American republican form of polity created by the Constitution of the United States. The legislative branch of government, Congress, articulates public policy through enacting laws arrived at after some level of debate. The executive branch, in the person of the President or through his cabinet officers, can establish public policy through the issuance of executive orders or the establishment of administrative regulations. In addition, the executive branch includes the investigative and prosecutorial arms of government, so that the level of enforcement can have an impact on the development of precedents. This is made even more complex by the existence of prosecutorial discretion that is inherent in this process. To that extent, the action or inaction of the executive branch of government can have a significant effect both on the development of new precedent and its evolution into the realm of *stare decisis*. In the case of legislation or executive orders, however, both are subject to review by the judiciary should their constitutionality be challenged. An example of this sort of review is the current litigation concerning the power of the president to limit immigration into the United States from certain countries, whose authority is derived both from the Constitution itself and the Immigration and Nationality Act of 1952.

Indeed, this "announcement of public policy" function cannot even be considered exclusively Anglo-American in origin. In the parliamentary form of government, which is characteristic of the United Kingdom and many civil law systems, the courts operate *de facto* as extensions of the legislative branch of government, rather than as a "separate, but equal" branch of government. The absence of a written constitution in effect puts courts in the position of simply enforcing acts of Parliament as written, with little discretionary interpretive authority in the court. In effect, they are announcing the public policy of the legislative branch through their decisions. In the American system, there are trial judges who from time to time, even when confronted with clear case authority, will disregard that authority if the outcome is a clear injustice, "distinguishing" that authority from the case at bar so as to allow the appellate court to uphold this change in direction. Such an outcome often is itself an affirmation of the evolutionary principle of *stare decisis*, rather than adherence to an established public policy, because of the subsequent action of the appellate court.

At its simplest, the trial court, whether state or federal, normally is bound by the pronouncements of the intermediate court of appeal, just as the intermediate court of appeal is bound by the opinions of the Supreme Court. It is not the function of the intermediate court of appeals to abrogate or modify established precedent or to mold the law as it may see fit. In the normal operation of the judicial process, that function lies solely with the Supreme Court to overturn the prior precedent or for the Legislature to supersede the prior precedent by statute[13]. Indeed, it is of the essence of the common law, because it is the mechanism by which the law evolves on a case-by-case basis through judicial decisions, instead of halting the judicial process while awaiting a reactive action by one of the other branches of government that might address the issue squarely. That said, it should be noted that, in some instances, both state and federal trial courts will ignore, or distinguish, appellate opinions that normally would be binding, if the facts or the policy should simply not lead to a just result.

For the attorney in private practice, the principle of *stare decisis* is of great practical importance in advising the client and preparing his case. If the judicial system has internal consistency as a primary feature, then the attorney can better advise the client, both as to the present state of the law, but also as to where it might be going. By careful observation of trends in the appellate courts' opinions, the attorney can help the client avoid pitfalls in business or personal planning that might otherwise end in litigation that consumes the resources of both the client and the state. Of course, the existence of *stare decisis* implies that the attorney has a professional responsibility to keep up with the changes in the law of the jurisdiction where he or she is practicing that come almost weekly from the appellate courts, and that can be very time consuming. Indeed, in some states in the United States it is considered on the borderline of legal malpractice for an attorney not to be aware of the latest case authorities in that state. For the judges, though there exists the legal presumption that the judge knows *all* the law, the reality is that judges must expend considerable effort to keep up with the law as it evolves, not only in their jurisdiction, but elsewhere should the case before them be of interstate or national significance. Some judges, quite honestly, are unwilling to engage in that level of effort, even at the risk of being reversed by a higher court, with the result that justice may suffer until corrected by the higher court or by the replacement of the judge.

---

13 See: *Texas Department of Public Safety v. Cox Texas Newspapers, LP,* 343 S.W.3d 112 (Tex. 2011) for an example of this aspect of *starte decisis* in the evolutionary process of legal development.

The "*law of the case*" is the clearest example of *stare decisis* applied internally to a single case as it moves through the system. This doctrine arises when a case is remanded back to a lower court, whether trial or appellate, from a higher appellate court after the higher court has decided part of the case. The "law of the case" doctrine is "that principle under which questions of law decided on appeal to a court of last resort will govern the case throughout its subsequent stages"[14]. It applies only to questions of law. In such an instance, that part of the case that was determined by the higher court may not be relitigated in the case and will, by definition, form part of the basis for the final judgment. Obviously, the parties to the lawsuit have from the appellate court a taste of *stare decisis* in their own case and, thus, a glimpse of the future of the case should it go back through the appellate process. In this instance, the law of the case doctrine combines for the parties the characteristics of consistency and finality in the subsequent life of the litigation, regardless of where it might go.

In the federal court system, it is common for both district [trial] and appellate judges to write opinions as part of announcing their decisions. The district court opinions, however, do not form a body of binding precedent that automatically obligates other federal trial courts to follow them. These opinions in many instances may however set a tone for trial courts nationwide such that in effect they become the standard by which an appellate court will review a district court decision. These opinions also perform the function of providing guidelines as to the decision in another, similar case for other trial courts in the same jurisdiction. This enhances uniformity throughout the jurisdiction at the various levels of the courts. It is true that it happens that subsequent federal district courts will sometimes disregard their brethren in the prior cases and render decisions that are qualitatively quite different. In such a case, the variation in opinions at the district court level virtually guarantees review by the circuit courts of appeal.

The opinions of the circuit courts range in length from a few sentences to many pages, depending upon the complexity of the case or the variations in the law that will be applied in the formulation of the decision. Often there is a split in the decision of the appellate court judges, and there will be a majority opinion and one or more dissenting opinions that recite the reasoning of the judges who disagree with the majority opinion. Similarly, when there is a conflict among the opinions of the federal circuit courts, the Supreme Court of the United States may, in its discretion, serve as the final arbiter. Prior to 1801, e.g., the Supreme Court of the United States followed the British practice of having each judge

14 *Briscoe v. Goodmark Corp.*, 102 S.W.3d 714 (Tex. 2003).

write his own opinion, and from a reading of all of them together, the "majority rule" would be discerned. After 1801, the number of opinions in most cases was reduced to one majority opinion and perhaps two or three dissents, which might include some elements of agreement with the majority.

By contrast, in some states, trial courts will occasionally write opinions that are published and are adopted by appellate courts to serve as precedent, but this is extremely rare. It is true that sometimes there are conflicts among the appellate courts within a state or within the federal system such that there could be more than one result from a given set of facts. In such a situation, the conflict will normally be resolved by the supreme court of the state in an effort to establish a uniform rule of decision for the state or country as a whole.

In the development of a body of jurisprudence, appellate courts tend to employ two primary approaches to the research of the case law. A cautionary note needs to be injected, however, in that some appellate courts from time to time seem to develop agendas that reflect a political, economic, or social bias on major issues, such as criminal punishment, plaintiff versus defendant, or sensitive political or social topics. In such cases, the approach of the development of the jurisprudence of that court may well be "result oriented", that is, the court will tend to research and cite as authority for the decision only those cases that tend to favor the result that the leading members of that court wish to have. The other approach that is most common for appellate courts to employ in their scholarship is that of allowing the decision to "emerge" from the authorities that exist. Put another way, if the case law or statutory authorities present a pattern or trend that is discernible, then the appellate court can either extend that trend one more step or simply follow the most recent decision.

Most recently, this discussion has revolved around the question of whether the Constitution of The United States is a "living document". The late Mr. Justice Antonin Scalia recently stated that those who believe that are "idiots" who do not understand that the document was written in 1789, and the Founding Fathers could not possibly have anticipated the many changes that have happened in the years since. If that were true, then *stare decisis* would become a Procrustean bed that would admit of no judicial innovation, and the case of *Gibbons v. Ogden*[15], which established the power of the federal government to regulate interstate commerce would never have come into being, because steamboats were not in existence in 1789. It is obvious that the concept of the evolution of the law through the action of the courts was not unknown in the earliest days of

15 9 Wheat. 1, 22 U.S. 1, 6 L.Ed. 23 (1824).

the United States. In modern times, this is sometimes referred to as "judicial activism", allowing the government to meet changes in the social and economic fabric of the country without doing violence to the existing Constitutional and statutory background. It is this "experiential" characteristic of *stare decisis* that validates the concept of a "living" Constitution as the standard against which to measure contemporary legislative or executive actions.

The contrast between these two scholarly approaches to research in the case law can be most clearly seen in the development of civil rights law in the United States. In either case, the system allows for an evolutionary outcome in most instances, since intermediate appellate courts do not generally engage in making public policy. At the level of the Supreme Court, whether state or federal, however, the difference in approach can result in quite revolutionary results, sometimes referred to as "social engineering". In such cases, the court will often cite changes in the social or economic background that justify a change regarding how the Constitution and laws are to be interpreted and applied.

At the federal appellate level, as noted above, there could be, and often is, a dissenting opinion. As a general rule the dissenting opinion does not become part of the precedential chain of authority. The passage of time, however, has caused many dissenting opinions to become the majority opinion because of changes in the social or legal circumstances that surrounded the case at the time when it was written.

A good example of how changes in the substantive law can come about from the shift in public policy with the passage of time appears in the dissenting opinion of Justice Thurgood Marshall in the Supreme Court of the United States case of *Regents of the University of California v. Bakke*[16]. A white, male student had been denied acceptance in favor of less qualified black and other minority students in order for the university to meet what it perceived was an appropriate racial balance in the student body. The majority of the Court ruled that, since there was no evidence that Mr. Bakke would have been admitted under a system that did not take race into consideration, there was no reason why this policy was un-Constitutionally discriminatory. The Court further noted that, since Mr. Bakke was already in his third year of medical school elsewhere, the case, for all practical purposes was moot. In his dissent in that case, Justice Marshall said that, mootness aside, there should be equality of treatment regardless of race in the admissions process to a state medical school. Later, in the case of *Hopwood v. State of Texas*[17], the majority of the circuit court held that a formal policy of

16 438 U.S. 265, 98 S.Ct. 2733, 57 L.Ed.2d 750 (1978).
17 236 F.3d 720 (5th Cir. 2000).

ranking applicants for the School of Law who were otherwise qualified based upon consideration of race, known as "affirmative action" or "reverse racial discrimination," was un-Constitutional, even though race could be considered *among other factors*. In effect, the Circuit Court adopted as its majority opinion the dissent of Justice Marshall written some twenty-five years earlier. As of this writing, there are currently pending before the Supreme Court of the United States two cases that may lead to a further revision of the law as it applies to the concept of "affirmative action", and those may well draw upon the dissents of those previous cases.

In the civil law system, in the absence of specific statutory authority, the court may find itself thwarted in its ability to render a decision that partakes of consistency with the existing statutory provisions, with the result that the decision is either unsatisfactory, delayed while awaiting legislative action, or does not happen at all. This would apply whether in the context of a court proceeding or an administrative one. When considering the applicability of *stare decisis* to the civil law system, it is important to recognize that the state-federal relationship in the American system, as a general matter, has no applicability. Most civil law systems are unitary in their structure, that is to say, one chain of relationship exists throughout the country from the trial court to the Supreme Court. There may be intermediate courts of appeal or higher appellate courts that have specialized functions, such as administrative tribunals, criminal appeals courts, or constitutional tribunals. The route of appeal to these courts from the trial courts also varies, but the court of last resort almost always retains discretion over what cases it chooses to hear, and there are very few appeals that are "of right" whether in a civil law system or a common law system. In both systems, the review at the intermediate level may consider the fact findings as well as legal rulings of the trial court, but in most instances the review at the highest level focuses on potential errors of law or possible changes in public policy.

In the common law system *stare decisis* actually allows the court in most cases before it, whether as a trial or as the review of administrative decisions, not only ultimately to consider the existing legislative background that underlies the dispute to be decided, but also to review the prior judicial history and then to move forward with a sense of continuity and order. In those relatively rare cases that do not have clear statutory or case law history to provide an immediate precedent which must be followed, the principles of equity, combined with a review of similar statutes and judicial decisions from other jurisdictions, and the intellect of the judge fill the interstices and, in the process, extend the scope of *stare decisis* to that group of cases. What is potentially of value for a civil law system by the application of *stare decisis* in its most common forms is that the doctrine provides the courts with the ability to adjust the application of statutes to meet changing conditions and, at the same time, liberates the legislative branch of government from micromanaging the day-to-day details of life.

One practical political effect of the American Revolution was to extend governmental power to a third branch of government, the judiciary, as an expression of the concept that this was to be a government of laws and not of men. Under the American form of the common law system, a law that is repugnant to the Constitution is "no law" by definition, and it is the duty of the court to make that determination as a *co-equal* branch of government. This participation in the Constitutional system of checks and balances distinguishes the American judicial system from that of the United Kingdom. It is *stare decisis* that lies at the base of that distinction and provides both consistency and finality in the operation of the judicial system. While there is no question that the parliamentary system serves very well in terms of application of law as the product of statutory enactments, the ability of the common law system to evolve through the use of court-created case law makes the entire system of government more responsive and relevant to the public at the moment that the government comes into contact with the public in court. A side benefit is that the government can function with less politically motivated disruption of the system at its foundation. As Bob Dylan said, "The times they are a-changin'", and it may be that it is useful for the civil justice system to consider the possibility of utilizing some components of *stare decisis* to make those changes smoother.

Leszek Leszczyński

Precedent in the Polish Jurisprudence (General Outline)

Abstract: The issue of the precedent is an important component of Polish analyses of judicial processes of application and practical (decision-making) interpretation of the law. The first step in this direction was a comprehensive concept of the role of precedent in the Polish legal system created in the 1960s by Jerzy Wróblewski. Within its framework, such issues found a special role as types of precedent (from strictissimo to largissimo sensu), differentiation of the practice of taking into account and following the precedent or different ways of justifying the use of another decision (per analogiam or per rationem decidendi). Subsequent considerations of the role of precedent in Polish literature included such issues as distinguishing a law-making and non-law-making, binding and non-binding, decision-making and interpretative precedents, as well as the legitimacy of taking over the properties of the Anglo-American practice in the context of recognising the potential of the precedent in the Polish legal system.

Keywords: Polish legal doctrine, J. Wróblewski's concept, types of precedents, potential of precedential practice

Precedent-related issues are present in the Polish legal doctrine in the form of definitions of the term and its types or as independent issues discussed while analysing the manner precedents operate in court practice and determining their role in making judgments. Some attempts are made at determining the potential of precedents in the Polish legal order.

1 Jerzy Wróblewski's Concept

J. Wróblewski is the author of the most comprehensive study of case law already back in the 1960s[1]. Besides the definition of the

---

1 Cf. Wróblewski's works: *Podstawa normatywna i reguła decyzji w sądowym stosowaniu prawa*, "Studia Prawno-Ekonomiczne" 1969, vol. 3, *Precedens i jednolitość sądowego stosowania prawa*, "Państwo i Prawo" 1971, iss. 10, *Sądowe stosowanie prawa*, Warszawa 1972, *Wartości a decyzja sądowa*, Wrocław 1973, *Uzasadnienie i wyjaśnienie decyzji sądowej*, "Studia Prawno-Ekonomiczne" 1976, vol. 16, *Decyzja sądowa a koncepcja systemu prawa*, "Acta Universitatis Lodziensis, Zeszyty Naukowe Uniwersytetu Łódzkiego, Nauki Humanistyczno-Społeczne" 1978, iss. 28.

precedent[2], the scholar focuses on the manner of justifying references to the precedent (*per analogiam* and *per rationem decidendi*[3]), the types of links between decisions (precedents *sensu strictissimo, stricto, largo and largissimo*)[4] and the quality of these links (making references to a prior decision as an additional argument and implementing a prior decision to indicate its influence on the content of a decision at hand)[5].

J. Wróblewski builds a collection of jurisdictional situations within which a named decision that normatively or actually affects another decision is the precedent[6]. As it seems, determining the link between decisions as an influence allows for further distinctions related to its intensity (depth of links)[7]. The precedential links are included in this concept, most of all within the distinction of the motivation criterion of the decision-maker and the fact of making a decision[8]. Hence, three conditions must be met: (1) conviction of the decision-maker that under the current conditions the D2 decision must be made which is identical or similar to the precedent D1[9], (2), making the D2 decision and (3), occurrence of one of four types of links between D1 and D2: (3a) repetition of D1 in D2, (3b) deriving D2 from D1 according to the accepted reference rules, (3c) justifying D2 with the same rules or applying the same or identical measures used to justify D1, and (3d) justification of D2 by referring to D1 in a different manner than in situation 3b and 3c. Particular variants of links allow for the separation of *strictissimo sensu* (3a), *sensu stricto (3b)*, *sensu largo* (3c) and *sensu largissimo* (3d) precedents.

---

2 See: J. Wróblewski, *Precedens…*, op. cit., p. 525, where precedent is defined as decision that normatively or factualy impacts the taking of other decisions ("decyzja, która normatywnie lub faktycznie wpływa na podejmowanie innych decyzji").

3 Cf. ibidem, p. 526 et seq.

4 Cf. ibidem, pp. 525–526.

5 Cf. ibidem, p. 529 et seq.

6 Cf.: ibidem, p. 525.

7 However, the distinction between the normative and actual influence indicates a certain link with the concept of *de iure* and *de facto* precedent, and directing the influence on the decision-making process means a possibility to situate it both apragmatically (in the content of the decision) and pragmatically (within the decision-making process).

8 Com. J. Wróblewski: *Precedens…*, op. cit., p. 525–526.

9 Excluding the factor referring to the conviction of the decision-maker allows for differentiation between the functional and objective precedent in this concept (the difference involves excluding the psychological factor from the objective term of the precedent - com. Ibidem, p. 525).

As it seems, the link between D1 and D2 in the last three situations (3b-3d) is referred in this concept to the justification of the decision (D2 has to be derived or justified), however within the link between 3c and 3d, the justification is treated as a place where the establishment of precedent links takes place. While, in situation 3b the justification plays the role somehow indirectly as the focus of the link on the possibilities to derive D2 from D1 links the justification with the actually performed reasoning based on which the content of the decision was built, and not only the content of the justification (or actually, maybe even more the content of the decision than the content of its justification). Furthermore, using the term "justifying" in this concept allows reasoning aimed at making the decision to be linked with arguments used to justify it. At the same time the author, preferring the approach to the precedent in the light of justification, links it in the specific scope with the context of heuristics, in particular by underlining the decision-maker's concept and reasoning.

The above divisions are accompanied by the differentiation of two types and scopes of the link between D1 and D2 of which one is determined as consideration, and the second – as being guided by the precedent. Consideration of the precedent (corresponding with its objective term) takes place when in the justification of D2 there is a reference to D1, however it is treated as an additional argument justifying one's own position (without which compliance between D2 with D1 could be stated at most). While, being guided by the precedent (corresponding with its functional term, including conviction of the decision-maker to use D1) occurs when it is possible to establish the role a reference to D1 plays in the motivation of D2[10]. Consequently, within this alternative not so much the scale of the link between the decisions is unambiguous, but the scale of the depth of the justification of the link.

In this concept, determination of the depth of links between decisions is not affected by the manner of justifying the link between the decisions which may be based either on classical *per analogiam* reasoning or *per rationem decidendi* reasoning[11], which according to J. Wróblewski may be connected with each other in a sense.

2 Other Approaches and Distinctions

In the works of other authors the notion of a precedent and its types usually appears in the context of analysing Anglo-Saxon legal practice (mostly

10 Ibidem, p. 529 et seq.

11 Com. Ibidem, p. 526 et seq.

American)[12] or without direct connection to the jurisprudence and *common law* practice. The latter usually focus on "dogmatic" issues[13] or on developing more complex theoretical approaches to the application of law[14]. Comparative studies whereby *common law* practices are superimposed on the continental statutory law orders constitute a significant part of such analyses[15]. Other studies compare "classical" precedential practice with the judicial decisions in various European legal orders[16], including the legal system in Poland[17]. It seems, however, that comparative studies regarding the role of the precedent are more common than attempts at a more comprehensive analysis of the matter in question[18].

---

12 Cf. A.M. Ludwikowska, *System prawa Stanów Zjednoczonych. Prawo i prawnicy, struktura władzy, spory prawne*, Toruń 1999, pp. 49–90; R. Tokarczyk, *Prawo amerykańskie*, 6th ed., supplemented, Kraków 2003, pp. 30–44; M. Koszowski, *Anglosaska doktryna precedensu. Porównanie z polską praktyką orzeczniczą*, Warszawa 2009, pp. 13–110.

13 Cf. A. Stelmachowski, *Prawotwórcza rola sądów (w świetle orzecznictwa cywilnego)*, "Państwo i Prawo" 1967, iss. 4–5, passim; R. Hauser, J Trzciński, *Prawotwórcze znaczenie orzeczeń Trybunału Konstytucyjnego w orzecznictwie Naczelnego Sądu Administracyjnego*, Warszawa 2008, passim.

14 Cf. J. Wróblewski, *Precedens…*, passim; T. Stawecki, *Precedens w polskim porządku prawnym. Pojęcie i wnioski* de lege ferenda, [in:] *Precedens w polskim systemie prawa. Materiały z konferencji Zakładu Praw Człowieka Wydziału Prawa i Administracji Uniwersytetu Warszawskiego, zorganizowanej 24 czerwca 2008 r.*, eds. A. Śledzińska-Simon, M. Wyrzykowski, Warszawa 2010, pp. 60–73; M. Zirk-Sadowski, *Tzw. prawotwórcza decyzja sądowego stosowania prawa*, "Studia Prawnicze" 1980, no. 1–2, p. 255 et seq.; L. Morawski, *Główne problemy współczesnej filozofii prawa. Prawo w toku przemian*, Warszawa 1999, pp. 197–244, L. Leszczyński, *Precedent and the Judge's Axiological Choices: Remarks on Polish Legal Culture, w: Unity of Civil Procedural Law and Its National Divergences*, ed. M. Sawczuk, Lublin 1994, p. 255 et seq.

15 Cf. M. Koszowski, *Norweska doktryna precedensu w zarysie*, "Zaszyty Naukowe Sądownictwa Administracyjnego" 2012, no. 3, p. 195 et seq. Such an analysis in the context of judicial law-making activity can be found in: A. Stelmachowski, op. cit., pp. 624–626.

16 Cf. B. Greczner, *Precedens jako przykład konwergencji kultur prawnych w obszarze prawa Unii Europejskiej*, "Acta Erazmiana" 2011, passim; A. Orłowska, *Precedens w systemach prawnych różnych krajów europejskiej kultury prawnej*, "Radca prawny" 2000, no. 5, passim.

17 Cf. M. Koszowski, *Anglosaska…*, op. cit., p. 111 et seq.

18 A significant article which summarises the state of the doctrine and the Polish practice of the day written by L. Morawski and M. Zirk-Sadowski and entitled "*Precedent in Poland*", was included in *Interpreting Precedent. A Comparative Study* (eds. D.N. MacCormick, R.S. Summers); this work is a comprehensive comparative analysis of precedential practice in different legal orders; the general image can be also found in the

Another key point highlighted by Polish legal scientists is the proposed distinction between the law-making precedent and that which lacks this aspect[19]. Besides this distinction, different types of precedents are collated such as those that have a binding force and those that don't[20], *de iure* and *de facto* precedents[21], specific and abstract ones[22] or decision-making (prevalent) and interpretation-developing precedents[23]. At the same time, the need for a more "casual" approach to precedent defining features in the statutory law order fosters a different

---

work by M. Król, *Precedent and the Law*, [in:] *Precedent and the Law*, ed. E. Hondius, Bruxelles 2007, passim.

19 Cf. L. Morawski, *Główne…*, op. cit., p. 214; Z. Ziembiński, *Teoria prawa*, Warszawa-Poznań 1974, pp. 83–85; J. Stelmachowski, op. cit., passim; idem, *Zarys…*, op. cit., pp. 434–456; R. Hauser, J. Trzciński op. cit., specifically pp. 10–13, 31–32; M. Zirk-Sadowski, *Precedens a tzw. decyzja prawotwórcza*, "Państwo i Prawo" 1980, iss. 6, passim, specifically pp. 69 et seq., 73.

20 The distinction of a binding precedent is frequently associated with an express statement that such precedents are absent in the Polish legal system (cf. J. Wróblewski: *Precedens…*, op. cit., pp. 528–533). Such a division on the construction level is suggested in numerous works, including: L. Morawski, *Czy precedens powinien być źródłem prawa?*, [in:] *W kręgu problematyki władzy, państwa i prawa, Księga jubileuszowa w 70-lecie urodzin Profesora Henryka Groszyka*, ed. J. Malarczyk, Lublin 1996, p. 199; L. Morawski, *Główne…*, op. cit., pp. 208. 212; *idem*, *Precedens a wykładnia*, "Państwo i Prawo" 1996, iss. 10, pp. 5–12 (where this issue is treated separately from the law-making activity – p. 5); M. Król, op. cit., pp. 425–426; A. Orłowska, *Moc wiążąca precedensu*, "Przegląd Sądowy" 2000, no. 7–8, passim; D. Dąbek, *Między precedensem a źródłem prawa (o uchwałach Naczelnego Sądu Administracyjnego)*, [in:] *Orzecznictwo w systemie prawa*, eds. T, Bąkowski, K, Grajewski, J. Warylewski, Warszawa 2008, p. 194 et seq. Various aspects of the binding nature of precedents in the *common law* countries are discussed in, e.g., N. Duxbury, op. cit., p. 58 et seq.; M.J. Gerhardt, op. cit., pp. 151 et seq., 177 (where the notion of the "super-precedent" appears understood as precedents that are practically immune to reversal or reconsideration). More information on various precedent-related practices in selected statutory law countries, including Italy, France, Germany, and Finland, can be found in: R. Siltala, *A Theory of Precedent. From Analytical Positivism to a Post-Analytical Philosophy of Law*, Oxford-Portland 2000, pp. 127–150.

21 Cf. M. Zirk-Sadowski, *Precedens…*, op. cit., p. 71; L. Morawski, *Główne…*, op. cit., p. 212. Based on the "actual binding force", resolutions of the Supreme Administrative Court are sometimes treated as de facto precedents (Cf. D. Dąbek, *Między…*, op. cit., p. 198 et seq.). M. Król (cf. *Precedent…*, op. cit., p. 426 et seq.) makes a somewhat similar distinction between formal and informal precedents.

22 Cf. L. Morawski, M. Zirk-Sadowski: *Precedent…*, op. cit., p. 229.

23 L. Morawski, *Główne…*, op. cit., p. 214; M. Zirk-Sadowski, *Precedens…*, op. cit., p. 73.

approach to the presence of roles of prior decisions in statutory law systems and leads, at times, to replace the term of "precedent" with the notion of "a prior decision"[24]. This shift is most visible where the role of such decisions in current decision-making processes and in the reasoning employed is carefully analysed.

The place and role of precedents in the court practice is discussed in Polish jurisprudence pragmatically (an analysis of elements of a decision-making process) and non-pragmatically (focusing on the content of a precedential decision as a result of a decision-making process). Both approaches lead to findings in the context of heuristics, i.e. discovering the rationale behind the decision taken, and in the context of justification, i.e. developing arguments which rationalise the link between various decisions and the reasoning processes behind them[25].

An analysis of the elements and course of the decision-making process helps determine the places in which prior decisions appear in the decision-making process and the type of reasoning on various stages of statutory interpretation. This, in turn, entails a particularly important distinction among three stages, i.e. validation findings, reconstruction of behavioural patterns, and establishment of a normative basis for a decision. Once the three stages are earmarked, the degree of independence of prior decisions implemented can be measured as a source of reconstruction of the normative basis for the current decision and subsequently positioned relative to binding legal provisions, open criteria, and the manner of conducting a test for the applicability of other decisions. Such positioning also includes the specific nature of the reconstruction process of the *ratio decidendi* deriving from the decision and its justification, and determination of meanings of phrases used therein, as well as the effects of the implementation of a prior decision on the course of formulating the grounds for the current decision. In addition to the above, a detailed scrutiny of the process in question entails analysing the manner of combining prior decisions with legal provisions and open criteria, with due consideration for conflicting and inference reasoning as

24 Stressing 'prior decisions' may be connected with the caution relating to the adoption of the term 'precedent' in the statutory law order, as expressed in the Introduction to this volume. Such considerations are particularly visible in the views held by T. Stawecki (*An Alternative in the Judicial Precedent in the Civil Law Countries*, [in:] *Peace Based on Human Rights. XXVIII World Congress on the Philosophy of Law and Social Philosophy*, Lisboa 2017, pp. 305–306) and M. Novak (*The Misty Skies of Jurisprudence Constante*, [in:] *Peace Based on Human Rights…*, op. cit., pp. 306–307).

25 J. Wróblewski's concept presented above seems to be the common denominator for both these viewpoints and contexts.

well as for the manner of adapting the normative basis of prior decisions to the current one[26].

In the context of justifying the need for references to prior decisions, scholars analyse the manner in which such references are made regarding the type of decisions selected as well as the identification of the reasoning processes behind them. Naturally, the content of a prior decision and the formulation of arguments indicating the implementation of prior decisions remain particularly important[27].

The adoption of the classic Anglo-American understanding of the precedent triggers an interest in the problems common to that legal culture and may, in consequence, lead to some scepticism concerning the practical role of the precedent[28] and to the presence of the precedent (as a separate legal category) in the statutory law order, let alone the mere use of the term of precedent in the context of such a legal order. Despite such scepticism, making references to or implementing prior decisions in court practice or even admitting their binding effect is not entirely undermined.[29]

The considerations outlined above may be accompanied by an analysis of classic issues relating to precedential practice in the theory of law. These include inter alia the effect of precedential practice on the axiology of the application of law and, in particular, on the uniformity and certainty of application of law[30],

26 Cf. L. Morawski, *Główne…*, op. cit., p. 208 et seq.; L. Leszczyński, *Zagadnienia teorii stosowania prawa. Doktryna i tezy orzecznictwa*, Kraków 2004, pp. 301–310; idem, *Precedens jako źródło rekonstrukcji normatywnej podstawy decyzji stosowania prawa*, [in:] *Prawo a wartości. Księga jubileuszowa Profesora Józefa Nowackiego*, eds. I. Bogucka, Z. Tobor, Kraków 2003, pp. 149–162; idem, *Rola wcześniejszych decyzji w procesie stosowania prawa. Szkic modelu i wybrane czynniki różnicujące*, [in:] *Prawo w XXI wieku*, ed. W. Czapliński, Warszawa 2006, p. 458 et seq.

27 Cf. J. Wróblewski, *Uzasadnienie i wyjaśnienie decyzji sądowej*, "Studia Prawno-Ekonomiczne" 1976, vol. 16, p. 7 et seq.; M. Matczak, *Teoria precedensu czy teoria cytowania? Uwagi o praktyce odwołań do wcześniejszych orzeczeń sądowych w świetle teorii wielokrotnych ugruntowań*, [in:] *Precedens w polskim systemie prawa*, op. cit., p. 99 et seq.; D. Dąbek, *Między precedensami…*, op. cit., p. 198 et seq.; A. Jakubowski, S. Gajewski, *Argument z linii orzeczniczej w orzecznictwie sądów administracyjnych*, Warszawa 2015, passim.

28 Cf. M. Zirk-Sadowski, *Precedens…*, op. cit., p. 71 et seq.; T. Stawecki, *Precedens jako zadanie dla nauk prawnych*, [in:] *Precedens w polskim systemie prawa…*, op. cit., specifically p. 247 et seq.

29 Cf. L. Morawski, M. Zirk-Sadowski, *Precedent…*, op. cit., p. 245 et seq.

30 J. Wróblewski, *Precedens…*, op. cit., specifically pp. 521–525, 532–533; idem, *Wartości a decyzja sądowa*, Wrocław 1973, p. 129 et seq.; L. Leszczyński, *Precedent…*, op. cit.,

general relations between precedents and legal provisions, a comparative analysis of the *per rationem decidendi* and *per analogiam legis* reasoning[31], an analysis of the law-making nature of precedent decisions[32] or the role of the precedent in the cause and effect based relations to the social and political environment of the law (specifically where the social environment undergoes a major change)[33].

As a result of expansion of theoretical analyses to cover the areas indicated above, acceptance of the viability to implement certain classic precedential solutions, with due caution and realism indicated in this volume may well be recommended at the cost of putting somewhat aside the *stare decisis* principle. This approach will consist in determining initial conditions required to implement prior decisions and developing criteria with which to measure the "depth" of links between decisions and their respective reasoning processes. Such an attitude of researchers may lead to the establishment of a model for the implementation of prior decisions as precedents and, as a result, an assessment of the precedential potential (precedent-based court practice) in the statutory law order.

In this context, a juxtaposition suggested by T. Stawecki[34] is of interest. He distinguishes four approaches in the Polish legal theory, i.e. traditional (as propounded by J. Wróblewski[35]), sceptical, pragmatic, and radical. The sceptical

---

passim; idem, *Ujednolicanie orzecznictwa a precedens w sądowym stosowaniu prawa*, [in:] *Jednolitość prawa sądowego cywilnego a jego odrębności krajowe*, ed. M. Sawczuk, Lublin 1997, passim; L. Leszczyński, *Dyskrecjonalność a jednolitość stosowania prawa. Rola argumentu per rationem decidendi*, [in:] *Dyskrecjonalność w prawie*, eds. W. Staśkiewicz, T. Stawecki, Warszawa 2010, p. 136 et seq.

31 Cf. J. Nowacki, *Analogia legis*, Warszawa 1966, passim; M. Koszowski, *Rozumowanie per analogiam w prawie precedensowym. Dwa ujęcia analogii*, "Rocznik nauk prawnych" 2015, vol. 25, no. 1, p. 7 et seq.

32 Cf. A. Stelmachowski, op. cit., passim; M. Zirk-Sadowski, *Tzw. prawotwórcza…*, op. cit., passim; Z. Ziembiński, op. cit., p. 83 et seq.; L. Morawski, *Główne…*, op. cit., p. 197 et seq.; R. Hauser, J. Trzciński, op. cit., passim; Z. Kmieciak, *Prawotwórstwo sędziowskie w sferze jurysdykcji sądów administracyjnych*, "Państwo i Prawo" 2006, iss. 12, passim; A. Gomułowicz, *Aspekt prawotwórczy sądownictwa administracyjnego*, Warszawa 2008, p. 10 et seq.

33 Cf. L. Morawski, *Główne…*, op. cit., p. 220 et seq.; L. Leszczyński, *Praktyka precedensowa w porządku prawa stanowionego. Podstawowe czynniki warunkujące*, "Acta Universitatis Wratislaviensis. Przegląd Prawa i Administracji" 2017, CX, p. 159 et seq.

34 Cf. T. Stawecki, *Precedens w polskim…*, op. cit., pp. 74–98.

35 Cf. J. Wróblewski, *Precedens…* and other works by the same author including: *Wartości…*, op. cit., pp. 133–149, *Sądowe stosowanie prawa*, Warszawa 1972, pp. 359–363, *Sądowe stosowanie prawa*, Warszawa 1988, pp. 371–375, *Podstawa normatywna i reguła decyzji w sądowym stosowaniu prawa*, "Studia Prawno-Ekonomiczne" 1969, vol. 3, p. 7 et seq.

approach[36], which refers to the Anglo-American practice (and, specifically, to the concept of the precedent), negates the notion of adaptation of said practice also in view of the problems connected with determining the normative and law-making character of a precedent-based decision. The pragmatic approach is based on linking case law with "the actual law-making function of the courts", which is related to judgment in civil[37], constitutional, and administrative cases[38]. Finally, the fourth approach or the radical one[39] treats the precedent as a genuine source of law on the basis of arguments relating to the division of power, the interpretation of law, and the effectiveness of court practice.

Irrespective of particular assumptions, the facts that courts resort to prior decisions and there are no statutory provisions that would prohibit such a practice seem to be the common denominator of the approaches listed above. All these approaches contain an element of observation-based pragmatism, albeit the essence of justification provided is somewhat different. It seems that the author of this juxtaposition tends to favour the sceptical approach, as far as the adaptability of the notion of precedent and precedent-based reasoning employed in the application of law in the Anglo-American legal order are taken into account[40].

3 Concluding Remarks

Accepting some arguments in favour of the sceptical approach does not, however, exclude accepting the pragmatic approach, which the author of this study supports, especially if the precedential practice is not linked with strong judicial activism alone and the court interpretation contains elements of universal reasoning of statutory law order and *common law*. What should be generally

---

36 Cf. M. Zirk-Sadowski, *Precedens…*, op. cit.; idem, *Tzw. prawotwórcza…*, op. cit., passim.

37 Cf. A. Stelmachowski, op. cit., passim (specifically p. 616 et seq., where the author binds law-making activity with the construction of the law); idem, *Wstęp do teorii prawa cywilnego*, Warszawa 1984, p. 434 et seq.; idem, *Zarys teorii prawa cywilnego*, Warszawa 1998, p. 295 et seq.

38 R. Hauser, J. Trzciński, op. cit., passim; D. Dąbek, *Prawo sędziowskie w polskim prawie administracyjnym*, Warszawa 2010, pp. 450–462; W. Jakimowicz, *Wykładnia w prawie administracyjnym*, Warszawa 2006, p. 356 et seq.

39 Cf. L. Morawski, *Główne…*, op. cit., p. 197 et seq.; idem, *Czy precedens…*, op. cit., p. 187 et seq.

40 Cf. T. Stawecki, *Precedens w polskim…*, op. cit., passim; idem, *Precedens jako zadanie…*, op. cit., passim; idem, *An Alternative…*, op. cit., passim.

accepted (especially for the present Polish legal order) are those elements which are related to the constitutional grounds for courts judgments, positive social effects which court activity may generate, notably in the area of human rights protection, reinforcement of rule of law, and the need for such activity in view of a state of higher necessity brought about by legislation of some procedural solutions in order to strengthen the efficacy of court practice in shaping the legal order[41]. It should be underlined that precedents may play a genuinely useful role if not essential for the quality of the statutory law order, at least in some of its aspects. Adapting the classical notion of the precedent and determinants of the precedential practice allows for establishing more effective judicial decision-making processes and later the development of a "theory of precedents" for the sake of the statutory legal order, including the Polish one.

41 Such development trends in precedential practice are discussed at length by D.N. MacCormick, R.S. Summers, *Further General Reflections and Conclusions*, [in:] *Interpreting Precedent…*, op. cit., pp. 531 et seq., 546–550.

Iwona Rzucidło-Grochowska

The Style of Judicial Opinion and the "Precedential" Potential of the Judicial Decision

Abstract: Judicial opinion has (full) potential for precedence when it combines two features (aspects): it is drafted in a way that makes the use of the decision of other courts possible and it makes a reference to the previous decisions in an appropriate way (explains evocatively the use of other judgments). An appropriate way in this sense is a way which allows a judicial decision to maintain a proper quality (especially, when it provides wide argumentation, is easily understandable and uses language in a proper way). Those two abovementioned sides of that potential are in fact the core of the style of the judicial opinion. Hence, it is the style of the judicial opinion that influences the potential for precedence of the court's judgment.

Keywords: style of judicial opinion judicial opinion legal argumentation precedent

1 Introductory Remarks

The concept of precedent has been derived in the culture of case law. For many years there has been a scholar and "practical" discussion on implementation of various elements of the precedent doctrine to the statutory law culture. It is motivated by, among others, the desire to get the advantages from using the case law as judges in the common law culture do. The most important advantage in this regard is the possibility to treat previous decisions (at least in part) as a source of legal norms. It provides also a useful point of reference for elaborating a more systematic description of the phenomenon of various degrees of "precedential power", enjoyed by judicial decisions also in the continental culture. The reflection over the role of precedent in the continental jurisdictions results also from an attempt to reconcile the two worlds of legal culture: the continental European and the Anglo-American one.

Continental judges try to borrow elements of the doctrine of precedent from the case law culture in three main ways: (a) treating the court's decisions as a source of law; (b) considering them as a source of legal interpretation or (c) as a source of a novelty (new legal problem) in the case law. In the first way, the continental culture attempts to take over the concept of precedent in its classical understanding – i.e. as a carrier of normative content. The previous judicial decisions may, hence, constitute a legal source even where the *stare decisis* doctrine is not officially binding. In those cases, other judgments may be treated as a source of law as far as they fulfill their persuasive role as an argument in a judicial opinion[1]. In the second meaning, one can point at the understanding of a precedent as an interpretative guideline and rhetorical support (i.e. in the ways which are more characteristic for the culture of statutory law). In the third way, the precedent can be perceived as a judgement that has a feature of novelty in terms of, final or particular, decision or argumentation (involving new law, new facts or the new interpretation). This is an effect of common understanding the precedent by statutory law culture judges.

The use of the court's decision as a precedent in each of the meanings mentioned above is based on solutions and circumstances that differ between the culture of case law and the continental law. They have, however, in common one basic and seemingly the most effective tool – the judicial opinion. It is not only a carrier of the court's decision itself but, first of all, expresses motives that stand behind the decision. The judicial opinion facilitates comprehension of the decision's grounds, understanding them and, followingly, helps to establish associations between this decision and the factual or legal circumstances of the case decided beforehand. As a result, by reference to the judicial opinion, previous decisions can be used as precedents to support deciding upon the subsequent cases. It is a judicial opinion that allows to identify the intention of the court in referring to the particular previous decision.

The implementation of all of the three modes of precedential use of judicial opinions is an effect of the precedential potential of the particular judicial decision and its degree (understood as the ability to be used as a precedent in, at least, one of the three meanings). The judicial opinion has (full) potential for precedence when it combines two features (aspects): it is drafted in a way that makes the use of the decision of other courts possible and it makes reference to the previous decisions in an appropriate way (explains evocatively the use of other judgments). An appropriate way in this sense is a way which allows a judicial decision to maintain a proper quality (especially, when it provides wide argumentation, is easily understandable and uses language in a proper way).

The judicial opinion allows to use the court's decision when motives for the judgement are easy to be understood. It means that grounds for court's decision

---

1 F.P. Shecaira, *Legal Scholarship as a Source of Law*, Dordrecht 2013, pp. 3, 14; A. Jakubowski, S. Gajewski, *Argument z linii orzeczniczej w orzecznictwie sądów administracyjnych*, Warszawa 2015, p. 47.

are presented and they are prepared in a way that enables the addressees of the judicial opinion to learn at least about the main reasons that led to the judgement. Referring to other court's decisions in an appropriate way builds on making comments on them (or involving in other sorts of discourse), which has a substantial meaning for the decision (i.e. does not only serve as an "empty" argumentative ornament). In this case, in other words, the previous judgments appear as arguments – particular one or a selection of judgments. The use of this kind of argument is quite similar to the use of "the argument from legal scholarship", when the court treats legal literature as a reference point in its opinion.

The basic and crucial category here is, thus, the style of the judicial opinion – i.e. the way in which grounds for the court's decision (in a written form) are presented[2]. The chosen style pre-determines to substantial extent, whether particular elements of the case and the judicial reasoning as well as various arguments are revealed in the opinion and how it has been done. Those two abovementioned sides of that potential are in fact the core of the style of the judicial opinion. Hence, it is the style of the judicial opinion that influences the potential for precedence of the court's judgment. The judicial opinion and the style that it is drafted in play a substantial role for facilitating the enhancement of the "culture of precedent" in the particular legal order, as well as the possibility to use particular judgments as precedents in the future.

It should be also noted that the term "style of the judicial opinion" is not understood uniformly in all legal orders. Most often, the style of the judicial opinion defines the manner of formulating statements in the opinion – the way of passing on thoughts, putting them into words, sentences, and constructing thereby a communication with the opinion's addressees.

As follows from these conclusions, there is an interrelation between the style and the potential for precedential power of the judicial opinion and, in consequence, of the court's decision. There is a correlation between fulfillment of the two aspects of the precedential potential of the specific style of judicial opinion, which have been described above, and the degree of this potential. Which may be pointed out intuitively here is that the more references to other judgments in the judicial opinion are made, the more the opinion favors the use of it the more potential for precedence has. In addition, the subject of further considerations will be also what style of judicial opinion is the most susceptible to the use of

2 For interesting remarks on the style of the judicial opinion see: R.A. Posner, *Judges' Writing Styles (And Do They Matter?)*, "University of Chicago Law Review" 1995, no. 62, p. 1421 et seq.

arguments from the "precedent" – which results from the initial assumption that the more favorable conditions for the use of other judgments by courts, the more the references to case law are exposed in court's opinions.

2 "National" Style of the Judicial Opinion

The style appropriate for a given legal system is a consequence of legal, historical and cultural circumstances related to the application of law. There are generally three basic styles of judicial opinion drafting that differs from each other – French, German and Anglo-American[3].

2.1 French Style

The judicial opinion of French court is the shortest one. It has a peculiar structure and presents motives of a decision in a specific way. In particular, it typically limits itself only to presenting rather short communicates, "announcing" reasons that lead to a judgment. Under the French approach, judicial opinions do not present the whole course of reasoning of the judges that decide the matter, but rather resemble a summary, a description of the result of the reasoning. The opinions of the French courts are more concealable, rather than show the course of judge's reasoning. They do not record any doubts or struggling with reaching the final outcome (e.g. by discussing a few concurring ways of reasoning or by arguing with statements of the parties). In the case of these opinions, it is particularly clear that there is no argument in favor of the position adopted by the court revealed in them. In the French style of judicial opinions, no attention is paid to legal interpretation – which takes place beyond the arguments revealed by a court. It is typically replaced by the most often resounding sound, like a voice from behind the wall, a statement that the law is clear and the case resolved has an obvious nature[4]. This, in turn, is related to the belief that the court's reasoning

3 See: E. Łętowska, *Pozaprocesowe znaczenie uzasadnienia sądowego*, "Państwo i Prawo" 1997, no. 5, pp. 3–5.

4 See among others: decision of the tribunal for Montpellier issued 22 July 2016, no. 15/0019 (Tribunal de grande instance de Montpellier, 1ère chambre b – chambre de la famille, 22 Juillet 2016, no. de RG: 15/0019), [online:] https://www.legifrance.gouv.fr/affichJuriJudi.do?oldAction=rechJuriJudi&idTexte=JURITEXT000034046791&fastReqId=401207292&fastPos=2; decision of the Court of Appeal for Paris issued 16 December 2016, no. 15/04964 (Cour d'appel de Paris pôle 4 – chambre 1, no. de RG: 15/04964, [online:] https://www.legifrance.gouv.fr/affichJuriJudi.do?oldAction=rechJuriJudi&idTexte=JURITEXT000033641983&fastReqId=851895202&fastPos=71.

is not making a decision, but rather revealing the outcome that preexisted in the legal order (i.e. the only right decision that is available in the case). Such judicial opinions resemble at most the presentation of the basic circumstances of the matter with the language of law, rather than the thorough opinion of the decision taken by the court. The court does not attempt to discuss the nature of the statute, but mostly the nature of the facts[5].

Under the French approach, the pursuit for applying law to facts is also clearly visible. This is a consequence of the positivist approach to the law, which leads to a conviction that the actual role of judge in interpreting and applying law should not be disclosed in the official argumentation produced by a court (rather marginalizing it, which results from the judge's concept as a mouth of law). In this picture, the application of law is considered in terms of a deductive logic and put in the frames of the syllogistic model of judicial application of law[6]. In this view, the court applies abstract premises to the facts of the case, focusing on the clarity of formulated sentences and the logical correctness of the argument[7].

Due to the fact that a judicial opinion is limited to simple statements about facts and law, there are no references to the legal scholarship and the case law, as it was mentioned above. Hence, in a judicial opinion there are, in principle, no quotations from other judgments or statements of academics or researchers[8]. Such references are considered as undesirable, as they may lead to excessive extension of the judges' power – contrary to the general principles of the relation between lawmaking and adjudicating that is adopted in the French legal tradition.

However, the lack of references to the legal literature or case law is just a veil for the actual shape of judicial reasoning. In fact, they influence judicial decision-making to a significant extent and provide a significant point of reference for judges – who only refrain from disclosing it in their reasoning. Hence, the argumentation based on precedents (grounded not only in the previous judgments, but

5 M. Troper, Ch. Grzegorczyk, *Precedent in France*, [in:] *Interpreting Precedent. A Comparative Study*, eds. D.N. MacCormick, R.S. Summers, Dartmouth 1997, p. 107.

6 J.L. Goutal, *Characteristics of Judicial Style in France, Britain and the U.S.A.*, "The American Journal of Comparative Law" 1976, vol. 24, no. 1, p. 45; M. Wells, *French and American Judicial Opinions*, "Yale Journal of International Law" 1994, vol. 19, iss. 1, p. 92.

7 M. Wells, op. cit., pp. 92–99.

8 G. Helleringer, *Judicial Melodies and Scholarly Harmonies – The Music of French Legal Interpretation*, "Rabels Zeitschrift für Ausländisches und Internationales Privatrecht" 2013, no. 77, pp. 345–367.

also in interpretation provided by the scholarship) is present in the process of judicial application of law. Judges look for normative content and interpretative guidance also in previous decisions. Furthermore, it is possible to be consistent with the case law. Courts not only use other judgments but it is also recommended[9].

Therefore, there is a clear and fundamental discrepancy between the actual use of the other judgments by the French courts and the arguments revealed in the judicial opinion. The use of other decisions, which exist in practice, is concealed in the linc of reasoning which is communicated officially by a court[10].

2.2 German Style

The situation is quite different in the case of the German style of judicial opinion. It developed a more discursive and argumentative style. Dependable on the complexity of the problem that emerges in a particular case, courts can be inclined to supply even very long and extended opinions, highly discursive and argumentative. This attitude is especially typical for decisions of the courts of higher instance. Their judgments enjoy higher precedential impact within the legal order and, hence, are expected to be supported with especially meticulous and deepened reasoning[11].

German style of judicial opinions provides not only the ultimate result of judicial reasoning in a given case, but also the way that led to this conclusion and argumentation in favor of individual partial interpretations of the judge. They do not only fulfill the function of describing the reasons behind the decision but also the beliefs about the accuracy of the chosen solution.

This style has developed, among others, thanks to the assumption that – although in each case there is usually one right answer only – there may be several solutions competing with each other, and the court's task is to choose the most appropriate, and therefore the most-argued and they have the most importance (relevance). This is clearly visible if the court's doubts and the manner in which they were dealt with were justified.

In their opinions, the German courts use various techniques of argumentation. The starting point is the interpretation and application of the statutory law. In addition, courts in their opinions refer both to the case law and the statements

9 A. Jakubowski, S. Gajewski, op. cit., p. 126.

10 I. Rzucidło-Grochowska, *Wcześniejsza decyzja sądowa jako argument uzasadnienia orzeczenia sądowego*, [article in preparation].

11 R. Alexy, R. Dreier, *Precedent in the Federal Republic of Germany*, [in:] *Interpreting Precedent…*, op. cit., pp. 21, 23–24.

of representatives of the legal scholarship. Although the use of other judgments or legal literature varies in terms of depth – sometimes judgments are quoted without a broader comment, sometimes in a more discursive way – their use is frequent and clearly noticeable[12]. The earlier case law is used as a mere illustration of a particular view or as an example of an established practice[13]. The "precedent" argumentation here refers rather to references to the view established in the jurisprudence, rather than to specific, individual judgments. This results from the assumption that the adjudicating court should present a view consistent with the position shaped thus far by the judiciary (i.e. the particular line developed in the case law)[14].

The conditions of the German legal culture indicate that the practice of using other judgments in the application of law process, as well as disclosing this fact in the judicial opinion, is accepted and desirable. For this reason, in the opinion of the German courts, open quite a broad room from developing "argumentation from precedent".

2.3 Anglo-American Style

The view that there are two aspects of the potential for precedent is fully supported by the Anglo-American style of judicial opinions. This issue is hard to be described in complete coherence with the previously discussed French and German styles due to substantial differences in court decision-making in the common-law and the statutory law culture. The notion of style, as discussed at the beginning, provides however a feasible conceptual framework for comparing the operation of precedential reasoning in judicial opinions.

In the Anglo-American style of judicial opinions there is, in principle, no clash between the actual use of case law and its creation (disclosure) in opinions. References to other judgments, both in the opinion and in the judicial reasoning,

---

12 Ibidem, pp. 23–24.

13 B.M. Markesinis, *A Matter of Style*, "The Law Quarterly Review" 1994, no. 110, p. 296.

14 See among others: decision of the administrative court of the first instance (Verwaltungsgericht) in Berlin issued 6 February 2017, no. VG 11 K 339.16, [online:] https://www.google.com/url?sa=t&rct=j&q=&esrc=s&source=web&cd=1&cad=rja&uact=8&ved=0ahUKEwjVvL6FsKvaAhXSmeAKHbBFAY0QFggnMAA&url=http%3A%2F%2Fwww.muenster.de%2F~lucas%2Fjura%2FVerwaltungsurteil.pdf&usg=AOvVaw1wtdSuxU2t3MftBbwsQrrm and decision of the Higher Regional Court in Düsseldorf (Oberlandesgericht Düsseldorf) issued 6 August 2015, no. I-2 U 11/15, [online:] https://openjur.de/u/867591.html.

are inscribed in the nature of this legal culture. The use of the previous case law in judicial reasoning is perfectly obvious.

Courts therefore in decision-making widely use, which reflect their opinions, previous court statements in other cases, as well as from statements made by legal scholarship representatives. As the essence of precedent judicature shows, the court presents in the opinion the quintessence (containing a normative element) of the used judgment and points to similarities or differences in relation to one's own case, commenting on them and creatively adapting. The use of other court decisions is therefore clearly discursive.

In addition, the manner in which courts formulate their statements clearly favors the use of this opinion by other courts in subsequent cases as a reference point (especially as a carrier of normative content). Judicial opinions provide a broad discussion of the case history and the relevant legal issues, resembling to some extent a structured and extended essay. As has been observed, "[t]he English opinion, in which reasoning appears only after a lengthy introduction, is a discursive process, incidentally integrating various forms of reasoning"[15]. As in the German style, but to a much deeper degree, court shows possible solutions for the case and argues for them, giving reasons for the ultimate choice.

In the style in question, court engages the reader in the court's reasoning process[16] and uses various arguments to motivate its decision. Inductive reasoning prevails in this style of writing judicial opinions; courts also commonly use reasoning by example and by analogy[17]. They also try to demonstrate the compliance of the ruling with the policy. The arguments used in writing have different origins – not only legal, but also social and cultural. This is due to the fact that the judicial opinion can always become in the future a point of reference for another ruling. In addition, court must scrupulously and properly legitimize judicial creativity in the case resolution. Hence, the opinion of Anglo-American style is not just a simple court statement as to the basis of the decision issued[18]. This style of judicial opinion is mostly individualistic-oriented – it reveals the impact of the judge's own style of writing on the content of court opinion[19].

15 J.L. Goutal, op. cit., p. 46.

16 R.S. Summers, *Precedent in the United States (New York State)*, [in:] *Interpreting Precedent…*, op. cit., p. 361.

17 Ibidem, pp. 47–49.

18 M. Wells, op. cit., pp. 85–91.

19 Decision of the United States Court of Appeals, First Circuit issued 23 December 2017, no. 16–2222, United States v. Alejandro-Rosado, [online:] https://law.justia.com/cases/federal/appellate-courts/ca1/16-2222/16-2222-2017-12-22.html; decision of the United States Court of Appeals, Seventh Circuit issued 30 December 2015, no. 14–2514,

2.4 Preliminary Conclusions

The considerations mentioned above lead to three conclusions. First of all, theoretically, the potential for precedent depends on the style of the judicial opinion in terms of its degree (intensity). Practically, not always the more "open" style of the judicial opinion and revelation of the use of other judicial decisions in the opinion – that is an element of the potential for precedent – are strictly correlated with each other. Thus, not in every situation it is possible to obtain a full precedential potential. This dependence is disturbed by the other factors, in particular whether the use of the previous decisions in the judicial opinion is easily comprehensible by external recipients or not.

The other conclusion is that the national style of the opinion and its potential for precedent do not influence the development of precedential practice. In the French style, characterized by not revealing the court's decisions used by the opinion's author, judgements are used anyway in the application of law (moreover, it is required for a court to comply with earlier judicial decisions, despite non-disclosing this point of reference in the opinion). There is no strong relation between the style (and its precedential potential) and the real development of precedential practice (the use of other judgements in judicial decision-making and in judicial opinions). Certainly, the right style helps to develop the practice of the precedent because of the coexistence of all the components (aspects) of the precedential potential at the same time, as in the style of the case law countries opinions.

The third conclusion is that the "common-law" style of the judicial opinion proves that the nature of the potential for precedent encompasses two abovementioned aspects. That style of the judicial opinion clearly shows that in case of the most "precedential" style (Anglo-American), judicial opinions reveal the use of other judgements and are prepared in a way that allows them to be used as a reference point in other forthcoming judgments.

Summing up, if the category of the style of the judicial opinion is perceived with regard to particular countries (as a style proper for national courts), there is no strong, distinct dependence between the style and the degree of precedential potential of the judicial opinion in every case.

United States v. West, [online:] https://law.justia.com/cases/federal/appellate-courts/ca7/14-2514/14-2514-2015-12-30.html.

3 "Internal" Style of the Judicial Opinion

Quite the opposite situation is when the category of style is considered in a different, more general sense – as a feature of the style of judicial opinion that appears in every "national" style within its framework (inside a style characteristic for a given state). In addition to the style of judicial opinion appropriate to a given law system, it is also possible to distinguish a more universal category of style, which functions within a specific legal system. There are two basic styles in this regard: magisterial (deductive, legalistic) and argumentative-discursive. They appear in principle in each of the national styles of judicial opinion and create – in combination with them – a different, specific subtype of the style of judicial opinion. In each national style, both distinguished internal styles can be used by courts. They are a more detailed national style and at the same time something more universal in that they appear in every national style – they are common to all of the national styles. That category of "internal" style is a more general concept, being at the same time more universal, since it appears, in principle, in every national style. It also has an "internal" character, because any kind of style can locate itself within the national style. The internal style can therefore be perceived as two oppositional and extreme attitudes towards the judicial decision in a given country, which not always appear in an ideal form (sometimes are mixed with each other) and which function despite the general determinants of the style in a given national system. Notwithstanding the general practice of the national style, sometimes imposed quite rigidly, the judge, however, has some freedom in constructing opinions even despite this practice.

3.1 "Magisterial" Style

The judicial opinion drafted in the magisterial style is a more rigid statement than a sophisticated and exhaustive statement of the court on the reasons behind the decision. This style of an opinion follows from the belief that the court is not obliged to explain its decision or, in a less radical form, that the reasons in question can be significantly limited. Information about the motives of a ruling (more than justifying the latter) is based on deductive reasoning. Under this view, the judicial opinion takes the form of a report (which content is dominated by descriptive elements) and it does not lead to a broader rationalization of a decision. The fragmentary arguments are purely legalistic – the court bases its argumentation on the reference to the content of legal rules[20]. By sticking to

20 M. Zirk-Sadowski, *Wykładnia i rozumienie prawa w Polsce po akcesji do Unii Europejskiej*, [in:] *Polska kultura prawna a proces integracji europejskiej*, ed. S. Wronkowska, Kraków

the literal content of legal provisions, the court refrains from adopting broader perspectives on the background of the case and does not attempt to weight reasons (also those extratextual ones).

The judicial opinion drafted in this style does not show reasoning as a discourse of arguments, but as just a way to the right decision. The court only reveals the arguments for the viewpoint it has adopted, not against it. In this case, the polemical-discursive elements appear rarely. There are basically no references to legal literature or other judgments, especially in a deepened sense. This results from the conviction that the resolution of the case is obvious and can be revealed merely by reading the provisions of law in a direct way (under this view the wording of which is clear and does not raise doubts as to the interpretation of the court).

3.2 "Argumentative-Discursive" Style

The argumentative-discursive style is located in an utter opposition to the magisterial style. Its basic characteristic feature is a dialog-oriented nature. The judicial opinion prepared in this style presents a polemic discourse with views expressed by parties to the proceedings, as well as external actors (such as other courts, in the previously decided cases, and the legal literature). By following this style, an opinion is feasible to be treated as a reference point for other judgments, which are to be decided in the future. Such an opinion is an act of court's communication with other entities.

The discursive style manifests itself in the relatively broad presentation of the motives of the judgment. The wording of the legal provisions is usually only a starting point for taking into account other perspectives of the court's decision – social, cultural or economic. The court demonstrates reasoning that leads to the decision, often pointing to problematic issues. Partial decisions made in the application of law process are argued with various reasons, often with reference to categories of broader meaning, as well as values. In the opinion of this kind, the court tries to explain to the addressees the motives that support the judgment and convince them to the decision. The judicial decision created in the argumentative-discursive style is also characterized by emphasizing the individuality of the interpreter who tries to show that the content of the decision is the result of her own reflection – weighing the arguments and presenting the way that led to the decisions (including also the opposite arguments). Importantly,

---

2003, p. 94 et seq. See also: L. Morawski, M. Zirk-Sadowski, *Precedent in Poland*, [in:] *Interpreting Precedent…*, op. cit., pp. 225–226.

this style of judicial opinion shows that the court's decision was worked out through the discourse of the court with other actors (such as parties and other courts), as well as that the opinion was drafted in a way that would take into account the cognitive needs of these entities[21].

3.3 Preliminary Conclusions

As it follows from this part of considerations, the stronger precedential aptitude can be associated with the argumentative-discursive style, not the magisterial one. Judicial opinions prepared in this style explicitly show the way how the other court decisions have been used, often commenting on them. They are also easy to use in the future cases, because they reveal the way of reasoning in the case, present argumentation – which allows that they will become reference points for other judgments. It can therefore be concluded that the precedential potential increases, where the author of the judicial opinion, having more freedom within the frames of the "general" style that dominates nationally, chooses an interior argumentative-discursive approach.

4 Conclusions

As it results from the presented considerations, the style of judicial opinion shows a connection with the precedential potential of the court decision. Between these two categories, however, there is no such close and clear relationship as one might assume at the first glance. Obviously, the greatest precedential potential is demonstrated by the opinion formulated in the Anglo-American style (which in this respect is to some extent paradigmatic for other legal cultures). In the case of the other two national styles, standing somewhat in opposition to each other, the situation is not entirely unambiguous. The assumed regularity consists in the fact that the more "discursive" opinion is, the greater precedential potential it has is not confirmed in practice. The example of the French style clearly shows that the precedential potential of the decision may be independent from the style of the judicial opinion, and may build rather on the universal acceptance for use of the previous judgments in deciding future cases. Theoretically, the French style of judicial opinion has weak precedential potential, but in judicial practice other decisions are commonly used, with strong preference in the legal order for maintaining coherence of the earlier and later judgments.

---

21 See remarks on argumentative and discursive style of judicial opinions in chapters dedicated to judicial opinions in selected states in the *Interpreting Precedents...*, op. cit.

Therefore, it is not possible to establish a strong dependence between the style of judicial opinion and the actual development of the precedential practice (using in fact other judgments) in every case. Undoubtedly, the right style of judicial opinion generally helps to obtain a stronger and more comprehensive precedential potential of the court decision, e.g. because it facilitates the use of the decision through a clear and comprehensive explanation of the motives, and indicates the place of the decision against the background of the cases decided previously.

Certainly, however, there is a relationship between the "internal" style in the sense described above and the precedential potential of the court decision formulated in it. Bearing in mind the two aspects of the potential for precedential reasoning – the ability to use the judgment in the future by its proper construction and the appointment in the opinion of other judgments – it should be concluded that this category corresponds closely with the argumentative-discursive style. The magisterial style, in turn, shows a negligible potential for precedents, not satisfying its determinants.

Aleksander Jakubowski

Precedent Argumentation and Settled Case Law Argumentation in the Context of Technological Development of Artificial Intelligence[1]

Abstract: The paper discusses the changes in the global model of application of law in the light of the potential developments of precedent argumentation and settled case law argumentation caused by the use of artificial intelligence (AI). Similarities between the settled case law argument and the classical precedent model provide a space for convergence which will result from the widespread – as it is anticipated – use of the AI software. In both types of legal systems AI will draw conclusions as to the content of applicable law, based on analysis of previous case law. AI will alter the judiciary factors, replacing the previous case law and doctrine practice in common law and statutory law systems with a new, universal method. The role of a lawyer will not be to independently interpret the law and substitute the factual condition against the hypothesis of a particular rules, but to supervise the reasoning carried out in this respect by AI from the perspective of human values (the axiological-humanistic perspective). The courts of higher instance will be exposed as those that fill the system with axiology and human sensitivity, modifying thereby the work of AI based on their case law.Development of AI will most probably result in homogenization of the models of application of law, the works of lawyers and the systems of administration of justice, as well as in change of the role of judiciary. As it seems, a new unified model of application of law will be of precedent character.

Keywords: artificial intelligence, precedent settled case law argumentation judiciary interpretation process the legal decision-making process

1 This paper was prepared as a part of the project titled "Settled Case Law Argument in the Case Law of Administrative Courts" financed by the National Science Centre under the PRELUDIUM programme on the basis of decision no. DEC-2012/07/N/HS5/01710 and in cooperation by implementation of the project titled "Potential of Precedent Argumentation in the Polish Legal Order (A Theoretical and Comparative Approach)" financed by National Science Centre under the OPUS programme (no. DEC-2013/11/B/HS5/03821).

1 Introduction

Reflections on development and influence of future technology should be very cautious; reading of publications from the past demonstrates how quickly the observations made therein were dealt with by time and technological progress[2]. Presently these observations mainly have historical value. Nonetheless, one should not shy away from the prophetic role of science, bearing in mind the uncertainty and risks of such prospects[3]. In the context of law, any attempt to describe how future technology could affect the present paradigm of application of law triggers reflections on possible approach to prognosed developments of lawyers themselves. This paper will discuss the changes in the global model of application of law in the light of the potential developments of precedent argumentation and settled case law argumentation caused by the use of artificial intelligence (AI).

2 Development of AI in the Scope of Legal Services

AI is considered as one of the most significant challenges of the modern world. It is connected with constant improvement of computing power that doubles about every 1.5–2 years (the so-called Moore's law)[4]. It is anticipated that by 2024 AI will be more proficient than humans in translating languages, by 2026 it will write better school essays, by 2027 it will drive trucks better, by 2031 it will more efficiently carry out retail sale, by 2049 it will write better books, and by 2053 it will be a more proficient at surgery[5]. What is more, scientists estimate that there is a fifty percent probability that within the next 45 years AI will outdo humans in all tasks, and within 120 years it will be able to replace humans in all professions[6].

---

2 See: F. Pasquale, G. Cashwell, *Four Futures Of Legal Automation*, "Ucla Law Review Discourse" 2015, no. 26, p. 28. The debate on a use of AI in law started in the 1970s. See: E.L. Rissland, K.D. Ashley, R.P. Loui, *AI and Law. A Fruitful Synergy*, "Artificial Intelligence" 2003, no. 1–2, p. 6.

3 The good example of such analysis from the past is: F.R. Dickerson, *Electronic Computers and the Practical Lawyer*, "Journal of Legal Education" 1962, vol. 14, p. 488.

4 See: J.O. McGinnis, R.G. Pearce, *The Great Disruption. How Machine Intelligence Will Transform the Role of Lawyers in The Delivery of Legal Services*, "Fordham Law Review" 2014, no. 6, pp. 3043–3044.

5 K. Grace, J. Salvatier, A. Dafoe, B. Zhang, O. Evans, *When Will AI Exceed Human Performance? Evidence from AI Experts*, [online:] https://arxiv.org/pdf/1705.08807.pdf [available: 20.04.2018].

6 Ibidem.

It is therefore no surprise that it is predicted that such robotization will alter the shape of law, institutions and legal education[7]. It is noteworthy that recently an Internet robot has been developed that assists in simple legal matters in the USA and Great Britain, e.g. in matters connected with parking fee challenges[8]. New legal programs based on AI are being invented[9], and moreover the already existing cognitive computer systems (e.g. Ross) are being further developed[10]. The possibilities are impressive. It is expected that soon computers will use network analysis to assess the strength of precedent by considering the degree to which other cases and briefs rely on certain decisions. Some search engines, such as Ravel Law, already graphically display how much a particular precedent affected the subsequent course of law. As search progresses, then, AI not only will identify precedents, it will also guide a lawyer's judgment about where, when and how to cite them[11]. Today's search capabilities still require people to identify the legal issues at stake in a given matter, but search engines will eventually do this by themselves, and then go on to suggest the case law that is likely to prove relevant to the matter[12].

The recent years have brought harbingers of these tendencies. Software that is able to weigh up legal evidence and moral questions of right and wrong has been devised by computer scientists at University College London, and used to

---

7 See: R. Calo, *Robotics and the Lessons of Cyberlaw*, "California Law Review" 2015, no. 3, p. 513.

8 K. Johson, *DoNotPay Bot Expands its Free Legal Services across the U.P. and U.K.*, [online:] https://venturebeat.com/2017/07/12/donotpay-expands-its-free-legal-services-across-u-s-and-u-k/ [available: 20.04.2018].

9 J. Sobowale, *Beyond Imagination. How Artificial Intelligence is Transforming the Legal Profession*, [online:] http://www.abajournal.com/magazine/article/how_artificial_intelligence_is_transforming_the_legal_profession [available: 20.04.2018].

10 J. Gray, *University of Toronto's Next Lawyer. A Computer Program Named Ross*, [online:] https://www.theglobeandmail.com/report-on-business/industry-news/the-law-page/university-of-torontos-next-lawyer-a-computer-program-named-ross/article22054688/ [available: 20.04.2018]. See also: K. Turner, *Meet 'Ross,' the Newly Hired Legal Robot*, [online:] https://www.washingtonpost.com/news/innovations/wp/2016/05/16/meet-ross-the-newly-hired-legal-robot/?noredirect=on&utm_term=.966a2742cfa2 [available: 20.04.2018]. The current information about the development of AI in the field of law can be found at https://www.artificiallawyer.com/ [available: 20.04.2018].

11 J.O. McGinnis, *Machines v. Lawyers*, [online:] https://www.city-journal.org/html/machines-v-lawyers-13639.html [available: 20.04.2018].

12 Ibidem.

accurately predict the result in hundreds of real life cases. The AI "judge" has reached the same verdicts as judges at the European Court of Human Rights in almost four in five cases involving torture, degrading treatment and privacy. The algorithm examined English language data sets for 584 cases relating to torture and degrading treatment, fair trials and privacy. In each case, the software analysed the information and made its own judicial decision. In 79 % of those assessed, the AI verdict was the same as the one delivered by the Court[13].

Programs analysing the US Supreme Court case law got similar results[14]. These programs are more efficient in predicting the rulings of this Court than experts[15].

These results are confirmed by a recently organized competition between lawyers and computer software. Humans lost it. The research method applied was developed by professors of law. Competitors had 4 hours to analyse five non-disclosure agreements and to identify 30 legal issues, among others from the field of arbitration, confidentiality of relations and damages. 20 lawyers from leading American law firms had on average a 85 % accuracy in the experiment, whereas the result of the AI was 94 %. On top of that, AI completed the task in only 26 seconds, whereas the lawyers on needed 92 minutes average. The probability that the above research result is random is equal to only 0.68 %[16].

In the opinion of J.O. McGinnis and R.G. Pearce, AI will completely change the legal labour market, adversely affecting above all the situation of those with narrow specialties or those performing routine tasks[17]. Machines will be more efficient in finding relevant provisions, carrying out legal literature and case law searches, develop templates and documents, make short notes and predict court rulings[18]. Consequently, one should expect an increasing stratification into a small group of lawyers generating considerable income and a mass of lawyers

13 See: N. Aletras, D. Tsarapatsanis, D. Preoțiuc-Pietro, V. Lampos, *Predicting Judicial Decisions of the European Court of Human Rights. A Natural Language Processing Perspective*, "PeerJ Computer Science" 2016, DOI: 10.7717/peerj-cs.93, https://peerj.com/articles/cs-93.pdf [available: 20.04.2018].

14 D.M. Katz, M.J. Bommarito II, J. Blackman, *A General Approach for Predicting the Behavior of the Supreme Court of the United States*, DOI: 10.2139/ssrn.2463244 [available: 20.04.2018].

15 See: J.O. McGinnis, R.G. Pearce, op. cit., p. 3053.

16 See: *Comparing the Performance of Artificial Intelligence to Human Lawyers in the Review of Standard Business Contracts*, [online:] https://images.law.com/contrib/content/uploads/documents/397/5408/lawgeex.pdf [available: 20.04.2018].

17 J.O. McGinnis, R.G. Pearce, op. cit., p. 3042.

18 Ibidem, pp. 3043, 3045–3066.

with earning difficulties[19]. At the same time there are no mechanisms that could counteract these processes; in fact they are not even at the disposal of lawyers' professional organizations[20]. Optimists might indicate that in the past technological changes contributed rather towards development of legal market than towards its reduction (e.g. transition from typewriters to computers). However, the present situation seems different for two reasons. Firstly, the developed technology is starting to perform the basic tasks of a lawyer, and it no longer only copies or transforms[21]. Secondly, the speed of computer science development, and thus the speed of development of tools replacing lawyer's work is greater than ever before.

It is anticipated that as the first step the developed legal programs will make it possible to more efficiently assess the force and role of a given ruling (precedent), however a lawyer will retain the function of defining the problem in a given case. The second step will deprive the lawyer of this role as well – AI will be able to independently determine legal problems present in given factual conditions, tying them to relevant case law[22]. Another consequence of development of the AI based legal programs will be a greater willingness to resolve disputes amicably, as the parties will be more aware of the chances they would have in court[23]. Furthermore, what will be next put into doubt is the necessity to keep professional organizations of legal advisers or advocates, as legal services provided by specialist programs will be commonly available, and thus the current monopoly of "lawyers" will be overcome[24]. However, the anticipated software will further continue to rely on previous data, and therefore its efficiency will depend on the achievements of case law and legal literature, etc. This way, a special niche will exist in those regulations that are entirely new and deprived of case law[25].

On the other hand, one should note analyses indicating that the hitherto technological changes have affected the legal labour market only to a small extent, and that future changes do not necessarily need to be revolutionary[26]. Some

---

19 See: ibidem, pp. 3054, 3065.

20 Ibidem, pp. 3042–3043, 3065.

21 Hence the arguments that were to reassure lawyers in the past no longer apply – see: F.R. Dickerson, op. cit., p. 488.

22 J.O. McGinnis, R.G. Pearce, op. cit., p. 3050.

23 See: ibidem, p. 3053.

24 See: ibidem, p. 3057.

25 See: ibidem, p. 3055, 3057.

26 See: D. Remus, F.P. Levy, *Can Robots Be Lawyers? Computers, Lawyers, and the Practice of Law*, [online:] http://law.typepad.com/files/can-robots-be-lawyers.pdf [available: 20.04.2018].

researchers include the legal profession in the group of "low risk" professions in terms of being replaced by automatization, at least in comparison to other professions threatened thereby[27]. It is also argued that classic values, such as due process, are not easily coded into software language[28], similarly to legal subtleties[29]. It is observed that AI will be most proficient at work in simple cases, in which there already exists a settled and uniform case law[30]. However, as those cases are not profitable, it may translate into a lower profitability of purchase of AI systems resulting in restrain its development. In such case, there is a risk of adverse feedback loophole – low profitability resulting from AI support in simple and low-profit cases will restrain the development of AI, making it impossible for AI to be used in hard cases, which will further sustain the low profitability of AI use. This vicious circle will be first broken, when AI is used in simple but mass cases which will provide funds for AI development.

Nonetheless, AI will for a long time have problems with hard cases, unclear and boarder situations, as well as cases that have never been considered in the case law before, e.g. new areas of law[31]. In the opinion of some authors, digital programs will not replace humans in the legal profession, since they will not be able to predict every situation or – due to the nature of their functioning – will not be inclined to undertake untypical actions, which are indispensable in non-standard cases[32]. This could be advantageous: it will be possible to delegate to AI actions belonging to legal routine[33], making the work of a lawyer more creative and satisfactory[34]. At the same time AI may present new problems that will need to be resolved by lawyers, contributing thereby towards increase and not towards reduction of the demand for legal services.

Against this background, one is certain: the AI software which derives information about application of law mainly from the previous rulings will participate

---

27 F. Pasquale, G. Cashwell, op. cit., p. 28.

28 D.K. Citron, *Technological Due Process*, "Washington University Law Review" 2008, vol. 85, note 12 at p. 1249.

29 F. Pasquale, G. Cashwell, op. cit., p. 44.

30 Ibidem, pp. 42, 47.

31 F. Pasquale, G. Cashwell, op. cit., pp. 42–45, 47.

32 See: ibidem, pp. 43–44.

33 See: ibidem, pp. 28, 39; D. Kennedy, [in:] G. Monahan, *How Automation is Changing the Legal Profession*, [online:] https://www.americanbar.org/news/abanews/publications/youraba/2015/october-2015/5-questions-on-automation/ [available: 20.04.2018].

34 It needs to be noted that similar advantages for the work of a lawyer from the use of computers were indicated already more than a half a century ago: F.R. Dickerson, op. cit., p. 488.

in modern lawyering. This will reinforce the role of case law in the process of application of law, which needs to be considered from the perspective of the system of precedent and the system based on settled case law.

3 Settled Case Law Argumentation

Although in the culture of statutory law, codified legal provisions are the principal source of argumentation in the process of application of law, nowadays we can observe the growing significance of argumentation made on the basis of other decisions[35]. It became culturally accepted to use argumentation taken from previous decisions of application of law, which follows both from the qualities of such argumentation, as well as from the increasing knowledge of case law and the ease to get hold of it[36]. A particular demonstration of this phenomenon is the use of the so-called settled case law argumentation, which is a kind of the so-called factual precedent[37]. It is very well-developed in Poland, although it is possible to observe similar phenomenon also in German legal system (*Linien der Rechtsprechung*; *Gefestigte Rechtsprechung*; *einheitliche Rechtsprechung*; *einheitliche Entscheidung*)[38].

Settled case law argumentation is an operation carried out in the process of application of law. Its essence is to rely on the model of interpretation of particular provisions of law established in previous court rulings or on a principle derived therefrom[39].

A settled case law argument can have a primary or secondary dimension. We deal with the latter, when the discussed argumentation consists in reliance on previously issued rulings in order to share the results of interpretation contained therein. Such operation does not attest to interpretation being carried out through the prism of the settled case law but is a means of embedding of a currently issued ruling into the already existing case law. In such case a legal norm is not discovered in the light of the existing settled case law but is accepted within

35 L. Leszczyński, *Rola wcześniejszych decyzji w procesie stosowania prawa. Szkic modelu i wybrane czynniki różnicujące*, [in:] *Prawo w XXI wieku. Księga pamiątkowa 50-lecia Instytutu Nauk Prawnych Polskiej Akademii Nauk*, ed. W. Czapliński, Warszawa 2006, pp. 458–459.

36 Ibidem, p. 459.

37 A. Jakubowski, S. Gajewski, *Argument z linii orzeczniczej w orzecznictwie sądów administracyjnych*, Warszawa 2015, pp. 48–50.

38 Ibidem, pp. 113–116.

39 Ibidem, pp. 9, 16.

the meaning established therein. One therefore applies a norm already established in the case law with respect to presented factual circumstances[40]. It seems that use of the settled case law argument in the secondary dimension will first be mastered by AI (specialist computer programs), since the degree of creativity is smaller than required to use the primary dimension.

The settled case law argument in the primary dimension is of autonomous character and constitutes an independent means of decoding a ready-to-use rule based on a given provision of law. In this perspective, the court does not only rely on the meaning of a provision established in the settled case law, but on a system of values and functions, including social values and functions, that the settled case law represents[41]. This specificity requires that the user of settled case law argumentation demonstrates a certain social sensitivity, which might initially prove difficult for AI. However, on cannot exclude that in the future relevant self-educating electronic systems – disposing of an enormous amount of data, including data from previous rulings – will be able to accurately determine socially desirable values and functions, and then through their prism to make a relevant selection of case law or even propose a resolution of the case.

The primary aim of using the settled case law argumentation in the reasons of a ruling is to convince not only the parties to a proceeding but also the appellate body which will view review it that the legal assessment made in this ruling is correct[42]. The settled case law argument is perceived as a manifestation of certain internal interpretational rule binding for the courts[43]. By relying on settled case law the court expresses a willingness to not cause tensions in the process of application of law, to construct a coherent, uniform, certain, stable and axiology-saturated legal order.

Settled case law argumentation is connected with the concept of the so-called factual precedent. Court's reliance on settled case law argumentation indicates that a particular view contained in the first ruling expressing a particular rule has the value of a precedent, and the rulings following it, comprising the so-called line of settled case law, reinforce the binding force of this rule. As a result of interpretation presented in a particular ruling having been relied on multiple

40 Ibidem, p. 32.

41 Ibidem, p. 33.

42 Ibidem, p. 16.

43 See also: E. Bojanowski, *Utrwalona linia orzecznictwa (kilka uwag na marginesie orzecznictwa sądów administracyjnych)*, [in:] *Między tradycją a przyszłością w nauce prawa administracyjnego. Księga jubileuszowa dedykowana Profesorowi Janowi Bociowi*, ed. J. Supernat, Wrocław 2009, p. 53.

times, an individual specific rule contained therein gains a general and abstract character, becoming a basis for issue of individual rulings in similar cases[44]. In other words, existence of settled case law means that a rule expressed in an individual and particular ruling, gains the property of being binding in the course of practice of application of law, motivated by the authority of the court formulating it or opportunism of other adjudicating panels[45]. This is however not a legal but a factual binding force, which comes down to a certain unwritten principle ordering judges to consider each new case in the context of the previous case law[46], with the reservation that the more adjudicating panels share a given view (thus the use of the phrase "settled case law", "established case law"), the less tolerable is any divergence therefrom. In this sense it is possible to argue that settled case law and argumentation relying thereon constitute a typical example of the law of precedent in the system of statutory law[47]. Precedents that settled case law relies on *(de facto)* are not binding and have non-law-making, interpretational character.

What is noteworthy is that the difference between classical precedent-based system and a system based on settled case law argumentation is that in the latter system one first looks for cases identical in terms of the legal condition, and then one possibly analyses their factual circumstances, whereas in common law systems the situation is opposite[48]. E. Łętowska emphasizes that any precedent should be accompanied by a reflection on the differences between factual circumstances of particular significant cases, and not by – as it is the case in Poland – by a practice of automatic quoting of rulings, additionally reinforced by the process of computerization[49]. A similar observation is made by M. Matczak, who argues that in Poland we do not have a precedent system as such, but a system of quotations[50]. Such practise leads to the situation when settled case

---

44 See: D. Dąbek, *Prawo sędziowskie w polskim prawie administracyjnym*, Warszawa 2010, p. 456.

45 See: ibidem, pp. 495–496.

46 See: ibidem, p. 494.

47 See: ibidem, p. 495; M. Koszowski, *Anglosaska doktryna precedensu. Porównanie z polską praktyką orzeczniczą*, Warszawa 2009, p. 139.

48 T. Stawecki, *Precedens jako zadanie dla nauk prawnych*, [in:] *Precedens w systemie prawa*, eds. A. Śledzińska-Simon, M. Wyrzykowski, Warszawa 2010, p. 249.

49 See: E. Łętowska, *Czy w Polsce możemy mówić o prawie precedensowym?*, [in:] *Precedens w systemie prawa*, op. cit., pp. 9–13.

50 See: M. Matczak, *Teoria precedensu czy teoria cytowań? Uwagi o praktyce odwołań do wcześniejszych orzeczeń sądowych w świetle teorii wielokrotnych ugruntowań*, [in:] *Precedens w systemie prawa*, op. cit., p. 99.

law, and to be precise, the legal rule contained therein, "detaches itself" from the factual circumstances of the case, based whereon it has been developed, and functions similarly to a provision of statutory law with all consequences for its interpretation, as well as for the possibility of such interpretation being carried out by electronic legal programs. Without the necessity to take into account the nuances of factual circumstances, in the system based on settled case law argumentation, AI will more efficiently search for a judiciary legal rule to be used in a decided case. Therefore, such system will be more easily influenced by development of technology than the system based on legal precedent.

It is worth noting that empirical studies have confirmed a clear relation existing between case law availability (an IT base) and the frequency of relying on settled case law argument and the significance that is attached to it. As it follows from the analyses conducted, since the introduction in 2007 in Poland of the Internet-accessible Central Base of Administrative Courts' Rulings, containing reasons of administrative courts' rulings issued since 1980, the frequency of administrative courts' reliance on settled case law argumentation has doubled (0.98 % in 2007 as compared to 2% in 2012)[51]. The more comprehensive and accessible a collection of rulings is, the more eager law-interpreting entities are to rely on it. At the same time, the scope of knowledge of the past rulings affects the courts' reliance on contrary views presented in the judicature, affecting thereby the discursiveness of application of law[52].

Bearing the above in mind, it is possible to expect that development of AI in the field of legal services will cause further facilitation of searching and analysing the previously issued case law, and thus will result in progressive growth of significance of settled case law argumentation, i.e. the role of factual precedent in the states with statutory law systems.

4 Precedent

Given the fact that both the court model using settled case law argumentation as well as the model based on *stare decisis* (in the common law legal systems) are of precedent character, one may wonder wheatear there is a chance for convergence of civil law and common law systems based on unification of the methodology of legal work as influenced by AI.

It should be clarified that a precedent is a court decision that constitutes a model for later decisions in the sense that the general *de iure* or *de facto* principle

51 A. Jakubowski, S. Gajewski, op. cit., pp. 94–96.
52 Ibidem, pp. 93–94.

contained therein becomes a basis or a template by resolution of similar cases in the future[53]. In other words, a precedent is any court ruling whose direct or indirect force exceeds the context of the particular case in which it has been issued[54]. Any instance of a ruling being based on another ruling, i.e. on an act of application of law, will make it possible to say that such ruling has the character of a precedent[55]. The essence of a precedent is therefore the capability of a given court ruling to influence the practice of application of law in such way that the normative basis of a future court decision is determined by borrowing of a certain rule, contained however not in the provisions of law, but in a previously issued ruling (precedent)[56].

Based on the binding force criterion, precedents are divided into two kinds. Firstly, there are *de iure* precedents, i.e. precedents that are an autonomous source of law and thus can constitute an independent basis of a court decision, whose violation would mean a violation of the applicable law. Secondly, there are *de facto* precedents, i.e. precedents with actual influence on the content of future court rulings, which however are not formally binding for the law applying authority. Due to that they cannot constitute an autonomous basis of normative court decisions. A factual precedent is therefore not binding, but in fact it constitutes a significant argument, excluding to a considerable extent a standpoint to the contrary resulting from deliberations of an applier of law[57].

In the common law system, the fundamental form of lawmaking is a court decision, and the *stare decisis* doctrine applies with respect to any general rule formulated by a court in a ruling *(ratio decidendi)*, which means that *ratio decidendi* of rulings of higher courts is binding not only towards the parties, but also – towards courts of lower instance[58], whereby such precedent may be overruled only by the court that has issued it or by a hierarchically higher court[59]. The basis of development of the American law is the precedent, understood as a binding ruling of a court of higher instance within the same jurisdiction or of

53 See: L. Morawski, *Główne problemy współczesnej filozofii prawa. Prawo w toku przemian*, 3rd ed., amended and supplemented, Warszawa 2003, p. 255.

54 See: J. Komárek, *Judicial Lawmaking and Precedent in Supreme Courts*, "Law, Society and Economy Working Papers" 2011, no. 4, p. 4.

55 See: D. Dąbek, op. cit., pp. 452–453.

56 See: ibidem, p. 453.

57 Ibidem, p. 497.

58 Ibidem, p. 66.

59 See: L. Morawski, op. cit., p. 258.

the same appellate court[60]. The essence of the *stare decisis* rule is the requirement of sustainability of precedent rulings (*let the decision stand*), if the following case under consideration is similar to the precedent ruling[61]. In this understanding it is possible to assume that precedents in those countries can be formally binding[62]. A consequence thereof is in particular that a violation of a precedent is considered in those countries a violation of law and constitutes a basis for overruling of a court decision in an appellate proceeding[63]. It is therefore possible to argue that precedent in the *common law* system is generally a *de iure* precedent[64].

The *stare decisis* rule has two dimensions: vertical and horizontal[65]. The former means that a court of lower instance is bound by the decision of a court higher instance (within the same jurisdiction). On the other hand the latter dimension constitutes the obligation of the court that issued a ruling in a precedent case to sustain its own decision[66]. Horizontal precedent is treated unorthodoxically to allow development of law and avoid preservation of erroneous views. This is assured by the right of relevant courts to overrule precedents. It is however limited to situations of "clear" and "obvious" unlawfulness of a given precedent[67]. Another method to avoid being bound by a precedent consists in distinguishing of cases (demonstration of factual differences), this however decreases the level of predictability of court rulings[68].

What is important, also in the common law system it is possible to find argumentation based on previous case law, which however is not of precedent character. It is based on (1) *obiter dicta*, i.e. the non-binding part of a precedent court judgement (contrary to the binding *ratio decidendi*) and (2) persuasive

60 R.P. Summers, *Precedent in the United States*, [in:] *Interpreting Precedent. A Comparative Study*, eds. D.N. MacCormick, R.P. Summers, Dartmouth 1997, p. 364.

61 See: F.H. Easterbrook, *Stability and Reliability in Judicial Decisions*, "Cornell Law Review" 1988, no. 73, p. 423; R. Tokarczyk, *Prawo amerykańskie*, 11th ed., supplemented, Warszawa 2011, p. 36. See also: D. Dąbek, op. cit., p. 68.

62 See: L. Morawski, op. cit., p. 257.

63 See: ibidem, p. 255.

64 See: ibidem.

65 J. Komárek, *Judicial Lawmaking…*, op. cit., pp. 8–9.

66 T. Stawecki, op. cit., p. 233.

67 G. Lamond, *Precedent and Analogy in Legal Reasoning*, The Stanford Encyclopedia of Philosophy, [online:] http://plato.stanford.edu/entries/legal-reas-prec/ [available: 20.04.2018].

68 T. Zych, *W poszukiwaniu pewności prawa. Precedens a przewidywalność orzeczeń sądowych w tradycji prawa anglosaskiego*, Toruń 2017, p. 478.

authorities[69], i.e. rulings of a character persuasive (convincing) for the court, despite their non-binding nature[70].

In the practice of application of law in the American system, these *dicta* are regularly quoted in parties' submissions in support of their argumentation, as well as taken into account by judges by issue of rulings. Courts rely on previous rulings in order to demonstrate the established presence of certain rules or principles in the legal system and to formulate conclusions concerning the *ratio* of a particular legal solution[71]. If *obiter dicta* derive from a court with a higher position in the instance hierarchy, their significance might in practice not be any different from the status of *ratio decidendi*. Courts of lower instances seldom take the liberty to not act in line with the standpoint of appellate courts or the Supreme Court, even if such standpoint is not binding[72]. Even if it happens that a court of a lower instance rejects a *dictum* deriving from a higher court, it usually tries to demonstrate lack of its binding force and the rationality of argumentation contrary to the argumentation of the *dicta*[73].

Persuasive authorities on the other hand are rulings – even if of precedent character –that were issued outside of the jurisdiction of a given court, and thus are not binding for it[74]. Additionally, the so-called unpublished opinions are also treated as persuasive authorities. This does not at all mean – as their name would suggest – that this specific group of rulings is unavailable to the general public. They are made public, but not as landmark rulings. Distinction of this kind of rulings is connected with the fact that they do not create a precedent[75].

These properties clearly demonstrate that unpublished opinions have in the American practice of application of law a function similar to settled case law argumentation, however in that system one cares less for the mere "continuity" thereof. Argumentation based on *unpublished* opinions, like settled case law argumentation, resembles precedent based on analogy, distinguished from

---

69 Also called as "persuasive precedents".

70 G. Lamond, *Persuasive Authority in the Law*, "Harvard Review of Philosophy" 2010, vol. XVII, pp. 16–17. See: D.N. MacCornick, *Rhetoric and the Rule of Law. A Theory of Legal Reasoning*, Oxford 2009, pp. 153, 160.

71 G. Lamond, *Persuasive Authority…*, op. cit., pp. 16–17.

72 M. Koszowski, *Anglosaska doktryna precedensu…*, op. cit., p. 23.

73 G. Lamond, *Persuasive Authority…*, op. cit., p. 25.

74 Ch. Flanders, *Toward a Theory of Persuasive Authority*, "Oklahoma Law Review" 2009, vol. 62, p. 64.

75 R.P. Arnold, *Unpublished Opinions. A Comment*, "Journal of Appellate Practice and Process" 1999, vol. 219, pp. 219–220.

precedent based on rules[76]. The conducted empirical analyses confirm the practice of the argumentation based on non-binding case law being relied on and considered in the American precedent-based system[77]. It is therefore no surprise that attorneys of parties believe that they should present persuasive authorities supporting their reasoning[78]. Courts also find that even if a binding precedent clearly expresses a legal rule, persuasive authorities may be used as rulings concerning factual circumstances more similar to those of the case under consideration than the precedent ruling[79].

It is also noteworthy that reliance on case law theses indicated in electronic legal programs separately from factual circumstances, mentioned in the context of settled case law argument, occurs also in the precedent law system. J. Komárek apart from classical reliance on case law due to similarity of factual circumstances (precedent) postulates reliance on a thought separated from the case law – in accordance with rules similar to the rules of application of a provision of a normative act[80].

What is important, limited time and ever more demanding, complex cases are indicated as factors stimulating the practice of relying on non-binding case law argumentation in the precedent model[81]. It is therefore possible to say that these are the same reasons as the reasons determining the will to use AI in legal work.

5 Conclusions

The above-mentioned similarities between the settled case law argument and the classical precedent model provide a space for convergence which will result from the widespread – as it is anticipated – use of the AI software. In both types of legal systems AI will draw conclusions as to the content of applicable law, based on analysis of previous case law. It will at the same time expand knowledge of rulings and their relevance, the motivation of adjudicating panels and of the mutual relations between rulings. But what is of key importance for a

---

76 M. Koszowski, *Rozumowanie per analogiam w prawie precedensowym. Reguła, konkurencja, poszukiwanie i uzasadnienie dla korzystania z analogii*, "Studia Iuridica Lublinensia" 2015, no. 4, pp. 41, 52–54.

77 A. Jakubowski, S. Gajewski, op. cit., pp. 136–137.

78 G. Lamond, *Persuasive Authority…*, op. cit., p. 26.

79 *Mack v. Strategic Materials, Inc.*, 270 F.Supp.2d 934, 937 (E.D.Mich.2003).

80 J. Komárek, *Reasoning with Previous Decisions. While beyond the Doctrine of Precedent*, "LSE Law, Society and Economy Working Papers 8/2012", p. 22, [online:] https://papers.ssrn.com/sol3/papers.cfm?abstract_id=2150133 [available: 20 April 2018].

81 G. Lamond, *Persuasive Authority…*, op. cit., p. 28.

turn in the continental practice of application of law towards "precedent" argumentation is the availability of knowledge about the history of court discourse[82]. L. Leszczyński argues, considering the mechanisms of shaping the precedent practice in the statutory law system, that:

> "what is important in the context of reliance on previous decisions in a given decision making process is […] that a technical condition from the borderline of the judiciary and cultural sphere, consisting in existence of an adequate »IT environment«, is satisfied. Expedient use of the achievements of case law in the form of previous court decisions must be based on existence of relevant measures enabling identification and factual use of their content, which is to be assured e.g. by availability of electronic and IT instruments. This means the need to be able to efficiently use the entire case law collected in this manner, but what is also important are certain specific issues connected with this general purpose, such as, e.g. the possibility to use decisions issued during the period prior to their publication"[83].

L. Leszczyński has divided the factors shaping of the precedent practice in the statutory law system into:

1) judicial factors (dependent on the judiciary practice and legal doctrine),
2) cultural-social factors, and
3) factors related to the political environment of the processes of application of law (the rules of the constitutional order, law-making policy, type of political regime)[84].

As it seems, development of AI systems in the scope of legal work will affect all three aforementioned areas which will cause adoption the practice of precedent in statutory law systems. The source of AI's "knowledge" is the case law, based whereon the system will either directly determine the content of the binding rule (in the classical precedent system) or the content of the rule resulting from the provision interpreted by this case law (in the continental system). At the same time it is difficult to expect that in one of those system lawyers will not make use of AI. Thus the method of a lawyer's work will be unified. Already now it is possible to

---

82 T. Grzybowski, *Między teorią a praktyką orzecznictwa sądów administracyjnych – uwagi na tle monografii "Argument z linii orzeczniczej w orzecznictwie sądów administracyjnych"*, "Zeszyty Naukowe Sądownictwa Administracyjnego" 2015, no. 6, p. 72.

83 Translated by Aleksander Jakubowski. See: L. Leszczyński, *Praktyka precedensowa w porządku prawa stanowionego. Podstawowe czynniki warunkujące*, "Przegląd Prawa i Administracji" 2017, no. 110, p. 164.

84 See: ibidem, p. 159.

observe a growing role of case law in the process of determination of the content of law – employment of AI will only significantly accelerate this process. What is more, employment of AI will not only speed up the interpretation process (to the speed of the creative work of a computer) and the legal decision-making process (determination of the legal condition and substitution of a given factual condition against the hypothesis of the rules will be carried out almost instantaneously by AI), but it will also limit the number of disputable cases based on differences between results of incomplete interpretations of law, since all systems of AI will be based on the same, possibly full database. Thus, the role of a lawyer will not be to independently interpret the law and substitute the factual condition against the hypothesis of a particular rules, but to supervise the reasoning carried out in this respect by AI from the perspective of human values (the axiological-humanistic perspective). This will expose the social and humanistic aspect of a lawyer's work.

AI will alter the judiciary factors, replacing the previous case law and doctrine practice in common law and statutory law systems with a new, universal method. What is more, it is possible to imagine that later in the future rulings of first instance will be issued by AI, and humans will only consider – also with application of AI systems – the challenges of such rulings. This process will accelerate, when it will have turned out that rulings issued by AI enjoy no smaller social recognition than rulings written by human hand. The role of the higher instances and legal literature will be to add contents on which the AI will rely, and to correct the results of its work from the perspective of human sensitivity.

AI's lawyering will undoubtedly result in social-cultural changes, which, as the development of AI systems and the support offered thereby will progress, will be connected with deepening of social trust in the system of administration of law, in which decisions in human matters will be made by electronic systems. In the political dimension, the idea of Montesquieu that the judiciary power should be "invisible and null" will come true, since AI will be perceived as "the mouths that pronounce the words of the law"[85]. On the other hand, the courts of higher instance will be exposed as those that fill the system with axiology and human sensitivity, having in this respect a norm-creating role, and modifying thereby the work of AI based on their case law.

Summing up, development of AI will most probably result in homogenization of the models of application of law, works of lawyers, the systems of administration of justice, as well as in change of the role of judiciary. As it seems, a new unified model of application of law will be of precedent character.

85 Monteskiusz, *O duchu praw*, transalated by T. Boy-Żeleński, Kraków 2003, pp. 150, 154.

Leszek Leszczyński

Potential of the Precedential Practice in the Statutory Legal Order. From Conditions to Prospects

Abstract: The study analyzes the potential of using earlier court decisions as precedents in the statutory law order in the context of dependence on several starting factors. Some of them have a social and political character, while others are related to the legal discourse in the dimension of the content of constitutional principles and attitudes of the legislature as well as the components of a specific process of law application (such as the similarity of facts or legal matters, the possibility of distinguishing the ratio decidendi, etc.). They may create an important role of precedents in the decision-making process, if the precedent reasoning is correctly shown in the justification of the decision. The precedential practice, by combining the value of flexibility with the value of uniformity and certainty in the judicial application of law, means autonomously shaped by the courts' reference to the argument of "wisdom from the past" in the statutory law order.

Keywords: conditions of using of precedents, role of the justification of decision, axiology of application of law

Analyzing the potential of the precedential practice (employing previous judicial decisions) in the statutory legal order, one should take into account factors that determine such practice, bearing in mind the grounds for adopting here certain features of the common law system[1].

---

1 For more on the features of this practice, see: A.L. Goodhart, *Case Law in England and America*, "Cornell Law Review" 1930, vol. 15, no. 2, pp. 173–193; J. Evans, *Change in the Doctrine of Precedent during the Nineteenth Century*, [in:] *Precedent in Law*, ed. L. Goldstein, Oxford 1991, passim; M.N.S. Sellers, *The Doctrine of Precedent in the Unites States of America*, "American Journal of Comparative Law" 2006, vol. 67, passim; L. Bell, *Comparing Precedent*, "Cornell Law Review" 1997, vol. 81, no. 5, pp. 1243 et seq.; N. Duxbury, *The Nature and Authority of Precedent*, Cambridge 2008, pp. 31 et seq.; L. Alexander, E. Sherwin, *Judges as Rule Makers*, [in:] *Common Law Theory*, ed. D.E. Edlin, Cambridge 2007, pp. 30 et seq.; J. Gardner, *Some Types of Law*, [in:] *Common Law Theory*, op. cit., pp. 66–75; E.G. Lee III, *Overruling Rhetoric. The Court's New Approach to Stare Decisis in Constitutional Cases*, "University of Toledo Law Review" 2002, no. 33, pp. 581 et seq. As regards such practice in Australia, see: M. Kirby, *Precedent – Report on Australia*, Materials of the International Academy of

There are basically two areas covered by the conditions for the use of previous legal decisions in court proceedings in the statutory law system. One area covers the social and political environment of the law and its application. It is linked with confidence the public puts in the system of justice and public consent for its independence in making judgments and with key principles on which the whole political system rests (separation of powers, rule of law, and democracy). The other area refers to broadly understood legal conditions including the law making policy and the maturity of court practice supported by the legal doctrine, as well as, in specific decision-making processes, the will of a given bench of judges, similarity between situations which require a decision and the possibility to employ the *ratio decidendi* approach in the justification to the decision.

1 Social and Political Conditions

(1) Confidence in the system of justice, perceived as a factor which shapes precedential practice, is linked with the approval of the discretionary power which judges enjoy. This discretionary power is seen, in turn, as "equitable adjustment" to the highly formalized results of law-making activity[2], without prejudice to the expected uniformity of judgments, which allows for the predictability of their content. Arguably, this practice is not dependent on the fulfillment of the requirement to become a judge as a result of election[3] (notably with respect to higher instance courts which have the biggest influence on judicial practice), albeit such election (invariably linked with first instance courts or their certain types) would surely not reduce the scope of this consent[4]. It seems that indirect democratic legitimacy, associated with the assessment of appointed judges, is sufficient.

Comparative Law Conference, Utrecht 2006, passim. M. Harding, I. Malkin, *The High Court of Australia's Obiter Dicta and Decision-Making in the Lower Courts*, "Sydney Law Review" 2012, vol. 34, no. 2, pp. 267 et seq.

2 For more information on *common law* see: S.J. Burton, *Judging in Good Faith*, Cambridge 2004, pp. 35–68.

3 The role of this argument is also discussed in: T. Stawecki, *Precedens jako zadanie dla nauk prawnych*, [in:] *Precedens w polskim systemie prawa. Materiały z konferencji Zakładu Praw Człowieka Wydziału Prawa i Administracji Uniwersytetu Warszawskiego, zorganizowanej 24 czerwca 2008 r.*, eds. A. Śledzińska-Simon, M. Wyrzykowski, Warszawa 2010, pp. 92–93.

4 For more information on the role of electing judges see: J.R. Nash, *Prejudging Judges*, "Columbia Law Review" 2006, no. 106, passim.

(2) The political aspect of resorting to previous judicial decisions is mainly connected with the division of power principle which does not negate precedential practice *per se*. This is probably best evidenced in the American judicial system. The separation of powers, which this principle establishes, especially when linked with the rule of law, reinforces the autonomy of the properly institutionally and organizationally developed[5] judiciary and is conducive to making references to its own prior decisions and justifying the efficacy of such a practice.

The use of previous judicial decisions is best supported by democracy[6], especially constitutional democracy which provides constitutional, statutory, and institutional guarantees of the independence of judges. *A rebours*, the self-autonomous use of prior judicial decisions by the judiciary is not supported by an autocratic political system. This is largely so because precedents that are shaped on the grass-root level in the course of decision-making processes retain their independence from the political center and may lead to making references to international or even foreign judicial practice. This way, they reduce supervision of the political center over the content of law perceived as a whole, which, not infrequently, may expose the true intentions of said center. Hence autocratic political systems have developed certain means that influence judicial practice such as various type of guidelines[7] put forward by supreme judicial authorities that are dependent on the political center.

What can significantly reinforce the desire to resort to previous judicial decisions is a social and political change, especially comprehensive, far-reaching

---

5 Cf. M. Taruffo, *Institutional Factors Influencing Precedents*, [in:] *Interpreting Precedent. A Comparative Study*, eds. D.N. MacCormick, R.S. Summers, Dartmouth 1997, pp. 437 et seq.; E.H. Caminker, *Why Must Inferior Courts Obey Superior Court Precedents*, "Stanford Law Review" 1994, no. 46, pp. 817 et seq.

6 A. Barak (*The Judge in a Democracy*, Princeton 2008, passim, and specifically pp. 99–112, 177–189, 213 et seq.) outlines the functioning of judges in a democratic system, also in the context of their discretionary power.

7 The guidelines concerning interpretation and application of law, which were binding in Poland prior to 1989, were abolished at the beginning of system transformations (Act of 20 December 1989 – Dz.U. 1989, no. 73, item 436). More on their role in passing judgments see: A. Stelmachowski, *Prawotwórcza działalność arbitrażu*, "Przegląd Ustawodawstwa Gospodarczego" 1959, no. 11, p. 615 and M. Zirk-Sadowski, *Precedens a tzw. decyzja prawotwórcza*, "Państwo i Prawo" 1980, iss. 6, pp. 73–74.

and democratic in its nature, under which judicial practice may set certain trends until a new legislative system is fully developed[8].

2 Conditions of the Legal Discourse

2.1 Attitudes of Legislators and of the Judiciary

(1) The implementation of prior judicial decisions in a statutory law system is also linked with certain "legislative consent". Contrary to the use of open criteria in the form of general referral clauses[9], making references to previous judicial decisions, is not only free from any special legislative authorization (the concept totally alien in *common law* countries) but also it is not usually perceived by legislators on the level of normative regulations[10]. It follows that precedential practice is not an element of a legislative policy as it happens where references are made to open criteria on a normative level.

The tendency of judicial practice to shape its independent legal solutions depends on the condition of legislation. A lower quality of legal provisions may simply require a deeper interference of judicial practice. There is, however, no connection with a specific legislative policy; otherwise, one would argue that legislators intend to lay down inconsistent or incomplete legal regulations. The policy of "legislative restraint" can occur only in the case of the afore mentioned thorough democratic social transformation, e.g. due to legal regulations currently in progress or an intention to oversee major appointments in the judiciary, opening up more opportunities for the judiciary.

(2) 'Maturity' of the judiciary is a general condition conducive to implementing prior judicial decisions in judicial processes. This maturity stands for an adequate attitude which assumes inter alia the will and the skill to employ the principle

---

8 The implementation of prior decisions and, as a result, the shaping of a fairly consistent jurisprudence could be then treated as "interim legislation" valid until a new intervention of the legislators.

9 Cf. J.W. Hedemann, *Die Flucht in die Generalklauseln. Eine Gefahr fur Recht und Staat*, Tubingen 1933, passim; L. Leszczyński, *Tworzenie generalnych klauzul odsyłających*, Lublin 2000, pp. 117–162.

10 The provisions of article 47 § 4 of the Polish Code of Civil Procedure make an exception in this respect; as a result the precedent is treated as the case adjudicated where no prior decisions apply (compare the Resolution of the Supreme Court of 18 December 2014, no. III SZP 3/14, in which a case acquires a precedential nature in the absence of changes to binding legislation or the appearance of decisions relating to the matter in question).

of autonomy and independence of the judiciary in a responsible manner, and proper balancing of arguments that come from normative regulations (legal provisions) and external criteria (social norms and values). Equally important is a strong resolve to follow universally accepted principles of operative interpretation while exercising judicial discretion in interpretation and in making decisions, to put into practice the principle of uniformity of judicial decisions, and to ensure that the decisions taken are properly justified. While leading to high standards in judicial practice, maturity of the judiciary makes it possible to deem prior judicial decisions a permanent and invaluable element of the judicial system. At the same time, the maturity discussed does not seem to cover the use of independence in making judicial decisions to enter an open "dispute" with legislators concerning the content of applicable law[11]. That said, in certain situations, where "equitable" adjustments are required, such a use of independence in making judicial decisions may not be ruled out altogether as precedential practice could acquire the features of judge-made laws[12].

In some sense, mature judicial practice fills up the void caused in the statutory law systems by the absence of the *stare decisis* principle[13]. The influence of judicial practice is somewhat weakened, since the implementation of prior decisions is not based on binding precedents (argument of power) but on the usability of

11 More information on these relations in the British system can be found in: R. Cross, *Precedent in English Law*, Oxford 1968, pp. 168 et seq. Also see: R. Alexy, *On the Concept and the Nature of Law*, Warszawa 2006, pp. 33–34 and M. Van Hoecke, *Law as Communication*, Oxford 2002, pp. 204 and 207–209.

12 Model relations between the judge and the legislator in the *senior – junior partnership* arrangement with respect to *common law* and conversely (*junior – senior*) with respect to the statutory law order are outlined in: A. Barak, op. cit., pp. 16–17 and 226–240. For more on the practical aspect of this relation in *common law* countries see: Z. Bankowski, D.N. MacCormick, *Precedent in the United Kingdom*, [in:] *Interpreting Precedent…*, op. cit., pp. 325 and 345 and R.S. Summers, *Precedent in the United States (New York State)*, in: Interpreting Precedent…, op. cit., p. 400.

13 Types and levels of links with precedents in comparative and theoretical variants are shown in the works gathered in the book *Interpreting Precedent…*, op. cit.; A. Peczenik, *Binding Force of Precedent* (pp. 461 et seq.); Z. Bankowski, D.N. MacCormick, L. Morawski, A. Ruiz Miguel, *Rationales for Precedent* [in:] *Interpreting Precedent…*, op. cit., pp. 486 et seq.; R. Alexy, R. Drier, *Precedent in Germany* (pp. 26, 29, where the link is described as "power of conviction of … reasons" as well as p. 32); M. Troper, C. Grzegorczyk, *Precedent in France* (pp. 115 et seq.); M. Taruffo, M. La Torre, *Precedent in Italy* (pp. 154 et seq.), A. Ruiz Miguel, F.J. Laporta, *Precedent in Spain* (pp. 272 et seq.).

a prior decision for the needs of a current decision-making process (power of argument). Nevertheless, it allows one to shape one's own model of precedential practice, albeit largely based on the experience of *common law* countries.

Factors in support of a mature judicial practice include legal doctrine and jurisprudence (in theoretical, dogmatic, and comparative aspects)[14] and the existence of a proper IT environment to enable courts to identify and to implement specific judgments or jurisprudence.

2.2 Elements of a Specific Judicial Process

The conditions which determine the implementation of prior judicial decisions – embedded in the decision-making process itself – include the intentions of a specific court and similarity, largely factual, between two decision-making situations as well as the efficacy of *the ratio decidendi* principle employed in the substantiation of the prior decision used and the quality of justification of the decision.

(1) Views held by a specific adjudicating bench[15] are updated simultaneously with a determination (always in the context of their own matter under consideration) of the significance of prior judicial decisions, a degree of insufficiency or inadequacy of regulations that stem from legal provisions or the nature of a legal problem at hand (e.g. the need to determine the content and role of an open criterion laid down in a general referral clause).

The similarity of adjudicated matters which determines the implementation of a prior judicial decision refers to the relations between factual circumstances, between elements of the legal materials or between the type of reasoning employed in the two decision-making processes (reference based and the current one). At the same time, by equipping the implementation of prior decisions with the characteristics of *per analogiam* action[16], analogy is no longer treated

---

14 The jurisprudential basis of precedential practice in *civil law* in connection with the idea of multi-faceted nature of law is presented in: R. Siltala, *A Theory of Precedent. From Analytical Positivism to a Post-Analytical Philosophy of Law*, Oxford-Portland 2000, passim, and specifically pp. 3–34, 151 et seq. The author also distinguishes and offers a theoretical approach to 12 types of the precedent ideology (pp. 67–78).

15 More on the role of judges' attitudes in the context of the manner of adjudicating see: J.R. Nash, R.I. Pardo, *Rethinking the Principal–Agent Theory of Judging*, "Iowa Law Review" 2013, vol. 99, no. 1, pp. 335–338; S. Perry, *Judicial Obligation, Precedent and the Common Law*, "Oxford Journal of Legal Studies" 1987, vol. 7, pp. 215 et seq.; L. Alexander, E. Sherwin, op. cit., pp. 46–49.

16 Cf. G. Lamond, *Precedent and Analogy in Legal Reasoning*, "The Stanford Encyclopedia of Philosophy", [online:] http://plato.stanford.edu/entries/legal-reas-prec/ [available: 26.10.2016].

as reasoning of an exceptional nature (as in the case of judicial decisions that are based on legal provisions) but as elementary type of reasoning properly linked with each implementation of a prior decision as a precedent in the sense of *per analogiam decisionis.*

That said, proper isolation of the *ratio decidendi*[17], from the justification to the judicial decision is but a preliminary step in precedent-based reasoning. Only after superimposing this *ratio* on a given material under judicial consideration and adapting the same to one's own reasoning, one can turn this *ratio* into a genuine precedent in the context of the adjudication process and the content of the final decision.

(2) The afore mentioned types of legal conditions refer to the quality of justifying the decision to apply relevant laws. It is the justification of the decision, especially its argumentation in writing, that becomes a focal point of the maturity of judicial practice and the resulting will of a specific bench of justices as well as the efficacy of the *ratio decidendi* adapted for the needs of the decision-making process at hand.

Justification of a judicial decision not only indicates the use of a prior decision in a given decision-making process – and, hence, developing the precedential nature of relations between these decisions and decision-making processes – but is also conducive to applying the adapted *ratio.* This gives rise to shaping precedential relations in subsequent decision-making processes[18]. There is no doubt that the precedential nature of judicial practice, if understood as a component of a legal culture also in a statutory law system, does not consist solely in claiming a one-off reference, whether to a large extent or not, to a previous decision or decisions, but it establishes a bond between more common practice or even some tendency in a given jurisdiction.

---

17 The role of identifying the *ratio* in the Anglo-Saxon legal practice is discussed inter alia in: R. Cross, op. cit., p. 31 et seq.; N. Duxbury, op. cit., pp. 58 et seq., and specifically pp. 67–110; L. Alexander, E. Sherwin, op. cit., pp. 45 et seq.; G. Marshall, *What is Binding in a Precedent*, [in:] *Interpreting Precedent…*, op. cit., pp. 510 et seq. For more on the role of reconstructing the *ratio* in the statutory law order see cf.: R. Siltala, op. cit., p. 85 et seq.

18 R.S. Summers and S. Eng discuss various approaches to precedents in court judgments in the context of departures therefrom; see: R.S. Summers, S. Eng, *Departures from Precedent*, [in:] *Interpreting Precedent…*, op. cit., pp. 519 et seq. (e.g. regarding non-overt argumentation – pp. 522–523). More on the role of justification in the context of Anglo-Saxon practise see: D. Dyzenhaus, M. Taggart, *Reasoned Decisions and Legal Theory*, [in:] *Common Law Theory*, op. cit., pp. 134 et seq. (specifically pp. 137, 146–167).

The precedential effects of judicial decisions are limited in the absence of links between the thesis proposed and the *ratio* employed. References to prior decisions are not likely to turn the same into a precedent where such references are merely limited to the prior decision case number without citing an excerpt from its justification. In fact, the presence of such a citation has little value in reinforcing the arguments used in a given justification. Only by linking the citation with an "adaptive" annotation, with particular stress on the latter, can the aim of reinforcing the argument be achieved. Even without the citation, said annotation should enhance the quality of the judgment. Such considerations also refer to the application of more than one decision or the entire jurisprudence within which a general (non-specific) reference to the judgment would have the smallest argumentative value.

Needless to say, the indication of the *ratio decidendi* applied in a given decision requires the inclusion of several features which, in fact, somewhat limits the reliability of ascertaining links between the current and precedential decisions. Such considerations must be based not only on perceiving the descriptive function in the justification (i.e. outlining the reasoning and the decision-making process) but also its eristic function (i.e. convincing the addressee of the justification to approve of the decision and its argumentation). This, in turn, may distort the scope of application of the decision indicated in the justification. Such considerations must also be based on perceiving the specific nature of the justification of collective decisions vested with, e.g., the reporting judge and constituting a well-balanced set of reasonable arguments which could, in the course of the decision-making process, clash against each other. Such clashes may not be fully recognized (for instance, due to the principle of secrecy which binds judges), and they may lead to establishing a different course of argumentation in the form of separate or dissenting opinions nd, by extension, restrict the precedential impact of such a decision.

(3) The components of the optimized model of justifying judicial decisions refer to formal and comprehensive justifications in writing regarding a given decision-making process and the actual decision taken. This entails the assumption of a precedential nature of a prior decision in a given decision-making process, and provided that the justification is properly developed, there is an opportunity that the current decision may be used in future decisions. Consequently, precedential practice in the statutory law order will continue to develop.

Firstly, references to a prior decision or decisions should be effected not by indicating the case number or numbers of a judicial decision, which can be perceived as merely ornamental, but by delving into the argumentation disclosed in that judgment. Rather than a direct citation (which is still better than merely making a reference to the case number), such a procedure should consist in precise explanation of the argument that led to the adaptation of the prior judgment to the current decision-making process. That said, focusing not so much on many decisions but rather on one or a few decisions at the most, indicated in the jurisprudence and its evolution and specifying their relation to the decision at hand offers the largest scope for the adaptation of prior decisions.

Secondly, while applying prior decisions, it is essential to specify the degree of compatibility of decision-making situations, and to identify the *ratio decidendi*, properly generalized and adequately adapted (i.e. the core of the justification where the content of the final decision is presented and the rationale behind it explained). The arguments in support of a given thesis should be clearly outlined, as they usually modify the applied *ratio*. Finally, the extent of adaptation of the prior decision or decisions to the current decision-making process should also be determined.

Thirdly, the most effective reference to prior decisions in which links between decisions are clearly exposed is such a reference to the arguments used in the justification of a decision which reflects the decision-making reasoning (i.e. the course of reasoning, the content of arguments and their role in arriving at the decision) and the decision itself with a view to determining the degree of "repetition" of the judgment. Both these aspects require annotations to the arguments disclosed in the justification to the prior decision in the light of the current decision-making process. Such annotations should indicate why a particular prior decision is referred to and how it applies to the current one.

Fourthly, the justification of the judgment which contains arguments with references to prior decisions should be expressed in the so-called discursive style[19]. Generally speaking, this style combines linguistic clarity and precision in formulating one's own thesis in the context of the jurisprudence heretofore

---

19 Cf. M. Zirk-Sadowski, *Wykładnia i rozumienie prawa w Polsce po akcesji do Unii Europejskiej*, [in:] *Polska kultura prawna a proces integracji europejskiej*, ed. S. Wronkowska, Kraków 2005, p. 94 et seq.; I. Rzucidło-Grochowska, *Strategia i taktyka formułowania uzasadnień orzeczeń sądowych*, "Ruch Prawniczy, Ekonomiczny i Socjologiczny" 2017, no. 2, p. 59 et seq. The US Supreme Court's decision in Planned Parenthood v. Casey is an example of complete discursivity of court judgment in the context of references to prior decisions, including Roe v. Wade as well as in the context of general statements and those which refer to a justified departure from the already well established precedent (cf. 505 US 1992, specifically pp. 854–855). Also see annotations to this decision by K. Yoshino, *What's Past is Prologue. Precedent in Literature and Law*, "The Yale Law Journal" 1994, no. 104, p. 471 et seq.

as well as a clear indication of the prior decision, reasoning behind it and arguments used which, for some reason, have not been adopted to the current decision-making process[20]. Furthermore, these annotations should precisely indicate the scope, causes, and effects of implementing prior decisions, reasoning processes or arguments used in the judgment in question (also in the context of "costs and benefits" of such references).

Fifthly, the "depth" of argumentation and the discursive nature of the style employed of the judgment may not thwart the general requirement of linguistic clarity and correctness. References to the arguments used in the justification of prior decisions must also encompass particular juridical precision particularly where such references are made to reasoning processes behind prior decisions as disclosed in relevant justifications. Since such a justification is to serve as the basis for future decision-making processes, the presence of "juridical style" is essential even at the cost of communicative clarity (transmission of the same) with respect to non-professional recipients of the judgment. That said, the scope of this restriction should be subject to careful scrutiny.

3 Potential of the Precedent in the Statutory Law Order – A General Perspective

3.1 Role in Judicial Process

A prior court decision may become a validation argument understood as a source of law in the decision-making approach (a carrier of a behavior pattern) in the statutory law order. Its use in the current decision-making process is based on several indicators.

Firstly, the use of other decisions is not linked with legislative authorization (as it is the case of general clauses referring to the open criteria). The legislator, even autocratic, usually does not prohibit courts from using their own jurisprudence, at most trying to influence the shape and effects of such use (e.g. by establishing the guidelines for adjudication issued by the Supreme Court, dependent on

20 One would, in particular expect some reference to the distinction between overruling a decision deemed as a precedent, which constitutes an established model of adjudicating in a given type of cases, and not implementing a given decision due to significant differences in the judicial decision-making situation (distinguishing or narrowing). More on references to the Anglo-Saxon practice see N. Duxbury, op. cit., p. 111 et seq.; M.A. Eisenberg, *The Principles of Legal Reasoning in the Common Law*, [in:] *Common Law Theory*, op. cit., pp. 93–96; R.M. Re, *Narrowing Precedent in the Supreme Court*, "Columbia Law Review" 2014, vol. 114, passim; E.G. Lee III, op. cit., p. 582.

political directives[21]). The methods and scope of using case law depend on the adjudicating entities themselves. The maturity of judicial practice plays a decisive role here as well as the current "need for decision-making", elements of which are both the degree of insufficiency of statutory regulations (which is not always related to the state of legislation) and the presence of judgments made in a similar decision-making situation (similarity of the facts, of the subjects of regulations or of reasoning made). It is also important that other decisions play a relatively small role when looking for sources of competence standards, growing when influencing the determination of the content of procedural standards and, in particular, substantive law standards, both qualifying and consequential.

Secondly, another decision cannot be an independent validation argument in the sense of the possibility of basing the judicial process of applying the law only on an earlier court decision (decisions). The need to base the process on legal regulations means that model role of other decisions should be determined as in fact supplementary or corrective in relation to legal provisions. The role grows however if a reference to the decision coincides with the validation use of open criteria contained in general reference clauses, or when the social environment of the processes of applying the law favors it.

Thirdly, the order of selecting validation arguments determined by the model role of legal provisions specified above does not place decisions in the role of a carrier starting with which the findings are commenced. In this context, other decisions complete the collection of validation arguments, being able to contribute to filling the gap in the normative regulation with content. However, it does not mean that considering the exclusion of other decisions should not take place early enough within this phase of operative interpretation, which favors the actual and deep use of their content in the entire decision-making process.

Fourthly, courts refer to decisions of the Supreme Court or a higher instance court most often, as well as to their own decision or that of "their own" court, or to the decision of international or supranational courts (under certain conditions). Such practice should be however extended through the referring to decisions of courts of the same instance or courts of other "judicial divisions" (which happens definitely less frequently) and referring to decisions of lower instance courts (which is the rarest). The importance and usefulness of judicial decisions of the supreme courts or "supranational" courts, that may be linked with a judicial pragmatism (and even opportunism) should be supplemented by

21 Cf. above: 1.

the will of the using any decision that is necessary for making actual decision and potentially, for establishing or keeping the rational line of jurisdiction.

3.2 Impact on the Legal Axiology

The potential of a precedent in the statutory law order, subject to the requirements, reasoning, and arguments of the decision-making process outlined above, does not depend strictly on the operation of the *stare decisis* principle. Lack of it does not mean that prior decisions are not implemented or that the link with a prior decision is not taken into account in decision-making processes in the statutory law order. Nevertheless, there is no doubt that the implementation of precedents leads to a major change whereby the implementation of a precedent is not obligatory but genuinely required and useful in taking a judicial decision (the power of the argument versus the argument of power)[22].

It is therefore essential to determine the scope of precedent-based judicial practice which is not associated with the demand for the law-making function of courts under which the rules would be formulated in isolation from the legislator or under which judicial activism would develop to openly oppose the legislator[23]. Such forms of activity of the judiciary would, in essence, become an element of a political discourse and an argument in determining the relation between the legislative and executive branches on the one hand and the judicial branch on the other. In statutory law countries with such a stand would shift the weight of the precedent from juridical argumentation (which, after all, is key) to political argumentation. The latter would rather blur than underline the real benefits prior decisions and judicial practice heretofore may offer to current decision-making processes.

---

22 Considerations on the reasons for not implementing precedents irrespective of the *stare decisis* principle can also be found in the Anglo-Saxon legal doctrine (cf. N. Duxbury, op. cit., p. 150 et seq.).

23 The precedent-based judicial decisions in the Anglo-Saxon doctrine are sometimes connected in this context with judicial activism, e.g. in determining the constitutionality of laws (see: L. Ringhand, *Judicial Activism. An Empirical Examination of Voting Behavior of the Rehnquist Natural Court*, [online:] http://ssrn.com/absrtract=765445 [available: 15.03.2015], passim; also see: C.L. Roberts, *In Search of Judicial Activism. Dangers in Quantifying the Qualitative*, [online:] http://ssrn.com/abstract=2003542 [available: 22.06.2016], passim; A. Barak, op. cit., p. 275 et seq. or E.J. Segall, *Reconceptualizing the Judicial Activism Debate as Judicial Responsibility. A Tale of Two justice Kennedy*, "Arizona State Law Journal" 2009, no. 41, p. 709 et seq. where interpretative activism is highlighted.)

With precedential practice the uniformity of the application of law is enhanced in a manner which is conducive to highlighting its flexibility, i.e. making adjustments to fairly formalized effects of legislative activity and relatively "rigid" precedents in view of current social needs as independent decisions or even case law. In certain situations involving the application of general referral clauses, principles of law, standards of political programs, human rights protection norms, etc. in which the discretionary power regarding decisions is by nature larger, precedential practice (even in its "soft" version where the *stare decisis* principle is absent) is a means of restricting this discretionary power in order to reach *iunctim* between flexibility and uniformity of the application of law and, by extension, underlining the principle of legal certainty.

Even if one accepts the legitimacy of reservations concerning effectiveness of adaptation of key aspects of *common law* precedential practice[24] in the statutory law order (largely pertaining to the differences between the two legal orders such as lack of tradition to resort to prior court decisions, lack of approval of judicial activism usually associated with court law-making processes, a certain degree of formalism and superficiality of argumentation indicating in court justifications that references to prior decisions) both the growing number of such references in actual practice and their role as an essential condition of continuity in law[25] cannot be neglected. If precedential practice fits the axiology and legal culture of a given legal order and contributes, irrespective of current legislation entangled in politics, to reinforcing the operative nature of law in the society, it is rather difficult to oppose a view that the set of precedents, which constitutes a major achievement of judicial practice, is, in fact, in the statutory law order genuine "wisdom from the past"[26].

24 A critical approach to US court decisions is shown in M.R. Levin, *Men in Black. How the Supreme Court is Destroying America*, Washington 2005, passim, specifically pp. 1–11, 23–34. A totally opposite view, i.e. defending the system, is presented by D. Herllman, *An Epistemic Defense of Precedents*, [in:] *Precedent in the United States Supreme Court*, ed. C.J. Peters, Dordrecht 2013, p. 63 et seq. Fairly optimistic predictions concerning the future of precedents in the *common law* are offered by M.J. Gerhardt, *The Power of Precedent*, Oxford 2008, pp. 199–204.

25 Cf. E.G. Lee III, op. cit., p. 583; W.A. Edmundson, *Law's Evolution and Law as Customs*, "San Diego Law Review" 2014, vol. 51, no. 4, p. 875 et seq.

26 Cf. D.N. MacCormick, R.S. Summers, *Introduction*, [in:] *Interpreting Precedent…*, op. cit., p. 1.

Authors affiliation

Leszek Leszczyński
Maria Curie-Sklodowska University
in Lublin (Poland)

Andrzej Korybski
Maria Curie-Sklodowska University
in Lublin (Poland)

Ewa Skrzydło-Tefelska
Kozminski University (Poland)

Bartosz Liżewski
Maria Curie-Sklodowska University
in Lublin (Poland)

Marzena Myślińska
Maria Curie-Sklodowska University
in Lublin (Poland)

Adam Szot
Maria Curie-Sklodowska University
in Lublin (Poland)

Paweł Sadowski
Maria Curie-Sklodowska University
in Lublin (Poland)

Andrzej Jakubecki
Maria Curie-Sklodowska University
in Lublin (Poland)

Ireneusz Nowikowski
Maria Curie-Sklodowska University
in Lublin (Poland)

John McClellan Marshall
Senior Judge, XIV District Court,
Dallas, Texas, Honorary Professor of
Maria Curie-Sklodowska University
in Lublin (Poland)

Iwona Rzucidło-Grochowska
European School of Law and
Administration in Warsaw (Poland)

Aleksander Jakubowski
Warsaw University (Poland)

Lex et Res Publica
Polish Legal and Political Studies

Edited by
Anna Jarón

www.peterlang.com

www.ingramcontent.com/pod-product-compliance
Ingram Content Group UK Ltd.
Pitfield, Milton Keynes, MK11 3LW, UK
UKHW021832100926
8556IPUK00004B/304

9 783631 790182